Decision Making under Uncertainty

Decision Making under Uncertainty

The Case of State-Dependent Preferences

Edi Karni

Harvard University Press
Cambridge, Massachusetts
and London, England
1985

Printed in the United States of America

10 9 8 7 6 5 4 3 2 1

This book is printed on acid-free paper, and
its binding materials have been chosen
for strength and durability.

Library of Congress Cataloging in Publication Data

Karni, Edi.
Decision making under uncertainty.

Bibliography: p.
Includes index.
1. Decision-making. 2. Uncertainty. 3. Risk
management. I. Title.
HD30.23.K28 1985 658.4′03 85-5478
ISBN 0-674-19525-6 (alk. paper)

To My Mother
and
In Memory of My Father

Preface

The research that led to this book was motivated by my belief that the dependence of the decision maker's preferences on the prevailing state of nature constitutes an indispensable aspect of many decision problems, and that the theory of decision making under uncertainty for state-independent preferences is not adequate for handling these problems. The objective of this book is to present analytical tools that can be applied in the study of decision making under uncertainty with state-dependent preferences, and to demonstrate their usefulness in the analysis of concrete problems. Its subject matter is preference structures and risky prospects and their properties as captured by their numerical representations.

The exposition in this book, much like the research that led to it, blends the development of theoretical concepts and ideas with analysis of concrete problems. If some of the problems seem contrived, it is only because of the need to isolate and thus clarify the role of the analytical tools involved in their analysis.

The area of decision analysis represents an intersection of several disciplines: economics, statistics, management science, and psychology. This book is intended for researchers whose main research interest is the field of decision making under uncertainty and for researchers and graduate students in relevant disciplines whose work requires an understanding of concepts and tools employed in the theory of individual decision making under uncertainty. The exposition is thus accessible to both audiences. The main results are presented and explained narratively and diagrammatically, while detailed proofs of the various propositions appear in the concluding section of each chapter. In the interest of fluency and in order to maintain the focus of attention I have refrained from using footnotes and from reviewing the related literature in the text itself. A brief review of the work most directly related to the content of each chapter appears in the penultimate section of that chapter.

Finally, the exposition is by and large self-contained. All propositions that appear in the text are proved. There is no attempt, however, to review mathematical concepts.

Two chapters of this book draw heavily on joint papers: Chapter 1 is based on "On State-Dependent Preferences and Subjective Probabilities" *Econometrica,* 51 (July 1983) by David Schmeidler, Karl Vind, and myself, and on an earlier, unpublished manuscript by David Schmeidler and myself entitled "An Expected Utility Theory for State-Dependent Preferences." Chapter 4 is based on two papers written jointly with Itzhak Zilcha, "Uncertain Lifetime, Risk Aversion, and Life Insurance" and "Risk Aversion in the Theory of Life Insurance: The Fisherian Model." I am indebted to my coauthors for these contributions and for many hours of enlightening discussions of issues related to the content of this book.

I am grateful to Mark J. Machina for many useful comments and suggestions regarding the content of Chapters 5 and 6. To David, Itzhak, and Mark I would like to express my gratitude for their comradeship and encouragement during the course of this research. Their support helped maintain my enthusiasm.

Two graduate students at Johns Hopkins University, Ailsa Röell and Michel Demers, took an interest in issues related to my work. Their contributions are mentioned in several places in this book and constitute portions of their Ph.D. dissertations. I should like to thank them for many helpful discussions. Ailsa Röell deserves special mention for her penetrating criticism, which helped me avoid several pitfalls in the course of this research.

My thanks go also to Joy Pankoff, who typed the various drafts of this book.

Contents

Decision Making under Uncertainty

Introduction

This book deals with the theory of decision making under uncertainty, where the decision maker's preferences depend on the prevailing state of nature. That is not to say that the book is concerned with a special case of a more general theory. In fact the theory explored in this book constitutes a generalization of the prevailing theory—the theory of decision making under uncertainty with state-independent preferences.

The essential feature that sets apart the problem of decision making under uncertainty with state-dependent preferences, as a subject for inquiry, is the unalterable character of the states of nature, which prevents the reallocation among decision makers of the risk intrinsic to the states of nature. This structure imposes certain prerequisites on the comparability of decision makers for the purpose of comparative statics analysis. Upon reflection, however, it becomes apparent that these restrictions are not particular to the case of state-dependent preferences. When the decision maker's preferences are state independent these prerequisites are intrinsic to the preference structure and consequently are implicitly satisfied. In the case of state-dependent preferences the increased complexity of the preference structure requires explicit consideration of the prerequisites. Once the requisite conditions for comparability are recognized, the analysis is by and large analogous to that of the state-independent preferences. Hence the comparative statics analysis, restricted as it may seem, constitutes an extension of the prevailing theory.

The general organization of this book is as follows. Chapter 1 is an exposition of an expected utility theory for state-dependent preferences. The theory consists of axioms that permit the joint determination of subjective probabilities and utilities when the decision maker's preferences depend upon the prevailing state of nature. In addition to the usual von Neumann–Morgenstern axioms, these axioms also include the requirement that the decision maker's actual preferences are consistent with his preferences contingent on a hypothetical probability distribution over the states of nature. Two versions of the consistency axiom are introduced and their significance in the context of Bayesian decision theory is discussed.

The key notion in developing a criterion for comparability of attitudes toward risk is the reference set—namely, the optimal distribution of wealth across states of nature that is obtained under fair insurance. The notion of the reference set is defined formally in Chapter 2. Utilizing this definition I introduce measures that permit the partial ordering of state-dependent utility functions according to their aversion to risk. These measures are shown to constitute a generalization of the Arrow–Pratt measures of risk aversion for state-independent preferences.

In Chapter 3 the aforementioned measures are employed in a comparative statics analysis of two decision problems involving state-dependent preferences: the optimal purchase of air travel insurance and the choice of optimal health insurance coverage. Flight insurance and health insurance models are presented, and the consequences of a higher degree of risk aversion are analyzed.

In Chapter 4 I conclude the discussion of risk aversion with a comparative statics analysis of the demand for life insurance. This problem differs from those of health and air travel insurance in that it involves multivariate utility functions. The definition of the relevant concept of interpersonal comparability of risk aversion uses the notion of the reference set. A comparative statics analysis of risk aversion is presented for two individuals at the same level of wealth, and for a given individual at different wealth levels.

In Chapter 5 I review the definition of increasing risk for state-independent preferences and, using the reference set as a basis for classifying individuals, I extend this definition to include state-dependent preferences. The generalized definition of increasing risk is then employed in the analysis of some economic problems. Finally, using the notion of mean utility-preserving increase in risk, I present another definition of the relation "more risk averse than" and demonstrate its equivalence to the definitions in Chapter 2.

The theory of risk aversion originally developed for state-independent univariate utility functions was extended to include state-dependent and multivariate utility functions. In Chapter 6 I offer a way of unifying these results by establishing the correspondence between multivariate risk aversion and risk aversion with state-dependent preferences. More specifically, I show that the prerequisite for comparability of risk aversion in the multivariate case—namely, identical ordinal preferences on the commodity space—corresponds to identical properly defined reference sets in the case of state-dependent preferences. For comparable decision makers the condition that the utility function of one is a concave transformation on the commodity space of the utility function of the other corresponds to the condition that the expected utility of one is a concave transformation on the reference set of the expected utility of the other.

1 A Theory of Choice under Uncertainty with State-Dependent Preferences

1.1 Introduction

The theory of rational choice under uncertainty deals with the manner in which decision makers ought to choose among alternative courses of action when the consequences of these actions are uncertain. The normative nature of the theory pertains to a set of consistency requirements that define rational behavior. Less clear and indeed much debated is the empirical or positive content of the theory. Systematic violations of the consistency discipline have been reported by numerous observers. Recognizing this difficulty, we nevertheless pursue the normative line of inquiry in the belief that it is not devoid of empirical content.

The problem of choice under uncertainty is conveniently described by the use of three basic notions: the notion of *states of nature,* which are portrayals of the world that leave no relevant aspect undescribed; the notion of *acts,* which are the objects of choice; and the notion of *consequences,* which describes anything that might happen to the decision maker. Each combination of an act and a state of nature determines a unique consequence. Uncertainty arises as a result of the lack of advance knowledge of the true state of nature—the state of nature that in fact obtains. Thus if the true state is independent of the act that is selected the decision maker does not know in advance the exact consequence that follows from a given act.

The decision problem is to choose an act that results in the most favorable consequences for the decision maker. The desirability of an act is a matter of judgment, presumably combining the decision maker's evaluation of the consequences that may follow from this act and his beliefs regarding the likely realization of these consequences or his beliefs regarding the likely realization of alternative states of nature. At any rate, postulating that decisions are determined by preference relations over acts, the expected utility theory is a hypothesis about the structure of preference relations that makes them quantifiable in accordance with the aforementioned presumption. In other words, the theory imposes certain consistency conditions on the preference relations over acts, which permit expression of the preference relations in numerical terms that separate tastes, which are represented by a utility function from beliefs, which are represented by a subjective probability distribution over states of nature.

The idea that preferences over acts may be represented by the mathematical expectation of some utility index dates back to Bernoulli (1738). However, only in this century has the link between expected-utility-maximizing behavior and rational behavior been established, through the work of Ramsey (1931), von Neumann and Morgenstern (1947), Savage (1954), and others. A basic premise common to all these contributions is that the preference relations over consequences are independent of the state of nature, or in Ramsey's terminology, are "ethically neutral."

The assumption of state-independence of preferences may be a reasonable characterization of many choice situations. There are circumstances, however, where the dependence of the preferences over consequences on the prevailing state of nature is an indispensable feature of the decision problem. Optimal choices of health and life insurance coverage are but two examples of decisions that involve state-dependent preferences.

If the probability over the states of nature is objectively known, then von Neumann and Morgenstern's expected utility theory can be easily modified to include state-dependent preferences. Such a modification requires only a redefinition of the consequences to include the state of nature itself as part of the definition of the outcome. The von Neumann–Morgenstern utility obtained assigns different real numbers to the same wealth, say, in different states of nature.

In the absence of objective state probabilities, however, the foundations of a decision theory that is based on expected-utility-maximizing behavior with state-dependent preferences are less straightforward. Since my concern throughout this book is the theory of choice under uncertainty with state-dependent preferences and some of its economic implications, it is only natural to begin the investigation by laying the foundations of the theory of expected-utility-maximizing behavior with state-dependent preferences. In so doing I draw heavily on Karni and Schmeidler (1981) and Karni, Schmeidler, and Vind (1983).

1.2 The Structure of the Problem

The primitive elements of our problem are three sets—the set of states of nature, the set of consequences, and the set of acts—and a preference relation over the set of acts. I shall now introduce these concepts in a more formal manner.

Let S be a finite nonempty set. The elements of S are referred to as *states of nature* and have the usual interpretation of a description of nature, that is, an object about which the decision maker is concerned, leaving no relevant aspect undescribed.

For each state s in S, let $X(s)$ be a finite set of prizes that are available if s obtains. It is not required that each prize be available under all states of nature; it is possible that $X(s) \neq X(t)$ for some s and t in S. The union of $X(s)$ over all $s \in S$ is denoted X.

A *consequence* is a lottery with objectively known (extraneous) probabilities over a finite nonempty set of prizes. The introduction of objective probabilities presupposes the existence of some device such as a die that generates random outcomes, the relative frequency of each of which is determined by the physical properties of the device and is known in advance. Let $f(s)$ denote a lottery over $X(s)$. Thus, $f(s)$ is an $|X(s)|$-dimensional vector in the nonnegative Euclidean space, with coordinates that sum to one. The entry $f(x,s)$ of the vector $f(s)$ has the interpretation of the objective probability of winning the prize $x \in X(s)$ if the state $s \in S$ is the true state of nature. We refer to $f(s)$ as a *consequence.* The set of all such consequences for a given $s \in S$ is denoted $F(s)$. An ultimate outcome is a prize–state pair $(x,s) \in X \times S$ such that $x \in X(s)$. The set of all ultimate outcomes is denoted Z.

An *act* in this context is a mapping from the set of states of nature into the set of consequences. In other words, to each $s \in S$ an act assigns a consequence $f(s) \in F(s)$. Hence by choosing an act the decision maker subscribes to a list of lottery tickets or consequences, one for each state of nature. Denoting $\Sigma_{s \in S}|X(s)|$ by D, we formally define the set of acts L as:

$$L = \{f \in R_{+}^{D} | \forall s \in S\; f(s) \in F(s)\}.$$

The set L is a mixture set. The definition of a mixture set is given in Herstein and Milnor (1953) as follows: A set S is said to be a *mixture* set if for any a, $b \in S$ and for any $\alpha \in [0,1]$ we can associate another element, which we write as $\alpha a + (1 - \alpha)b$, which is again in S, and where for all $\alpha, \beta \in [0,1]$ and all $a, b \in S$,

$$1 \cdot a + (1 - 1)b = a,$$
$$\alpha a + (1 - \alpha)b = (1 - \alpha)b + \alpha a,$$
$$\beta[\alpha a + (1 - \alpha)b] + (1 - \beta)b = (\alpha\beta)a + (1 - \alpha\beta)b.$$

One way of interpreting acts is to regard them as compounded games of hazard. According to this interpretation, in choosing an act the decision maker enters a two-stage lottery to determine the ultimate outcome. In the first stage an element, say s, from S is selected by some mechanism of chance. This entitles the decision maker to participate in a lottery $f(s)$ from a predetermined list of lotteries, which determines the prize x to be awarded to our gambler according to the outcome of some random process with objectively known probability. The position of the decision maker at the end of this game is described in every relevant aspect by the ultimate outcome (x,s).

The final basic component of the theory is the decision maker's preference relation over acts, denoted $\succsim$. A preference relation is a binary relation on L. In the present context $f \succsim g,\ \ f,g \in L$ has the interpretation "f is at least as desirable as g." Given such a relation we define the strict preference relation $\succ$ and the indifference relation $\sim$ as follows: for all $f,g \in L, f \succ g$ if and only if $f \succsim g$ and not $g \succsim$ f, and $f \sim g$ if and only if both $f \succsim$ g and $g \succsim$ f. The nature of this preference relation is the main concern of the theory of decision making under uncertainty.

1.3 The Three Basic Axioms of Rational Behavior and Their Implications

One of the tenets of decision theory is that choices between pairs of alternative courses of action in a given situation reflect the decision maker's unchanging preferences over the objects of choice. The notion of rational choice pertains to certain consistency conditions embedded in the structure of the preference relation. The following three axioms, due originally to von Neumann and Morgenstern (1947), are widely accepted as fundamental principles of rational behavior.

AXIOM (A.1) (WEAK ORDER). *(a) For all f and g in L: $f \succsim g$ or $g \succsim f$. (b) For all f, g, and h in L, if $f \succsim g$ and $g \succsim h$ then $f \succsim h$.*

AXIOM (A.2) (INDEPENDENCE). *For all f, g, and h in L and for all $\alpha \in (0,1)$: If $f \succ g$, then $\alpha f + (1 - \alpha)h \succ \alpha g + (1 - \alpha)h$.*

AXIOM (A.3) (CONTINUITY). *For f, g, and h in L: If $f > g$ and $g > h$, then there exist α and β in (0,1) such that $\alpha f + (1 - \alpha)h > g$ and $g > \beta f + (1 - \beta)h$.*

The first part of (A.1) asserts the pairwise comparability of all acts. The second part of this axiom asserts the transitivity of the preference relation. It follows from (A.1) that the transitivity property applies to the strict preference relation $>$, as well as the indifference relation $\sim$. Axiom (A.1) thus permits the ranking of all the elements of L according to their relative desirability, with ties occurring only within ranks.

Axiom (A.3) asserts infinite sensitivity of judgment on the part of the decision maker. This is demonstrated dramatically by the implication that there exist lottery tickets that offer the death penalty as one prize and a dollar and one penny as the other prize, which the decision maker would prefer to receiving one dollar with certainty. Perhaps the more important behavioral implication of (A.3) is that it rules out objection to gambling on moral grounds, as well as joy of gambling as such.

Axiom (A.3) assures the continuity of the preference relation. Taken together the role of (A.1) and (A.3) is to establish the existence of a continuous real-valued function over acts.

The independence axiom (A.2) constitutes the core of the theory. This axiom is responsible for the linearity of the functional that represents the preference relation on L. The axiom involves a comparison of two lotteries, both of which offer the same consequence in one event and the first of which offers a strictly preferred consequence if the event does not materialize. Hence if the first lottery is chosen the decision maker is at least as well off in all events and strictly better off in one event. The first lottery is then strictly preferred to the second, provided the aforementioned event does not have probability 0. Stated in these terms the axiom seems normatively compelling, yet as already mentioned, when presented with a choice among courses of action where the analysis along these lines is not immediately apparent, decision makers exhibit patterns of choice that systematically violate the axiom.

The set of preference relations on L satisfying (A.1), (A.2), and (A.3) is denoted Ω. Preference relations in Ω can be represented numerically by a real-valued linear function on the set of acts. Before we introduce this result, however, we define the notion of a null state. In the present context a null state represents an element of S such that the decision maker is indifferent between any acts whose consequences are the same in every other state in S. Formally,

DEFINITION 1.1. *A state $s \in S$ is said to be null if and only if $f \sim g$ whenever $f(t) = g(t)$ for every $t \in S$, $t \neq s$.*

Notice that in the present context the indifference among all acts that agree in terms of their consequences in each state other than *s* may be the result of all the prizes in *X*(*s*) being equally desirable, the result of the decision maker's belief that the realization of *s* is virtually impossible, or both.

With this in mind we present a theorem that is a minor extension of the von Neumann–Morgenstern expected utility theory.

THEOREM 1.1. *If $\succsim$ is a binary relation in Ω, then*

(i) *There exists a function $w \in R^Z$ such that for all f and g in L, $f \succsim g$ if and only if $\Sigma_{s \in S} \Sigma_{x \in X(s)} w(x,s) f(x,s) \geqq \Sigma_{s \in S} \Sigma_{x \in X(s)} w(x,s) g(x,s)$.*

(ii) *For every $v \in R^Z$ the relation "For all f and g in L, $f \succsim g$ if and only if $\Sigma_{s \in S} \Sigma_{x \in X(s)} v(x,s) f(x,s) \geqq \Sigma_{s \in S} \Sigma_{x \in X(s)} v(x,s) g(x,s)$" holds if and only if there exist a real number $b > 0$ and $a \in R^S$ such that for all $x \in X(s)$ and all $s \in S$, $v(x,s) = bw(x,s) + a(s)$.*

(iii) *$w(x,s)$ is constant on $X(s)$ if and only if s is null.*

For proof see Fishburn (1970), chap. 13.

Theorem 1.1 asserts the existence of a numerical representation of the preference relation $\succsim$ in Ω. This representation has the form of a sum across states of nature of the conditional mathematical expectation of a real-valued function on the set of ultimate outcomes with respect to the objective probability distribution over prizes in each state. This representation is unique up to a cardinal unit-comparable transformation (that is, a positive linear transformation with intercepts that may vary across states).

The significance of this result, which is the essence of the theory of rational choice under uncertainty, can hardly be overstated. In view of its importance it is worth noting that the above representation of preferences does not require the explicit separation of the decision maker's beliefs about the likely realization of alternative states of nature from his tastes for alternative ultimate outcomes. Both are implicit in the *evaluation function w*. Such a separation, however, has been a subject of great interest, for both decision theorists and statisticians. The remainder of this chapter is devoted to the exploration of the additional structure that must be imposed on the preference relation $\succsim \in \Omega$ that will permit the separation of probability beliefs from tastes in a *unique* manner.

1.4 State-Independent Preferences and Subjective Probabilities

It is not difficult to conceive of situations in which the preference relations are independent of the prevailing state of nature. A gambler, for instance, may be indifferent between stacking his bet on red or black when playing roulette. Similarly, an investor may be concerned with the fluctuations in the price of a stock insofar as it affects his wealth while presumably deriving no direct satisfaction from the event that produced the price changes. These examples are typical of many circumstances where the sole concern of a decision maker is the effect on wealth of the realization of a random event, and not the event itself. This lack of concern regarding the event or the state of nature that obtains is captured by the following axioms:

AXIOM (A.4). *There are prizes* x' *and* x'' *such that* $x', x'' \in \cap_{s \in S} X(s)$ *and* $f > g$ *when* $f(x',s) = g(x'',s) = 1$ *for all* $s \in S$.

This axiom asserts a certain degree of overlap among the prizes available under alternative states of nature. More specifically, at least two prizes that are not equally desirable are available under all states of nature.

AXIOM (A.5) (STATE-INDEPENDENCE). *If* $s, s' \in S$, s *and* s' *are nonnull,* $\tilde{f}, \tilde{g} \in F(s) \cap F(s')$, *and* $\Sigma_{x \in X(s) \cap X(s')} \tilde{f}(x,s) = \Sigma_{x \in X(s) \cap X(s')} \tilde{g}(x,s') = 1$, *then* $f \gtrsim g$ *where* $f(t) = g(t)$ *for all* $t \in S$, $t \neq s$, *and* $f(s) = \tilde{f}$; $g(s) = \tilde{g}$ *if and only if* $f' \gtrsim g'$ *where* $f'(t) = g'(t)$ *for all* $t \in S$, $t \neq s'$, *and* $f'(s') = \tilde{f}$, $g'(s') = \tilde{g}$.

This axiom asserts that the preference relations over consequences that may occur under any two distinct states of nature are independent of the states of nature. Thus the ranking of any two acts that agree, in terms of their consequences, in all states but one, say s, is the same as the ranking of any two other acts that agree in all states but one, say s', provided that the consequences of the first pair of acts in s are identical to those of the second pair of acts in s', respectively. In a sense this is a statement that the consequence $\tilde{f}$ is at least as desirable as $\tilde{g}$, independent of the state of nature.

Axioms (A.4) and (A.5) taken jointly imply that if a state is null it can only be the result of the decision maker's belief that the realization of this state is virtually impossible. The other possibility—that all the prizes available in a given state are equally desirable—is ruled out by (A.4) and the assertion in (A.5) that the preference relation over prizes is state-independent.

Axioms (A.1)–(A.5), in conjunction with L being a mixture set, enable a unique separation of the valuation function $w(x,s)$ of Theorem 1.1 into a product $p(s)u(x)$, where u is a real-valued function defined on X and p is a probability distribution on S. This result is contained in the following theorem.

THEOREM 1.2. *Suppose that the binary relation $\succsim$ on L satisfies axioms (A.1) through (A.5). Then:*

(i) *There exist $u \in R^X$ and a probability measure p on S such that for all f and g in L, $f \succsim g$ if and only if*

$$\sum_{s \in S} \sum_{x \in X(s)} p(s)u(x)f(x,s) \geqq \sum_{s \in S} \sum_{x \in X(s)} p(s)u(x)g(x,s).$$

(ii) *For every $v \in R^X$ and a probability measure q on S the relation: "For all f, $g \in L$, $f \succsim g$ if and only if $\Sigma_{s \in S}\Sigma_{x \in X(s)} q(s)v(x)f(x,s) \geqq \Sigma_{s \in S}\Sigma_{x \in X(s)} q(s)v(x)g(x,s)$" holds if and only if $p(s) = q(s)$ for all $s \in S$ and there are numbers $b > 0$ and c such that $v(x) = bu(x) + c$ for all $x \in \cup_{\{s: s \text{ not null}\}} X(s)$.*

(iii) *$p(s) = 0$ if and only if s is null.*

For a proof of this result see Fishburn (1970, theorem 13.2).

Theorem 1.2 asserts the existence of a utility function over the set of prizes and a probability measure over the set of states, which permit the representation of the preference relation over acts via an expected utility index. Furthermore, the subjective probability measure over the set of states is unique, and the utility function is unique up to a positive linear transformation. Finally, the utility function is state independent, reflecting the state-independent nature of the underlying preferences.

1.5 State-Dependent Preferences

There are circumstances in which the evaluation of prizes or consequences is not independent of the prevailing state of nature. Quite conceivably, a person who on a sunny day would prefer watching a football game in an open stadium would also prefer to stay home and watch the game on television if it rains. Similarly, even a dedicated skier may prefer a pair of symphony tickets over a paid vacation in a ski resort if he happens to suffer a fractured ankle. In these examples the state of nature—the weather conditions in the first instance and the state of the skier's health in the second—have a direct effect on the relative evaluation of the alternative consequences. The dependence of preferences on the states of nature has interesting implications for the analysis of a class of insurance problems involving irreplaceable objects, including life, health, and heirlooms. It may also prove relevant for the economic analysis of choice of criminal activities where the ultimate outcomes involve loss of freedom. The study of these phenomena requires a theory of choice under uncertainty that takes account of the dependence of preferences on the state of nature.

Proceeding along the traditional path, we shall develop an expected utility theory of choice for state-dependent preferences. This theory is founded on the notion that preference relations over acts have a numerical representation in terms of a unique subjective probability over the set of states of nature and a utility function over the set of ultimate outcomes representing intrinsic tastes for prize–state pairs. The utility assigned to two distinct prize–state pairs may differ even if the prize is the same in both. Obviously this would require forsaking the state-independence axiom and replacing it with an alternative restriction on the structure of the preference relation.

1.6 Prize–State Lotteries and Hypothetical Preferences

As a first step in developing our theory we introduce the notion of a prize–state lottery. A prize–state lottery is best thought of as a mechanism of chance with known physical attributes, which assigns objective (unanimously agreed-upon) probabilities to the elements of the set of ultimate outcomes $Z = \{(x,s) | x \in X(s), s \in S\}$. Let a prize–state lottery be denoted $\hat{f}$. It is formally defined by $\hat{f}\colon Z \to R_+$ and $\Sigma_{(x,s)\in Z}\hat{f}(x,s) = 1$. The set of all prize–state lotteries $\hat{L}$ is

$$\hat{L} = \left\{ \hat{f} \in R_+^Z \,\middle|\, \sum_{(x,s)\in Z} \hat{f}(x,s) = 1 \right\}.$$

As an illustration of the notion of a prize–state lottery, consider our football fan who must choose between staying at home and watching the game on television or going to the stadium and watching the game in the open air. Suppose that while deliberating his options he hears a weather forecast predicting a 20-percent chance of rain during the game. Suppose further that our hero believes this to be a correct assessment of the likelihood of rain. Analyzing the situation, the football fan realizes that he faces two prize–state lotteries corresponding to the acts of staying at home and going to the stadium. If he stays home, the prize–state lottery is described as *20-percent chance of watching the game on television while it rains and 80-percent chance of watching the game on television while the sun is shining.* If he goes to the stadium he participates in a lottery offering *20-percent chance of watching the game in the stadium while it rains and 80-percent chance of watching it in the stadium while the sun is shining.* This is a rather simple illustration of the notion of prize–state lottery, in that each act corresponds to a single prize; that is, staying home implies watching the game on television. The important observation is that the assignment of (hypothetical) objective probabilities to the alternative states transforms every act into a prize–state lottery.

Next we hypothesize the existence of preference relations over the set of prize–state lotteries, which satisfy the von Neumann–Morgenstern axioms. Let $\hat{\succsim}$ be a binary relation over $\hat{L}$ with the relation $\hat{\succ}$ and $\hat{\sim}$ defined for all $\hat{f}$ and $\hat{g}$ in $\hat{L}$ as "$\hat{f} \hat{\succsim} \hat{g}$ and not $\hat{g} \hat{\succsim} \hat{f}$," and "both $\hat{f} \hat{\succsim} \hat{g}$ and $\hat{g} \hat{\succsim} \hat{f}$," respectively. The preference relation $\hat{\succsim}$ is assumed to satisfy

AXIOM (Â.4) (WEAK ORDER). *(a) For all $\hat{f}$ and $\hat{g}$ in $\hat{L}$, $\hat{f} \hat{\succsim} \hat{g}$ or $\hat{g} \hat{\succsim} \hat{f}$. (b) For all $\hat{f}$, $\hat{g}$, and $\hat{h}$ in $\hat{L}$, if $\hat{f} \hat{\succsim} \hat{g}$ and $\hat{g} \hat{\succsim} \hat{h}$, then $\hat{f} \hat{\succsim} \hat{h}$.*

AXIOM (Â.5) (INDEPENDENCE). *For all $\hat{f}$, $\hat{g}$, and $\hat{h}$ in $\hat{L}$ and for all $\alpha \in (0,1)$: If $\hat{f} \hat{\succ} \hat{g}$, then $\alpha\hat{f} + (1-\alpha)\hat{h} \hat{\succ} \alpha\hat{g} + (1-\alpha)\hat{h}$.*

AXIOM (Â.6) (CONTINUITY). *For $\hat{f}$, $\hat{g}$, and $\hat{h}$ in $\hat{L}$, if $\hat{f} \hat{\succ} \hat{g}$ and $\hat{g} \hat{\succ} \hat{h}$, then there exist α and β in (0,1) such that $\alpha\hat{f} + (1-\alpha)\hat{h} \hat{\succ} \hat{g}$ and $\hat{g} \hat{\succ} \beta\hat{f} + (1-\beta)\hat{h}$.*

Let $\hat{\Omega}$ denote the set of all binary relations on $\hat{L}$ that satisfy (Â.4), (Â.5), and (Â.6).

We assume that in addition to having a preference relation $\succsim \in \Omega$ the decision maker has a preference relation $\hat{\succsim} \in \hat{\Omega}$. This assumption is crucial for our theory and merits some elaboration. Consider again our football enthusiast. Even without the weather forecast he is supposed to be able to choose between staying at home and going to the game. This choice is an expression of his preference relation over acts. The additional assumption that he also has a preference relation over prize–state lotteries means that the decision maker can predict his own behavior under any conceivable probability of rain. In other words, statements such as "If the probability of rain during the game does not exceed p, then I would prefer going to the stadium, otherwise I would rather stay home," are meaningful in the sense that they express the decision maker's plan of action once the probability of rain becomes known. The decision maker is able to assess hypothetical situations in the same way that he assesses actual choice situations.

The critical aspect of this assumption is its implication that the decision maker is able to compare alternatives that involve distinct, hence conflicting, probabilities over the states of nature. In particular this implies that the decision maker can rank degenerate prize–state lotteries such as "watching the game in an open stadium when it rains" and "watching the game on television when the sun is shining." The difficulty inherent in such comparisons is in imagining the circumstances that call for such choices. The intuition that comparisons of hypothetical situations involving distinct probability distributions over the states of nature are possible, however, is supported by the prevalence of moral hazard in many risk-sharing arrangements. Moral hazard is the phenomenon where, by omission or by commission, a decision maker changes the probability distribution over states of nature. The decision maker thereby reveals his preference for one probability distribution on S over another, given an act in L and the possible cost or benefit of his actions or inaction. This is an indication of the decision maker's ability to assess the relative desirability of acts under alternative probability distributions over the states of nature, which is essentially what is required by the assumption that he has preference relations over $\hat{L}$.

A preference relation $\hat{\succsim} \in \hat{\Omega}$ has a von Neumann–Morgenstern utility representation. Formally:

THEOREM 1.3. *There exists a preference relation $\hat{\succsim} \in \hat{\Omega}$ if and only if there exists a function $u \in R^Z$ such that for all $\hat{f}$ and $\hat{g}$ in $\hat{L}$:*

$$\hat{f} \mathrel{\hat{\succsim}} \hat{g} \text{ if and only if } \sum_{(s,x)\in Z} u(s,x)[\hat{f}(s,x) - \hat{g}(s,x)] \geqq 0.$$

Furthermore, for every $v \in R^Z$ the relation "for all $\hat{f}$ and $\hat{g}$ in $\hat{L}$, $\hat{f} \mathrel{\hat{\succsim}} \hat{g}$ if and only if $\Sigma_{(s,x)\in Z} v(s,x)[\hat{f}(s,x) - \hat{g}(s,x)] \geqq 0$" holds if and only if there is a $b > 0$ and $c \in R$ such that for all $(s,x) \in Z$ $v(s,x) = bu(s,x) + c$.

For proof see Fishburn (1970, theorem 8.2).

The role of the prize–state lotteries and the preference relations on such lotteries can now be explained using Theorems 1.1 and 1.3. First consider Theorem 1.1. The preference relation $\succsim \in \Omega$ is represented by the evaluation function $w \in R^Z$. If the preferences reflect probability beliefs regarding the likelihood of the realization of elements of S, then these probabilities are implicit in w. Next consider the preference relation $\hat{\succsim} \in \hat{\Omega}$. The probability of the realization of states of nature has already been incorporated into the definition of the elements of the set $\hat{L}$. More specifically, for each $s \in S$ the probability $p(s)$ incorporated into the definition of $\hat{f} \in \hat{L}$ is given by $p(s) = \Sigma_{x\in X(s)} \hat{f}(x,s)$. Thus the utility $u \in R^Z$, which according to Theorem 1.3 represents the preference relation $\hat{\succsim} \in \hat{\Omega}$, is purged of the effects of the decision maker's subjective probabilities over S. Consequently, u represents his intrinsic tastes for prize–state pairs, that is, his preferences over Z. It seems, therefore, that if these tastes can somehow be connected with the evaluation w, then the probability distribution on S implicit in w could be extracted. This link is provided by the consistency axiom, which asserts that the tastes implicit in w are the same as those represented by u.

1.7 The Axiom of Strong Consistency

Interest in the separation of subjective probabilities and utilities stems from the distinction between the transitory nature of probability beliefs and the unchanging nature of tastes. In particular, probability beliefs are subject to revision in view of new information, as in the case of Bayesian learning. Tastes, on the other hand, are not affected by new information. Because they incorporate both tastes and beliefs, preferences over acts do vary as a result of changes in probability beliefs and in tastes. If tastes remain invariant the preferences over acts may still change. The possible range of variation in such cases is restricted, however. This restriction, which captures the unchanging nature of tastes, is embodied in the notion of consistent preference relations and is expressed formally by the Axiom of Strong Consistency, stated below.

Intuitively speaking, two preference relations are consistent if they are induced by the same utilities and if the difference between them is explained solely by their different underlying subjective probabilities. A formal presentation of this notion requires some additional notation and definitions. A prize–state lottery $\hat{f} \in \hat{L}$ is said to be *nondegenerate* if and only if for every $s \in S$, $\Sigma_{x \in X(s)} \hat{f}(x,s) > 0$.

Denote by H a mapping from $\hat{L}$ to L such that $H(\hat{f}(x,s)) = \hat{f}(x,s)/\Sigma_{y \in X(s)} \hat{f}(y,s)$, for all $(x,s) \in Z$ and all nondegenerate $\hat{f}$ in $\hat{L}$. Every nondegenerate lottery $\hat{f}$ in $\hat{L}$ is transformed by the mapping H into an act in L by assigning to each $x \in X(s)$ the probability of obtaining x under $\hat{f}$ conditional on $s \in S$.

Given f and g in L and $s \in S$, we use the self-explanatory term *f equals g outside s* if for all $t \in S$, $t \neq s$, and all $x \in X(t)$, $f(x,t) = g(x,t)$. Likewise for $\hat{f}$ and $\hat{g} \in \hat{L}$.

Next consider the notion of a null state. When the preference relation over L is state independent and the preference relation $\gtrsim$ is nontrivial—that is, $>$ is nonempty—a state $s \in S$ is considered null if for all f and $g \in L$ such that f equals g outside s, $f \sim g$. In this case, as already mentioned, the indifference relation means that the decision maker regards the realization of s as virtually impossible. When preferences are state dependent, however, pairs of acts that are equal outside a given state may be equally preferred because all the prizes in that state are equally preferred. Thus in the case of death, for instance, a decision maker with no dependents may be indifferent regarding the size of his bequest. Consequently, a state $s \in S$ such that all pairs of acts that are equal outside s are equally preferred is definitely null only if we have independent evidence that not all the prizes in $X(s)$ are equally valued. This evidence can be obtained from another preference relation, such as $\hat{\succsim} \in \hat{\Omega}$.

DEFINITION 1.2: *A state of nature $s \in S$ is said to be obviously null if: (1) for all f and g in L such that f equals g outside s, $f \sim g$ and (2) there exist $\hat{f}$ and $\hat{g} \in \hat{L}$ such that $\hat{f}$ equals $\hat{g}$ outside s and $\hat{f} \hat{\succ} \hat{g}$.*

A state $s \in S$ is obviously nonnull if for at least one pair of acts in L that are equal outside s one of the acts is strictly preferred over the other. In between we have the case of states where all the prizes in $X(s)$ are equally preferred, where there is no way of inferring the belief of the decision maker regarding the likely realization of s from his choices among acts. The state s in this case is neither obviously null nor obviously nonnull. With this in mind we state the Axiom of Strong Consistency:

AXIOM ($\hat{\text{A}}$.7) (STRONG CONSISTENCY). *For all $s \in S$ and for all nondegenerate $\hat{f}$ and $\hat{g}$ in $\hat{L}$, if $\hat{f}$ equals $\hat{g}$ outside s and $H(\hat{f}) > H(\hat{g})$, then $\hat{f} \hat{\succ} \hat{g}$. Moreover, if s is obviously nonnull, then for all nondegenerate $\hat{f}$ and $\hat{g}$ in $\hat{L}$, such that $\hat{f}$ equals $\hat{g}$ outside s, $\hat{f} \hat{\succ} \hat{g}$ implies $H(\hat{f}) > H(\hat{g})$.*

The strong consistency axiom requires that the preference relation that guides the decision maker in his choice among any two acts that are equal outside any given state $s \in S$ be the same as that which would determine his choice between any two prize–state lotteries that are equal to one another outside that state. It is in this sense that the decision maker is said to be able to predict his own decisions when faced with choices between acts, given a hypothetical probability distribution on S.

Let $>_s$ denote the strict preference relation between pairs of acts that are equal outside $s \in S$. Similarly, let $\hat{\succ}_s$ be the strict preference relation between prize–state lotteries that are equal outside $s \in S$. With this notation the above discussion can be summarized as in Table 1.1.

Finally, we introduce the nontriviality condition, namely that not all acts in L are equally desirable.

AXIOM (A.8) (NONTRIVIALITY OF $\succsim$). *There exists f^* and g^* in L such that $f^* > g^*$.*

Table 1.1

	$\hat{>}_s \neq \emptyset$	$\hat{>}_s = \emptyset$
$>_s \neq \emptyset$	Obviously nonnull	$\emptyset$
$>_s = \emptyset$	Obviously null	Intermediate case

1.8 The Strong Expected Utility Theorem for State-Dependent Preferences

We are now in a position to state our first expected utility theorem for state-dependent preferences. The theorem consists of three parts: The first part asserts the existence of a numerical representation of the preference relation on the set of acts, expressed in terms of a real-valued function defined on the set of ultimate outcomes and a probability distribution on the set of states of nature. The second and third parts, respectively, assert the uniqueness properties of these functions.

THEOREM 1.4. *Let the binary relation $\succsim$ on L satisfy (A.1)–(A.3), (A.8), and let the binary relation $\hat{\succsim}$ on $\hat{L}$ satisfy (Â.4)–(Â.6). Suppose further that the two binary relations satisfy strong consistency. Then:*

(a) There exists a real-valued function u on Z and a (subjective) probability p on S such that, for all f and g in L,

(1) $$f \succsim g \text{ iff } \sum_{s \in S} \sum_{x \in X(s)} p(s)u(x,s)[f(x,s) - g(x,s)] \geqq 0.$$

and for all $\hat{f}$ and $\hat{g} \in \hat{L}$,

(2) $$\hat{f} \hat{\succsim} \hat{g} \text{ iff } \sum_{s \in S} \sum_{x \in X(s)} u(x,s)[\hat{f}(x,s) - \hat{g}(x,s)] \geqq 0.$$

(b) The u of part (a) is unique up to a cardinal unit-comparable transformation.

(c) For s obviously null, $p(s) = 0$, and if there exist f_s and $g_s \in L$ such that f_s equals g_s outside an obviously nonnull state and $f_s > g_s$, then $p(s) > 0$. Moreover, if for each state $s \in S$ there exist $\hat{f}_s$ and $\hat{g}_s \in \hat{L}$ such that $\hat{f}_s$ equals $\hat{g}_s$ outside s and $\hat{f}_s \hat{>} \hat{g}_s$, then the probability p of part (a) is unique.

The proof appears in Section 1.12 below. The implications of part (c) of Theorem 1.4 are summarized in Table 1.2.

As I show in the next section, the uniqueness of the utility function and of the subjective probability can be obtained under weaker assumptions than those included in the hypothesis of Theorem 1.4, with weaker implications.

1.9 Weak Consistency and a Second Expected Utility Theorem for State-Dependent Preferences

The representation of the preference relation over acts by a unique subjective probability distribution on the states of nature and a von Neumann–Morgenstern utility function on the set of ultimate outcomes does not require the existence of a preference relation over the whole set of prize–state lotteries. It suffices that such a preference relation exists on a subset of $\hat{L}$, which includes all the prize–state lotteries such that, given a strictly positive probability distribution p' on S, $\Sigma_{x \in X(s)} \hat{f}(x,s) = p'(s)$ for all $s \in S$. For a given strictly positive p' denote the set of such lotteries $L_{p'}$; then

$$L_{p'} = \left\{ \hat{f} \in \hat{L} \,\middle|\, \text{for all } s \in S \sum_{x \in X(s)} \hat{f}(x,s) = p'(s) > 0 \right\}.$$

Notice that $L_{p'}$ is a mixture set, and if $\hat{f} \in L_{p'}$, then the probability p' can be recovered by defining $p'(s) = \Sigma_{x \in X(s)} \hat{f}(x,s)$ for all $s \in S$.

Instead of assuming the existence of a preference relation $\hat{\succsim} \in \hat{\Omega}$, we impose the weaker condition that there exists a binary relation $\succsim'$ on at least one subset $L_{p'}$ of $\hat{L}$ that satisfies the weak order (A'.4), independence (A'.5), and continuity (A'.6) axioms. Let the set of all such binary relations be denoted $\Omega'(p')$. In addition, we restrict the strong consistency axiom to $\hat{f}$ and $\hat{g}$ in $L_{p'}$.

This last step constitutes the main weakening of our assumptions and therefore merits elaboration. To begin with, notice that since p' is strictly

Table 1.2

	$\hat{\succ}_s \neq \varnothing$	$\hat{\succ}_s = \varnothing$
$\succ_s \neq \varnothing$	$p(s) > 0$	$\varnothing$
$\succ_s = \varnothing$	$p(s) = 0$	$p(s) \in [0,1]$

positive, every element of the set $L_{p'}$ is nondegenerate. Second, the independent evidence required to identify null states must come from the preference relation $\succsim'$. Consequently we define a state $s \in S$ to be *evidently* null if $\succ_s = \varnothing$ and $\succ'_s \neq \varnothing$, where $\succ'_s$ denotes the strict preference relation between any pair of elements of $L_{p'}$ that are equal outside s. A state s is *evidently nonnull* if $\succ_s \neq \varnothing$. In between we have the intermediate case. These possibilities are summarized in Table 1.3.

If some state $s \in S$ is evidently nonnull—if $\succ_s \neq \varnothing$—then $\succ \neq \varnothing$. Note, however, that the opposite implication also holds. If the preference relation $\succsim$ is *nontrivial*—$\succ \neq \varnothing$—then the von Neumann–Morgenstern utility representation of $\succsim$, say w, is not constant for at least one $s \in S$. Since $w(\cdot, s)$ represents $\succsim_s$, $w(\cdot, s)$ not constant implies $\succ_s \neq \varnothing$. Hence there exists at least one nonnull state.

With this in mind we formulate the Axiom of weak consistency.

AXIOM (A′.7) (WEAK CONSISTENCY). *For all $s \in S$, a given strictly positive probability p' on S and for all f' and g' in $L_{p'}$, if f' equals g' outside s and $H(f') > H(g')$, then $f' \succ' g'$. Moreover, if s is evidently nonnull, then for all f' and g' in $L_{p'}$ such that f' equals g' outside s, $f' \succ' g'$ implies $H(f') > H(g')$.*

Axiom (A′.7) represents a weakening of the condition (Â.7) in that it requires consistency with a preference relation on a subset of $\hat{L}$. Thus it does not require that decision makers express preferences over prize–state lotteries with different, and thus incompatible, probability distributions over S. As was noted earlier, this may be a source of contention in accepting (Â.7) and consequently Theorem 1.4. Ridding ourselves of this condition, however, necessitates a certain weakening of the implications, as is made clear in Theorem 1.5.

THEOREM 1.5. *Given a binary relation $\succsim$ on L that satisfies axioms (A.1)–(A.3), (A.8), a strictly positive probability p' on S, and a binary relation $\succsim'$ on*

Table 1.3

	$\succ'_s \neq \varnothing$	$\succ'_s = \varnothing$
$\succ_s \neq \varnothing$	Evidently nonnull	$\varnothing$
$\succ_s = \varnothing$	Evidently null	Intermediate case

$L_{p'}$ that satisfies axioms (A'.4)–(A'.6), suppose that the two binary relations satisfy weak consistency. Then:

(a) There exists a real-valued function u on Z and a probability distribution p on S such that, for all f and g ∈ L, f ≿ g if and only if

$$(3) \qquad \sum_{s\in S} \sum_{x\in X(s)} p(s)u(x,s)[f(x,s) - g(x,s)] \geqq 0,$$

and for all f' and g' ∈ $L_{p'}$, f' ≿' g' if and only if

$$(4) \qquad \sum_{s\in S} \sum_{x\in X(s)} u(x,s)[f'(x,s) - g'(x,s)] \geqq 0.$$

(b) The u of part (a) is unique up to a unit-comparable transformation.
(c) For s evidently null, p(s) = 0, and for s evidently nonnull p(s) > 0. Furthermore, the probability p restricted to the event of all evidently nonnull states are unique.

The proof of Theorem 1.5 appears in Karni, Schmeidler, and Vind (1983). It can easily be reconstructed from the proof of Theorem 1.4. The implications of part (c) of Theorem 1.5 are summarized in Table 1.4.

1.10 Discussion

The theory of decision making under uncertainty summarized in Theorem 1.1 applies to a larger class of preference relations than the theories represented by the subsequent expected utility theorems. In view of the theory's generality, it is natural to question the need for imposing further restrictions on the preference relations to obtain the separation of subjective probabilities and utilities. One may be tempted to argue that this separation serves a purpose in allowing the processing of new information, by the application of Bayes's theorem to update the subjective probabilities. Insofar as decision theory is concerned, however, the purpose of updating the preference rela-

Table 1.4

	$>'_s \neq \varnothing$	$>'_s = \varnothing$
$>_s \neq \varnothing$	$p(s) > 0$	$\varnothing$
$>_s = \varnothing$	$p(s) = 0$	$p(s) \in [0,1]$

tions over acts in light of new information can be achieved without separating tastes from probability beliefs, by updating the valuation function in accordance with Bayes's theorem.

To see this suppose that, before choosing an act from the set L, a decision maker whose preferences over L satisfy the von Neumann–Morgenstern axioms is informed of the outcome of an experiment which contains information relevant to identifying the true state of nature. More specifically, let E be a finite set of possible outcomes of an experiment, and suppose that the decision maker knows the conditional probabilities $q(e|s)$, $e \in E$, $s \in S$, where $q(e|s) \geqq 0$ and $\Sigma_{e \in E} q(e|s) = 1$ for all $s \in S$. The decision maker's preferences are represented by the valuation function w, as implied by Theorem 1.1. The new information can be incorporated into the valuation function without imposing any further restrictions on the underlying preference ordering, by applying Bayes's theorem directly to the prior preferences, represented by w, and obtaining posterior preferences, represented by w'. The posterior preferences depend, of course, on the outcome of the experiment, but—and this is the crucial observation—are independent of the prior probability distribution p on S, provided that p is strictly positive. This idea is captured in Proposition 1.1.

PROPOSITION 1.1. *Given conditional probabilities q as above, a result of the experiment $e \in E$, and a prior preference represented by $w \in R^Z$, the posterior preference relation represented by $w' \in R^Z$, where w' is computed using Bayes's theorem, is independent of the prior probability p, provided that $p(s) > 0$ for all $s \in S$.*

Proof. Suppose an arbitrary p satisfying the condition of Proposition 1.1. Define, for each $s \in S$, $u(x,s) = w(x,s)/p(s)$. By Bayes's theorem, for each $s \in S$, $p(s|e) = p(s)q(e|s)/\Sigma_{t \in S} p(t)q(e|t)$. Since for all $s \in S$, $w'(x,s) = p(s|e)u(x,s)$, by substitution we get $w'(x,s) = q(e|s)w(x,s)/\Sigma_{t \in S} p(t)q(e|t)$.

The dependence of $w'(x,s)$ on p is through the coefficient $[\Sigma_{t \in S} p(t)q(e|t)]^{-1}$, which is independent of $s \in S$. Since the preference relation represented by w' is not changed when w is multiplied by a positive constant, we get the same posterior preference relation whatever the positive prior probability p.

According to Proposition 1.1 it is formally possible to obtain a posterior preference relation over acts from a prior preference relation, using Bayes's theorem. This is true regardless of whether the structure of the prior preferences is compatible with the existence of a unique prior probability distribution on *S*. Proposition 1.1, however, does not mean that decision makers actually revise their prior preferences according to Bayes's theorem. Neither does the assumption of the existence of unique prior probability beliefs imply the use of Bayes's theorem by decision makers, although the accepted practice is to use the uniqueness of the prior as evidence in support of the claim that decision makers are Bayesian. (A Bayesian decision maker is defined as an expected utility maximizer who, when facing new information, uses Bayes's theorem to revise his prior probability beliefs.)

The fact that the preference relation by itself does not imply the use of Bayesian procedures to absorb new information implies that different views on whether decision makers are Bayesian are possible. One view is to suppose that decision makers are Bayesian unless there is evidence to the contrary. In this case there is no apparent need for insistence on the uniqueness of the prior. The assumption that a decision maker is Bayesian, in conjunction with his prior preferences, is sufficient to determine his posterior references according to the procedure employed in the proof of Proposition 1.1. Further, insofar as the theory of decision making under uncertainty is concerned, this theory is fully characterized by Theorem 1.1. In other words, there is no need for restriction on the preference relations over acts beyond that implied by Axioms (A.1) through (A.3).

The viewpoint that is referred to as the accepted practice seeks to find a clue in the structure of the preferences themselves. More specifically, if the structure of the preferences determines a unique prior, then the decision maker is assumed to be Bayesian. Insistence on a unique prior restricts the class of preference relations that are compatible with Bayesian decision theory, either by the condition of state independence or by the condition of weak consistency with the auxiliary preferences on $L_{p'}$. According to this view the theory of decisions under uncertainty is represented by Theorem 1.2 or 1.5, respectively.

An even more stringent attitude merits attention in view of the possibility, not excluded by the existence of a unique prior when preferences are state dependent, that two distinct preference relations that incorporate two distinct conceivable posteriors will give rise to distinct priors. In other words, it is possible that a decision maker has prior preferences on the set of acts that satisfy the von Neumann–Morgenstern axioms, posterior preferences contingent on a posterior probability, say p', that satisfy the same axioms, and the condition of weak consistency. The same decision maker, when facing another conceivable posterior, say p'', has other posterior preferences that satisfy the von Neumann–Morgenstern axioms and the condition of weak consistency. Then, applying Theorem 1.5 twice, we obtain two unique but distinct priors. To exclude this possibility we need to impose the condition of strong consistency, with the corresponding auxiliary preferences on $\hat{L}$. The resulting decision theory is summarized by the implications of Theorem 1.4.

None of these tests can provide conclusive evidence concerning the issue of whether a decision maker is Bayesian. Under the postulated structure of preferences these issues must remain an independent tenet of the theory of decision making under uncertainty.

1.11 Related Work

The axiomatic approach to the derivation of subjective probability originated with the work of Ramsey (1931). The axiomatic approach to derivation of utilities from preference relations over probability distributions came from von Neumann and Morgenstern (1947). Savage (1954) presented a unified axiomatic approach to the derivation of subjective probabilities and utilities, under the assumption of state-independent preferences. Many authors elaborated on different aspects of the theory by offering alternative axiomatizations. Much of this work is summarized in Fishburn (1970).

Ramsey's method of deriving subjective probabilities, while not ruling out state-dependent or "ethically nonneutral" preferences, requires that there be some ethically neutral propositions. He did not pursue this issue in detail. An alternative axiomatization of expected utility theory with state-dependent preferences is offered in Fishburn (1973). Fishburn defines events as nonempty subsets of the set of states of nature and conditional acts as the set of acts conditioned on such events. He then assumes that decision makers have preference relations over the set of conditional acts that satisfy the von Neumann–Morgenstern axioms. In addition, Fishburn introduces the restriction that for every two disjoint events there is a preference overlap, which means that not all the consequences conditioned on one event are preferred to all the consequences conditioned on the other event. This axiom is irreconcilable with some applications that motivated the present work. In particular, in the context of flight insurance (see Chapter 2) the set of states of nature contains the states "life" and "death." Fishburn's axiom asserts that a rich passenger with no dependents may still prefer death over life if he takes out a large insurance policy. Since the set of consequences is not restricted, this implication seems untenable, as has been recognized by Fishburn (1974).

1.12 Proofs

Before proving Theorem 1.4 we introduce two lemmas. The first lemma is obvious and its proof is omitted.

LEMMA 1.1. *Suppose that the relation $\succsim$ on L and $\hat{\succsim}$ on $\hat{L}$ exist and $\succsim$ satisfies (A.1), (A.2), (A.3), and let $w \in R^Z$. If s is an obviously null state, then for all x and $y \in X(s)$, $w(x,s) = w(y,s)$.*

LEMMA 1.2. *Suppose that the relations $\succsim$ on L and $\hat{\succsim}$ on $\hat{L}$ exist and $\succsim$ satisfy (A.1), (A.2), (A.3), (A.8); then there exists an obviously nonnull $s \in S$.*

Proof. By way of negation, suppose that every $s \in S$ is obviously null. Then by Lemma 1.1, for all $s \in S$ and all x and y in $X(s)$, $w(x,s) = w(y,s)$. Hence for any f and $g \in L$; $\Sigma_{s\in S}\Sigma_{x\in X(s)} w(x,s)[f(x,s) - g(x,s)] = 0$; that is, $f \sim g$. This is a contradiction to (A.8).

1.12.1 Proof of Theorem 1.4.

(a) Let w and u be the functions obtained from Theorems 1.1 and 1.3, respectively. Choose an arbitrary nondegenerate $\hat{f} \in \hat{L}$ and let $f = H(\hat{f})$, $f \in L$. For any obviously nonnull $s \in S$ define the sets

$$L_s = \{g \in L | g \text{ equals } f \text{ outside } s\}$$

and

$$\hat{L}_s = \{\hat{g} \in \hat{L} | \hat{g} \text{ equals } \hat{f} \text{ outside } s\}.$$

Note that the mapping H restricted to $\hat{L}_s$ is one to one, and we can identify L_s with $\hat{L}_s$. Since s is obviously nonnull the relations $\succsim$ and $\hat{\succsim}$ restricted to L_s or $\hat{L}_s$ are identical. For the restricted relation $\succsim$, however, the function $w(\cdot,s)$ constitutes a von Neumann–Morgenstern utility function on $X(s)$. Similarly, for the restricted relation $\hat{\succsim}$ the function $u(\cdot,s)$ is also a von Neumann–Morgenstern utility function on $X(s)$. Hence $w(\cdot,s)$ is a positive linear transformation of $u(\cdot,s)$; that is, there is $c(s) > 0$ and $d(s)$ such that for all x in $X(s)$, $w(x,s) = c(s)u(x,s) + d(s)$. Invoking Theorem 1.1, we can rescale w so that for each such s we subtract from $w(\cdot,s)$ the constant $d(s)$. To avoid complicating the notation we also denote the rescaled function by w. Therefore, for each obviously nonnull s and each $x \in X(s)$ we have $w(x,s) = c(s)u(x,s)$.

Using Lemma 1.1 and Theorem 1.1 we assume, without loss of generality, that for all $x \in X(s)$ and for all obviously null s, $w(x,s) = 0$. Defining, for each obviously null $s \in S$, $c(s) = 0$, we have the equality $w(x,s) = c(s)u(x,s)$ for all $(x,s) \in Z$.

By Theorem 1.1 we have for all g and $h \in L$, $g \gtrsim h$ if and only if

$$\sum_{s \in S} \sum_{x \in X(s)} w(x,s)[g(x,s) - h(x,s)] \geqq 0,$$

which in turn is equivalent to $g \gtrsim h$ if and only if

$$\sum_{s \in S} \sum_{x \in X(s)} c(s)u(x,s)[g(x,s) - h(x,s)] \geqq 0.$$

By Lemma 1.2 there exists an obviously nonnull $s \in S$, so $\Sigma_{s \in S} c(s) > 0$, and we can define, for all $s \in S$, $p(s) = c(s)/\Sigma_{t \in S} c(t)$. In this case the previous inequality may be rewritten as $g \gtrsim h$ iff

$$\sum_{s \in S} \sum_{x \in X(s)} p(s)u(x,s)[g(x,s) - h(x,s)] \geqq 0.$$

p is the desired (subjective) probability distribution on S, and $p(s) = 0$ for obviously null s.

Part (b) follows from part (ii) of Theorem 1.1.

(c) Let s be a state for which the relation $\hat{>}$ restricted to s is nonempty; that is, there are $\hat{f}_s$ and $\hat{g}_s \in \hat{L}$ such that $\hat{f}_s$ equals $\hat{g}_s$ outside s and $\hat{f}_s \hat{>} \hat{g}_s$. Let p and u satisfy (1) and (2) of part (a); then $u(\cdot,s)$ is not constant on $X(s)$. Thus there exist $\bar{x}_s$ and $\underline{x}_s$ in $X(s)$ such that

$$u(\bar{x}_s,s) > u(\underline{x}_s,s).$$

If s is obviously null, then by definition $\hat{>}$ restricted to s is nonempty. Define g and h in L_s by $g(\bar{x}_s,s) = h(\underline{x}_s,s) = 1$. Then $p(s) > 0$ implies $p(s)[u(\bar{x}_s,s) - u(\underline{x}_s,s)] > 0$, which in turn implies $g > h$, a contradiction of the definition of obvious nullity of s. Hence for s obviously null, $p(s) = 0$.

If s is obviously nonnull and f_s and g_s are as in part (c), then by (1) of part (a) $\Sigma_{x \in X(s)} p(s)u(x,s)[f_s(x,s) - g_s(x,s)] > 0$. Thus $p(s) > 0$.

Next we shall prove that if for all s the relation $\hat{>}$ is nonempty, then the probability p of part (a) is unique. By way of negation, suppose that there exists a probability distribution over S, p' not equal to p. Using part (b) we may now write condition (1) of part (a) as

$$g \gtrsim h \text{ iff } \sum_{s \in S} \sum_{x \in X(s)} p'(s)u(x,s)[g(x,s) - h(x,s)] \geqq 0,$$

iff $\Sigma_{s \in S} \Sigma_{x \in X(s)} p(s)u(x,s)[g(x,s) - h(x,s)] \geqq 0$. We define lotteries in L such that the above inequalities contradict the assumption that for some t and $s \in S$, $p(s) > p'(s)$ and $p(t) < p'(t)$.

For r in [0,1] define

$$g_r(\bar{x}_s,s) = h_r(\underline{x}_t,t) = r,$$
$$g_r(\underline{x}_s,s) = h_r(\bar{x}_t,t) = 1 - r,$$
$$g_r(\underline{x}_t,t) = h_r(\underline{x}_s,s) = 1,$$

and outside s and t, g_r and h_r coincide.

Using condition (1) of part (a) as above,

$$rp(s)[u(\bar{x}_s,s) - u(\underline{x}_s,s)] + (1 - r)p(t)[u(\underline{x}_t,t) - u(\bar{x}_t,t)] \geqq 0$$

if and only if

$$rp'(s)[u(\bar{x}_s,s) - u(\underline{x}_s,s)] + (1 - r)p'(t)[u(\underline{x}_t,t) - u(\bar{x}_t,t)] \geqq 0.$$

The difference between the values of u in the first set of square brackets is positive and in the second set negative. The inequalities between the values of p and p' imply that $p(s)$ and $p'(t)$ are positive. Thus there exists $\bar{r}$ that turns the first inequality into an equality. Clearly for the same r the second inequality is false and the required contradiction has been obtained.

2 The Measurement of Risk Aversion

2.1 Introduction

It is common to classify attitudes toward risk into three categories—risk aversion, risk neutrality, and risk proclivity. Of these, risk aversion is by far the most prevalent. Participation in unfair gambles notwithstanding, many economic phenomena can be explained in terms of market response to the nearly universal desire to avoid bearing risk. Insurance, the issuance of common stock, cost-plus supply contracts, and long-term labor contracts are just a few examples of the wide range of arrangements whose purpose is to improve the allocation of risk bearing. The hypothesis of universal risk aversion is central to current perceptions of economic behavior and, in conjunction with the expected utility theory, it implies that utility functions display diminishing marginal utility of wealth.

Risk aversion may be sufficient to explain the existence of many observed practices and institutions. In itself, however, it is not sufficiently elaborate to permit the study of the full range of behavioral implications emanating from the desire to avoid bearing risk. This task requires more precise measures of the intensity of risk aversion.

An intuitively appealing measure of risk aversion is the risk premium, namely the maximum a decision maker would be willing to pay to avoid bearing risk. It is reasonable to expect that, *ceteris paribus,* the more risk averse the decision maker is, the more he would be willing to pay to avoid bearing a given risk. As a result of the seminal contributions of Pratt (1964) and Arrow (1965), we know that for absolute risks the partial ordering of decision makers according to the magnitude of the risk premium is equivalent to their ranking according to the magnitude of the negative of the ratio of the second derivative and the first derivative of their utility functions. (For risks that are proportional to the decision maker's wealth the analgous measure is the negative of the elasticity of the marginal utility of wealth.) Furthermore, these measures—and consequently the corresponding partial orderings—are invariant under positive linear transformations of the utility function—the class of transformations permitted according to the von Neumann-Morgenstern expected utility theory. I shall have more to say later about the Arrow-Pratt measures of risk aversion. At this point, it suffices to note that these measures were developed for state-independent preferences, and their usefulness is restricted to the analysis of problems involving such preferences. Here our main concern is to generalize the measurement of risk aversion to include state-dependent preferences.

The development of risk-aversion measures for state-dependent preferences raises a preliminary issue concerning the comparability of decision makers in terms of their atitudes toward risk. Unlike the case in which preferences are represented by a univariate, state-independent utility function, universal comparability of attitudes toward small risks does not obtain when the utility representation of preferences is either multivariate or state dependent. The first step in developing a measure of risk aversion for state-dependent preferences is thus to find a criterion for identifying comparable decision makers. This we do in the next section with the introduction of the reference set.

Traditionally the study of attitudes toward risk is concerned with the comparison of these attitudes among individuals who are identical in every respect except their risk aversion, and the comparison of attitudes toward risk of a given individual at different levels of wealth. In the case of univariate state-independent preferences these two lines of inquiry are not fundamentally different. In particular, the comparison of a given individual's risk aversion at different levels of wealth does not require the imposition of additional restrictions on the structure of the underlying preferences. When the utility function that represents the decision maker's preferences is either multivariate (for example, defined over many commodities) or state dependent, interpersonal comparison of risk aversion is fundamentally different from the comparison of risk aversion of the same individual at different levels of wealth. The latter comparison requires that the underlying preferences at distinct levels of wealth meet the prerequisite for comparability; the preferences must be self comparable. This implies certain restrictions on the structure of the ordinal preferences that are not required for the comparison of distinct decision makers at the same level of wealth. In this chapter I shall pursue both kinds of comparisons for state-dependent preferences. I shall have more to say about the correspondence between multivariate risk aversion and risk aversion for state-dependent preferences in Chapter 6.

Finally, in view of the severe restrictions on comparability imposed by my method of measuring risk aversion, my approach may appear overly limited. The reader should bear in mind, however, that this approach, limited as it may be, represents a generalization of the Arrow–Pratt theory.

2.2 The Reference Set

Interpersonal comparisons of attitudes toward risk require that the individuals being compared calibrate risks in the same manner. This implies that risk-averse individuals agree on what is the most preferred (least risky) distribution on the set of consequences in each situation. This is true whether the preferences are state dependent or not. We shall refer to the most preferred distribution within the set of all distributions with the same actuarial value as the *reference point* of this set. The set of all the reference points is the *reference set.*

2.2.1 Definition of the Reference Set

To define the reference set formally let a gamble on S, the finite set of states of nature, be a real-valued function on S—$\mathbf{w} \in R^S$ where for each $s \in S$, w_s denotes the payoff in s. Let W be the set of all gambles on S. Let P denote the set of all probability distributions on S. Thus $\mathbf{p} \in P$ is an $|S|$-dimensional nonnegative vector and $\Sigma_{s \in S} p_s = 1$. The expected utility functional V is a real-valued function on the Cartesian product $P \times W$, which is linear in the probabilities. For a given $\mathbf{p} \in P$ and $c \geqq 0$ let $B(\mathbf{p},c)$ be the subset of W such that for all $\mathbf{w} \in B$, $\Sigma_{s \in S} p_s w_s = c$. Thus $B(\mathbf{p},c)$ may be thought of as a budget set that includes all the elements of W with the same actuarial value c. Suppose that, given $\mathbf{p} \in P$ and c, a decision maker is allowed to choose his most preferred gamble in $B(\mathbf{p},c)$. Since he is an expected-utility maximizer, his choice is determined by the solution to

(P.1) $$\max_{\{\mathbf{w}\}} V(\mathbf{w},\mathbf{p}) \quad \text{subject to } \mathbf{w} \in B(\mathbf{p},c).$$

We define the *reference point* of V in $B(\mathbf{p},c)$ to be the solution to problem (P.1) and denote it by $\mathbf{w}^*(\mathbf{p},c)$. Holding $\mathbf{p}$ constant and letting c take any positive value, we obtain a set of reference points with distinct actuarial values. The set of all such points is the *reference set.*

DEFINITION 2.1 (THE REFERENCE SET) *For any* $\mathbf{p} \in P$, $RS_V(\mathbf{p}) = \{w^* \in B(\mathbf{p},c) \mid V(\mathbf{w}^*,\mathbf{p}) \geqq V(\mathbf{w},\mathbf{p}) \quad \forall \mathbf{w} \in B(\mathbf{p},c), c \geqq 0\}$.

Thus the reference set may be described as the optimal distribution of wealth across states of nature that is chosen by a risk-averse decision maker facing fair insurance. The nature of the reference set is determined by the structure of the expected utility functional. In many decision problems the reference set is independent of $\boldsymbol{p}$ (see Chapter 3). If the decision maker is strictly risk averse the reference set may be described as a vector of functions $\mathbf{f}(\cdot)$, where for each $s \in S, f_s(\cdot): R_+ \to R_+, f_s'(\cdot) > 0$ and for some $s \in S$, $f_s(\cdot)$ is the identify function.

In view of the crucial role of the reference set in the development of our ideas, it is worth considering in detail the reference sets of some specific decision problems.

2.2.2 State-Independent Preferences

Consider a risk-averse decision maker whose preferences are represented by the state-independent expected utility index $U(\boldsymbol{w},\boldsymbol{p}) = \Sigma_{s\in S} p_s U(w_s)$. Given $\boldsymbol{p}$ and c, the budget set is the hyperplane defined by $\Sigma_{s\in S} p_s w_s = c$. The necessary and sufficient conditions for the maximization of $U(\boldsymbol{w},\boldsymbol{p})$ are $U'(w_s') = U'(w_{s'})$ for all $s, s' \in S$. Since the utility function is state independent this implies that for all $s \in S$, $w_s = w^*$. Thus the reference set coincides with the certainty set; wealth is the same across states of nature. This is illustrated for the case of two states of nature in Figure 2.1. The indifference curve U_0 depicts a given expected utility. Its convexity is an implication of the assumption of risk aversion. The B_0 curve depicts the budget set. The slope of the budget set is $-p_1/p_2$. The tangency point of U_0 and B_0 is the optimal wealth distribution. It must always be on the certainty line. Hence RS_U coincides with the certainty line.

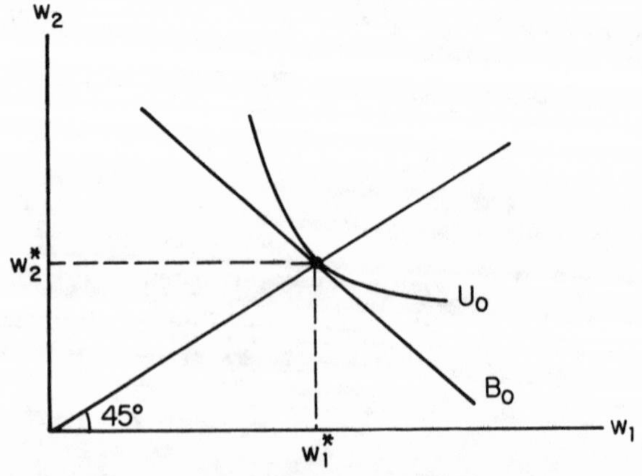

Figure 2.1 The reference set for state-independent preferences

When preferences are state-independent the main features of the reference set can be summarized by three observations. First, the reference set is independent of the probability distribution over the states of nature. This is an immediate implication of the definition of the reference set for this problem as the subset of W such that the marginal utility is equal across states of nature. Since the marginal utility is independent of $\boldsymbol{p}$, the reference set is independent of $\boldsymbol{p}$. In terms of Figure 2.1 this observation implies that changes in the probability distribution $\boldsymbol{p}$ tilt the budget set and the indifference curve so that their tangency point remains intact.

The second observation concerns the properties of the utility function on the reference set. Since the marginal utility of wealth is equal across states of nature and the utility function is state independent and strictly concave, the total wealth and the level of utility are equal across states of nature.

Finally, we observe the obvious fact that all decision makers whose preferences over $P \times W$ are state independent have identical reference sets. The significance of this observation becomes apparent once we show that the requisite condition for interpersonal comparison of risk aversion is that the reference sets of the persons being compared are the same. This may explain why early treatments of the issue of measurement of risk aversion, which were confined to state-independent preferences, failed to take explicit notice of the reference set. The prerequisites for comparability of attitudes toward risk were implicitly satisfied. Unfortunately, no such simple resolution of the requisite condition for comparability is possible when preferences are state dependent; an explicit consideration of the reference set is necessary.

2.2.3 State-Dependent Preferences

Consider a decision maker whose preferences on $P \times W$ are represented by the state-dependent expected utility index $U(\boldsymbol{w},\boldsymbol{p}) = \Sigma_{s \in S} p_s U_s(w_s)$. Suppose further that for all $s \in S$, U_s is strictly concave and twice continuously differentiable. Given the budget constraint $\Sigma_{s \in S} p_s w_s = c$, the necessary and sufficient conditions for the maximization of $U(\boldsymbol{w},\boldsymbol{p})$ are

$$(2.1) \qquad U_s'(w_s^*) = \lambda \qquad \forall\, s \in S$$

where $\lambda > 0$ is a Lagrangian multiplier whose value is independent of the state of nature. The reference set for a decision problem involving two states is illustrated in Figure 2.2. As in the previous example, the reference set is independent of the probability distribution $\boldsymbol{p}$. The positive slope of the reference set is a consequence of the strict concavity of the utility functions. Notice also that since $U_s'(\cdot)$ is monotonic decreasing and continuous, it

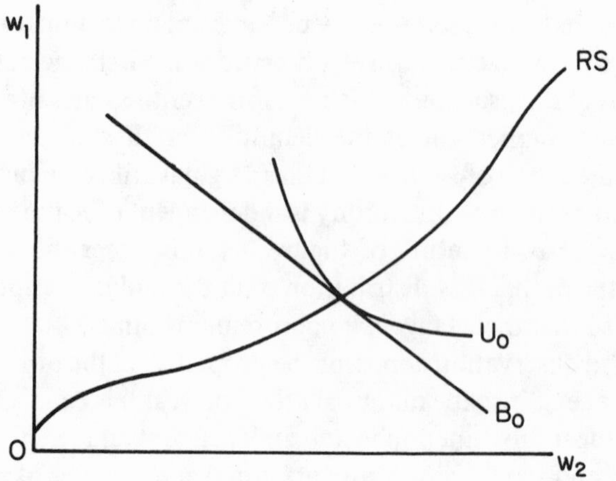

Figure 2.2 A reference set for state-dependent preferences

has an inverse, say $(U_s')^{-1}$. Thus the functions describing the reference set are given by $w_2 = (U_2')^{-1}[U_1'(w_1)] \equiv f_2(w_1)$, and $f_1(w_1) \equiv w_1$. Clearly, $f_2'(w_1) = [U_1''(w_1)]/[U_2''(w_2)] > 0$ and $f_1'(w_1) = 1$.

This example illustrates that when the preference relation on $P \times W$ is state dependent the equality of the marginal utility of wealth across states does not, in general, imply the equality of the utility or wealth across states of nature. Observe also that not all risk-averse expected-utility-maximizing decision makers have identical reference sets. Because it implies that interpersonal comparisons of aversion to risk must be restricted to groups of decision makers whose reference sets are identical, this observation cannot be overemphasized. While this condition is quite restrictive, it does enable us to generalize the theory of risk aversion to include decision problems involving state-dependent preferences, which could not be handled by the Arrow–Pratt theory. At the same time, the requirement of identical reference sets also makes clear the necessary limitations of this generalization.

2.2.4 Comparability

DEFINITION 2.2. *Let U and V be utility representations of the preference relations $\succsim_u$ and $\succsim_v$ on $P \times W$. U is said to be globally comparable to V if and only if $RS_U \subset RS_V$.*

Notice that comparability in the sense of Definition 2.2 is not symmetric. The significance of this observation will become apparent in Chapter 5. It is sufficient to note at this point that the reference set may be "thick" if the utility functions are not strictly concave. For instance, the reference set of a state-independent linear utility function coincides with the domain of the utility function. Consequently, every utility function is comparable to the state-independent linear utility function, but not vice versa. In the same vein, two distinct utility functions may be comparable to a third utility function but not to one another. Clearly, if two decision makers are strictly risk-averse and one of them is comparable to the other, then they are *mutually comparable.* Notice also that if the dependence of the preferences on the state of nature is represented by a shift in the level of utility across states but no change in the marginal utility, the prerequisite for comparability is still satisfied. It is the change in the marginal utility of a given level of wealth across states that accounts for the destruction of universal comparability of decision makers.

Equipped with the notion of the reference set, we are in a position to pursue the question of interpersonal comparison of risk aversion.

2.3 Risk Premiums

Consider two mutually comparable risk-averse decision makers. In what sense is it meaningful to say that one is more risk averse than the other? An intuitively appealing answer is that, other things being equal, the more risk-averse individual should be willing to pay more to avoid a given risk. The *ceteris paribus* caveat includes the initial allocation of wealth across states and the probability distribution over the states of nature. The idea of quantifying the relation "more risk-averse than" by a monetary measure was originated by Pratt (1964), who used the term "risk premium" to describe this measure.

2.3.1 Definition of Risk Premium

Generally speaking, a risk pemium is defined as the difference between the actuarial value of the decision maker's initial wealth and the smallest actuarial level of his wealth that yields the same level of expected utility. For a risk-averse individual the position on the reference set is, of course, the most preferred among all the positions that can be attained given the actuarial value of wealth. He should be willing to pay something, in terms of actuarial wealth, for the privilege of attaining a position in his reference set. The risk premium stands for the maximum reduction in actuarial value that the decision maker is willing to accept to attain a point on the reference set rather than bear actuarially neutral risk. Figure 2.3 illustrates this for the case of two states of nature. As before, the curve B_0 depicts wealth distributions of equal actuarial value. The point K represents the original wealth distribution across the two states of nature. Relative to position M, K represents an actuarially neutral risk. Point L depicts the element of the reference set that yields the same level of expected utility U_0 as the original distribution. Henceforth we refer to this position as the *reference equivalence.* The risk premium is the difference between the actuarial value of the position K and its reference equivalence, and is measured along the 45-degree line by π.

Formally, let $\boldsymbol{w}^0$ denote a position on RS_U such as M in Figure 2.3. Let $\boldsymbol{x}$ be a vector in $R^{|S|}$ such that $\Sigma_{s\in S} p_s x_s = 0$. Let $\pi^U(\boldsymbol{w}^0,\boldsymbol{x},\boldsymbol{p})$ be defined by the equation

$$\text{(2.2)} \qquad \sum_{s\in S} p_s U_s(f_s(w_t^0 - \pi^U)) = \sum_{s\in S} p_s U_s(w_s^0 + x_s).$$

Assuming the existence of the expectations of the right side of Eq. (2.2), the existence and uniqueness of π^U follows from the monotonicity of U_s and f_s and from the fact that, as a function of π^U, the expected utility functional covers its range. Let the risk premium vector $\boldsymbol{\pi}^U$ be defined as $\boldsymbol{\pi}^U(\boldsymbol{w}^0,\boldsymbol{x},\boldsymbol{p}) = \boldsymbol{w}^0 - \boldsymbol{f}(w_t^0 - \pi^U)$; in Figure 2.3 the position analogous to $\boldsymbol{f}(w_t^0 - \pi^U)$ is depicted by the point L. The risk premium π_U is defined as

$$\text{(2.3)} \qquad \pi_U(\boldsymbol{w}^0,\boldsymbol{x},\boldsymbol{p}) = \sum_{s\in S} p_s \pi_s^U(\boldsymbol{w}^0,\boldsymbol{x},\boldsymbol{p})$$

Clearly, if the preferences are state independent our definition of a risk premium is the same as that of Pratt (1964).

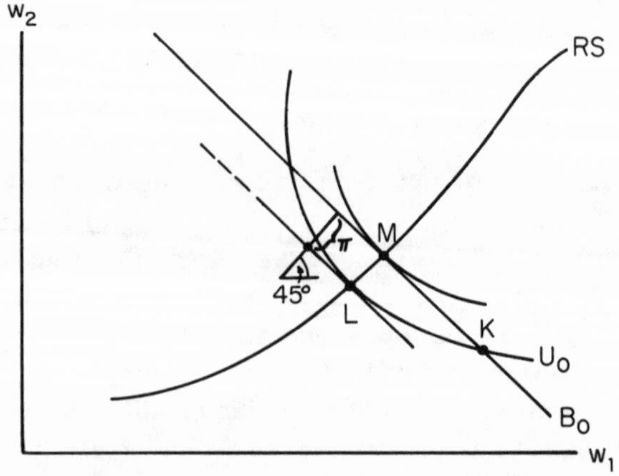

Figure 2.3 The risk premium

2.3.2 "More Risk-Averse"

DEFINITION 2.3. *Let U and V be mutually comparable, risk-averse, state-dependent utility functions. U is said to be more risk averse than V if and only if* $\pi_U(\boldsymbol{w},\boldsymbol{x},\boldsymbol{p}) \geqq \pi_V(\boldsymbol{w},\boldsymbol{p},\boldsymbol{x})$ *for all* $\boldsymbol{w} \in RS$, $\boldsymbol{p} \in P$, *and* $\boldsymbol{x} \in R^{|S|}$ *such that* $\Sigma_{s\in S} p_s x_s = 0$.

If U is comparable to V but not vice versa the same definition applies, provided that $\boldsymbol{f}(w_t)$ in the definition of $\boldsymbol{\pi}^U$ is in RS_U.

To relate the notion of risk premium to characteristics of the utility function, namely to identify the restrictions on the utility functions U and V that would make U more risk-averse than V in the sense of Definition 2.3, consider the case of small risks (let $|\boldsymbol{x}| < \epsilon \boldsymbol{i}$, where $\boldsymbol{i}$ denotes the unit vector and $\epsilon > 0$ is arbitrarily close to zero). Taking the Taylor expansion on both sides of Eq. (2.2) around $\boldsymbol{w}^0 \in RS_U$, we get

$$\sum_{s\in S} p_s U_s(f_s(w_t^0 - \pi^U)) \approx \sum_{s\in S} p_s U_s(w_s^0) - \pi^U \sum_{s\in S} p_s U_s'(w_s^0) f_s'(w_t^0) \tag{2.4}$$

and

$$\sum_{s\in S} p_s U_s(w_s^0 + x_s) \approx \sum_{s\in S} p_s U_s(w_s^0) + \sum_{s\in S} p_s U_s'(w_s^0) x_s + \frac{1}{2} \sum_{s\in S} p_s U_s''(w_s^0) x_s^2. \tag{2.5}$$

Equating (2.4) and (2.5) as required by (2.2) and using (2.1), we solve π^U to obtain

$$\pi^U \approx -\cdot \frac{1}{2A} \sum_{s\in S} p_s \left[\frac{U_s''(w_s^0)}{U_s'(w_s^0)}\right] x_s^2, \tag{2.6}$$

where

$$A = \sum_{s\in S} p_s f_s'(w_t^0).$$

From Eq. (2.3) and the definition $\boldsymbol{\pi}^U(\boldsymbol{w}^0,\boldsymbol{x},\boldsymbol{p})$ the first-order approximation for π_U is

$$\pi_U \approx \pi^U \cdot A. \tag{2.7}$$

Hence

$$\pi_U \approx \frac{1}{2} \sum_{s\in S} p_s \left(-\frac{U_s''(w_s^0)}{U_s'(w_s^0)}\right) x_s^2, \tag{2.8}$$

or in matrix notation,

$$\pi_U \approx \tfrac{1}{2} \boldsymbol{x}^t R_U(\boldsymbol{w}^0) \boldsymbol{x}, \tag{2.9}$$

where $R_U(\boldsymbol{w}^0)$ is a diagonal matrix whose typical element is $p_s[-U_s''(w_s^0)/U_s'(w_s^0)]$ and $\boldsymbol{x}^t$ is the transpose of $\boldsymbol{x}$.

The expression R_U is a matrix measure of local absolute risk aversion. Equation (2.9) reveals the properties of the utility functions that are relevant for interpersonal comparability of risk aversion. Referring back to Definition 2.3, we observe that if $\pi_V(\boldsymbol{w}^0,\boldsymbol{x},\boldsymbol{p}) \leqq \pi_U(\boldsymbol{w}^0,\boldsymbol{x},\boldsymbol{p})$ for all $\boldsymbol{p}$, it follows from (2.8) that

$$(2.10) \qquad -\frac{U_s''(w_s)}{U_s'(w_s)} \geqq -\frac{V_s''(w_s)}{V_s'(w_s)}, \qquad \forall s \in S.$$

That is to say that U displays a larger Arrow–Pratt measure of risk aversion than V for every $s \in S$.

2.4 Interpersonal Comparative Risk Aversion

For small risks the binary relation "more risk-averse than" is a complete ordering on sets of comparable risk-averse utility functions. Because attitudes toward risk may change with variations in wealth, some utility functions whose attitudes toward small risks can be ordered according to the relation "more risk-averse than" do not preserve this order in the face of large risks. Hence when no restrictions are imposed on the admissible risks, the binary relation "more risk-averse than" is a partial ordering. Utility functions that belong to this relation are only those that are comparable in the sense of Definition 2.2 and whose relative ranking according to their aversion to small risk is invariable along the reference set.

For utility functions that satisfy this condition the relation "more risk-averse than" may be defined in two other equivalent and useful ways.

THEOREM 2.1. *Let U and V be mutually comparable, risk-averse, state-dependent, twice continuously differentiable utility functions. The following conditions are equivalent in either the strong or the weak form:*

(i) $$-\frac{U_s''(w)}{U_s'(w)} \geqq [>] -\frac{V_s''(w)}{V_s'(w)} \qquad \forall s \in S \text{ and } w \geqq 0.$$

(ii) *For every $\boldsymbol{p} \in P$ there exists a monotonic increasing [strictly] concave transformation $T_{\boldsymbol{p}}$ such that $\Sigma_{s\in S} p_s U_s(f_s(w)) = T_{\boldsymbol{p}}[\Sigma_{s\in S} p_s V_s(f_s(w))]$ and $T'_{\boldsymbol{p}}[\Sigma_{s\in S} p_s V_s[f_s(w)]]$ is independent of $\boldsymbol{p}$.*

(iii) *$\pi_U(\boldsymbol{w}^0,\boldsymbol{x},\boldsymbol{p}) \geqq [>] \pi_V(\boldsymbol{w}^0,\boldsymbol{x},\boldsymbol{p})$ for all $\boldsymbol{w} \in RS_U$, $\boldsymbol{p} \in P$ and $\boldsymbol{x}$ such that $\Sigma_{s\in S} p_s x_s = 0$.*

The first definition states that a utility function U is more risk averse than a comparable utility function V if its Arrow–Pratt measure of risk aversion is larger than that of V in every state of nature and for every level of wealth. The second definition states that for every $\boldsymbol{p} \in P$ the expected utility of U is a concave transformation of the expected utility of V along the reference set. In particular, it implies the existence of concave transformations, one for each state of nature, such that for each state of nature U is a concave transformation of V. Finally, the last definition is a statement about the relative size of the risk premiums. The risk premium of U exceeds that of V for every actuarially neutral risk and every initial wealth distribution across states. Notice that if U and V are not mutually comparable, but $RS_U \subset RS_V$, Theorem 2.1 is still valid provided that $\boldsymbol{f}(w) \in RS_U$ for all positive w.

If the preference relation on $P \times W$ is state independent, then we have the following corollary of Theorem 2.1.

COROLLARY 2.1 (PRATT 1964). *Let U and V be state-independent, twice continuously differentiable utility functions. The following conditions are equivalent in either the strong or the weak form:*

(i) $-[U''(w)]/[U'(w)] \geqq [>] -[V''(w)]/[V'(w)]$ *for all* w *[and > for at least one* w *in every interval].*

(ii) *There exists a monotonic increasing and [strictly] concave transformation* T *such that* $U(w) = T[V(w)]$.

(iii) $\pi_U(w,\tilde{z}) \geqq [>] \pi_V(w,\tilde{z})$ *for all* w *and any random variable* $\tilde{z}$ *such that* $E\{\tilde{z}\} = 0$ *and* π_h, $h = V,U$, *is defined by* $h(w - \pi_h) = E\{h(w + \tilde{z})\}$.

Thus the measure of absolute risk aversion for the case of state-independent preferences is a special case of the measure of absolute risk aversion when preferences are state-dependent.

2.5 Changing Attitudes toward Risk

Attitudes toward risk may change systematically with the individual's wealth. Regarding the nature of this change, Arrow (1965) proposed the hypotheses of decreasing (with wealth) absolute risk aversion and increasing relative risk aversion. (The latter notion is a measure of aversion to risks that are proportional to the decision maker's wealth.) These hypotheses have interesting implications for individual behavior under uncertainty. In particular they imply that when there are two assets, one risky and the other risk-free, the optimal portfolio allocation of a risk-averse decision maker will be such that when his wealth increases the absolute investment in the risky asset increases but its relative share in the portfolio declines.

2.5.1 Autocomparability

It is tempting to try to generalize the notion of decreasing (constant, increasing) absolute risk aversion to the case of state-dependent preferences, by assuming that for each state of nature the corresponding utility function displays decreasing (constant, increasing) absolute risk aversion in the sense of Arrow and Pratt. As the following example from Röell (1983) shows, however, this is not a sufficient condition for decreasing absolute risk aversion in the presence of state-dependent preferences.

Example: Let $S = \{s,t\}, p_s = 0.1, p_t = 0.9$. The decision maker's preferences are represented by the utility functions $U_s(w_s) = 1 - e^{-w_s}$, $U_t(w_t) = \log w_t$; U_s displays constant absolute risk aversion and U_t displays decreasing absolute risk aversion. The reference set is given by the equation $w_t = e^{w_s}$. Let the initial wealth be given by the vector $(0, e + 0.9)$. The element on the reference set with the same actuarial value is $(1,e)$. The risk premium is 0.724. Now let the initial wealth increase to $(1,e^2 + 0.9)$. The corresponding point on the reference set is $(2,e^2)$. The risk, defined as the deviation of the actual wealth position from the reference set, is $(-1,0.9)$ in both instances. The risk premium that corresponds to the higher expected wealth is 1.462. Hence, although the underlying utility functions display constant and decreasing absolute risk aversion, respectively, the behavior of the risk premium indicates increasing absolute risk aversion.

The key to this puzzle is to be found in the nature of the reference set itself. Our study of interpersonal comparative risk aversion suggests that the requisite condition for comparing the attitudes toward risk of distinct individuals according to the relation "more risk-averse than" is that they have identical reference sets. To apply this approach to the behavior of a given individual at different levels of actuarial wealth we need to specify the sense in which his preferences are comparable across levels of actuarial wealth. In other words, we need to specify when the reference set of a given individual is identical at distinct levels of actuarial wealth. To do so, consider two distinct elements of the reference set, say $\boldsymbol{w}^0$ and $\boldsymbol{w}'$. Let N^0 and N' denote the disjoint neighborhoods of $\boldsymbol{w}^0$ and $\boldsymbol{w}'$ in the reference set.

Let M be mappings of W into itself, defined as follows: For all $\boldsymbol{w} \in W$, $M(\boldsymbol{w} | \langle \boldsymbol{w}^0, \boldsymbol{w}' \rangle) = \boldsymbol{w} + (\boldsymbol{w}' - \boldsymbol{w}^0)$. Using these notations we introduce a definition.

DEFINITION 2.4. *A preference relation on $P \times W$ is said to be autocomparable (across levels of wealth) if and only if for any two elements $\mathbf{w}^0$, $\mathbf{w}' \in RS$ and the corresponding neighborhoods N^0, N' in RS, $M(\cdot \mid \langle \mathbf{w}^0, \mathbf{w}' \rangle)$ maps N^0 into N' or $M(\cdot \mid \langle \mathbf{w}', \mathbf{w}^0 \rangle)$ maps N' into N^0.*

This discussion is illustrated in Figure 2.4. The mapping $M(\cdot \mid \langle \mathbf{w}^0, \mathbf{w}' \rangle)$ is depicted by the shift of the coordinate system. The image of N^0 is depicted by the dotted line. In panel (a) the preference relation is not autocomparable; in panel (b) it is.

As suggested by this illustration, the condition of autocomparability is equivalent to linearity of the reference set. In other words, autocomparability is equivalent to the condition that the functions $\mathbf{f}(w)$ describing the reference set are linear in w. Clearly, all state-independent preferences are autocomparable. Some, but not all, state-dependent preferences are autocomparable. In general, the class of autocomparable preference orderings on $P \times W$ has the following parametric representation (see Röell, 1983). Let U_t be a utility representation of the decision maker's conditional preferences in some arbitrary state $t \in S$. If, for all $s \in S$, $s \neq t$, the conditional preferences are represented by state-dependent utility functions U_s such that $U_s(w) = a_s U_t[(1/a_s)\, w_t - (b_s/a_s)] + k_s$, where $a_s > 0$ and b_s and k_s are arbitrary constants, then the reference set is represented by the vector of functions $\mathbf{f}(w)$ such that for all $s \in S$, $s \neq t$, $f_s(w) = a_s w + b_s$ and $f_t(w) = w$.

2.5.2 *Decreasing Absolute Risk Aversion*

DEFINITION 2.5. *An autocomparable preference relation on $P \times W$ is said to display decreasing (increasing, constant) absolute risk aversion if and only if*

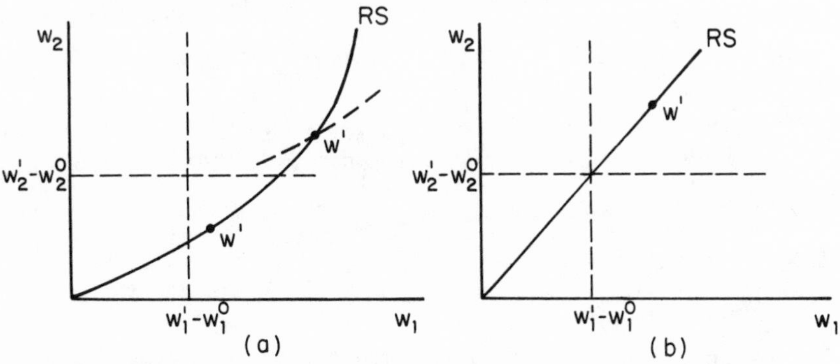

Figure 2.4 An illustration of autocomparable (b) and nonautocomparable (a) preference relations

for all $w \geqq 0$ *and* $a > 0$, *and any given* $\boldsymbol{p} \in P$ *and* $\boldsymbol{x} \in R^{|S|}$ *such that* $\Sigma_{s \in S} p_s x_s = 0$, $\pi(\boldsymbol{f}(w),\boldsymbol{x},\boldsymbol{p}) > (<,=) \pi(\boldsymbol{f}(w+a),\boldsymbol{x},\boldsymbol{p})$, *where* π *is the risk premium defined in (2.3) above.*

Equivalent and analytically useful characterizations of decreasing absolute risk aversion are given in Theorem 2.2.

THEOREM 2.2. *Let U be a twice continuously differentiable utility representation of an autocomparable preference relation on* $P \times W$; *then the following conditions are equivalent:*

(i) *For all* $s \in S$, $-U_s''(w)/U_s'(w)$ *decreases in w.*
(ii) *For every* $\boldsymbol{p} \in P$ *there exists a monotonic increasing concave transformation* $T_{\boldsymbol{p}}$ *such that for every* $w \geqq 0$ *and real number* $a > 0$, $\Sigma_{s \in S} p_s U_s(f_s(w)) = T_{\boldsymbol{p}}[\Sigma_{s \in S} p_s U_s(f_s(w+a))]$. $T_{\boldsymbol{p}}'[\cdot]$ *is independent of* $\boldsymbol{p}$.
(iii) $\pi(\boldsymbol{f}(w),\boldsymbol{x},\boldsymbol{p}) \geqq \pi(\boldsymbol{f}(w+a),\boldsymbol{x},\boldsymbol{p})$ *for all* $w \geqq 0$, $a > 0$, $\boldsymbol{p} \in P$, *and all* $\boldsymbol{x}$ *such that* $\Sigma_{s \in S} p_s x_s = 0$.

The proof of Theorem 2.2 follows from that of Theorem 2.1 upon defining, for all $s \in S$, $V_s,(f_s(w) + x_s) = U_s(f_s(w + a) + x_s)$. Notice that if for some $s \in S$ condition (i) holds, then by autocomparability it holds for all $s \in S$. Notice also that autocomparability is a sufficient condition for the equivalence of conditions (i)–(iii) in Theorem 2.2. It is also a necessary condition for the case of constant risk aversion. It is not yet clear whether it is also a necessary condition for the equivalence of conditions (i)–(iii) in the case of increasing and decreasing risk aversion. Since state-independent preferences are autocomparable, Theorem 2.2 implies a corollary.

COROLLARY 2.2 (PRATT 1964). *Let U be a state-independent, twice continuously differentiable utility function. Then the following conditions are equivalent:*
(i) The local risk aversion $-U''(w)/U'(w)$ *is decreasing in w.*
(ii) The risk premium $\pi(w,\tilde{z})$ *is a decreasing function of w for all* $\tilde{z}$, *where* $\tilde{z}$ *is a random variable.*

2.6 Related Work

The measures of absolute and relative risk aversion for state-independent utility functions were developed independently by Arrow (1965) and Pratt

(1964). Arrow developed his ideas within the context of a concrete economic problem, namely the optimal portfolio allocation between a risky and a riskless asset (money). Pratt's approach is more formal. He was the first to introduce the notion of risk premium as a formal measure of risk aversion and to relate it to the aforementioned properties of the utility function. The inequalities involved in Pratt's main result (Corollary 2.1) were not new, however, having appeared in Hardy, Littlewood, and Polya (1934). Stronger measures of risk aversion were introduced by Ross (1981) to resolve a difficulty in portfolio selection theory. The problem is that the Arrow–Pratt measures of risk aversion do not imply that a more risk-averse individual chooses a less risky portfolio position when there are two risky but no riskless assets to choose from.

A common feature of these measures is that they characterize risk aversion in the case of univariate state-independent preferences. Thus the requisite conditions for comparability of attitudes toward risk, either among individuals or for a given individual among distinct levels of actuarial wealth, are implicitly satisfied. The case of multivariate, state-independent preferences was studied by Kihlstrom and Mirman (1974, 1981) and Diamond and Stiglitz (1974). They concluded that the prerequisite for comparability of risk aversion is that the individuals being compared have identical ordinal preferences on the commodity space. In Chapter 6 I shall consider the correspondence between these restrictions on comparability and those implied by the identity of the reference set in detail.

Yaari (1969) suggested a way of measuring risk aversion for state-independent utility functions in the context of the state–preference approach.

2.7 Proofs

2.7.1 Proof of Theorem 2.1

Before proving the main theorem we establish the following result.

LEMMA 2.1. *For any given* $\mathbf{p} \in P$ *and all* $\mathbf{x}$ *such that* $\Sigma_{s\in S} p_s x_s = 0$ *and* $\mathbf{w}^* \in RS$,

$$\sum_{s\in S} p_s T_s[V_s(w_s^* + x_s)] \leqq T_{\mathbf{p}}\left[\sum_{s\in S} p_s V_s(w_s^* + x_s)\right],$$

where $T_s \equiv T_{\mathbf{p}}$ *for* $\mathbf{p} \in P$ *such that* $p_s = 1$, $p_t = 0$, $\forall t \in S - \{s\}$.

Proof. Define the following functions:

$$G(h) = \sum_{s \in S} p_s T_s[V_s(w_s^* + hx_s)],$$

$$H(h) = T_p\left[\sum_{s \in S} p_s V_s(w_s^* + hx_s)\right].$$

Since $U_s(w) = T_s[V_s(w)]$ for all $s \in S$, $G(0) = H(0)$. By concavity of V_s we have, for all $s \in S$,

$$V_s(w_s^* + hx_s) - V_s(w_s^*) \geqq h \cdot V_s'(w_s^* + hx_s)x_s \equiv h \cdot \beta_s \tag{2.11}$$

and

$$V_s(w_s^* + hx_s) - V_s(w_s^*) \leqq hV_s'(w_s^*)x_s \equiv h \cdot \alpha_s. \tag{2.12}$$

From Eqs. (2.12) and (2.11) we obtain, for all $s \in S$,

$$V_s(w_s^* + hx_s) > V_s(w_s^*) \Rightarrow \alpha_s > 0,$$
$$V_s(w_s^* + hx_s) < V_s(w_s^*) \Rightarrow \beta_s < 0.$$

Next we shall show that for all $s \in S$, $\beta_s \leqq \alpha_s$.

$$\begin{aligned}\beta_s &= V_s'(w_s^* + hx_s)x_s = V_s'(w_s^*)x_s + hV''_s(w_s^* + \theta x_s)x_s^2 \\ &\leqq V_s'(w_s^*)x_s \equiv \alpha_s,\end{aligned}$$

where $\theta \in [0,h]$, and the concavity of V_s is used. Since T_s is concave,

$$\beta_s > 0 \Rightarrow T_s'[V_s(w_s^* + hx_s)] < T_s'[V_s(w_s^*)].$$

Thus for all β_s and all $s \in S$,

$$T_s'[V_s(w_s^* + hx_s)]\beta_s \leqq T_s'[V_s(w_s^*)]\beta_s. \tag{2.13}$$

Differentiating $G(h)$ with respect to h and using (2.13), we get

$$\begin{aligned}G'(h) &= \sum_{s \in S} p_s T_s'[V_s(w_s^* + hx_s)]\, V_s'(w_s^* + hx_s)x_s \\ &= \sum_{s \in S} p_s T_s'[V_s(w_s^* + hx_s)]\beta_s \leqq \sum_{s \in S} p_s T_s'[V_s(w_s^*)]\beta_s \\ &= \sum_{s \in S} p_s T_p'\left[\sum_{s \in S} p_s V_s(w_s^*)\right]\beta_s \\ &\leqq T_p'\left[\sum_{s \in S} p_s V_s(w_s^* + hx_s)\right]\sum_{s \in S} p_s \beta_s,\end{aligned}$$

where use has been made of the facts that, since $\boldsymbol{w}^* \in RS$, $\Sigma_{s\in S} p_s V_s(w_s^*) \geqq \Sigma_{s\in S} p_s V_s(w_s^* + hx_s)$ and $T_s'[V_s(w_s^*)] = T_p'[\Sigma_{s\in S} p_s V_s(w_s^*)]$. The last statement is proved below as part of Theorem 2.1.

Differentiating $H(h)$ we have

$$H'(h) = T_p'\left[\sum_{s\in S} p_s V_s(w_s^* + hx_s)\right] \cdot \sum_{s\in S} p_s V_s'(w_s^* + hx_s)x_s$$
$$= T_p'\left[\sum_{s\in S} p_s V_s(w_s^* + hx_s)\right] \cdot \sum_{s\in S} p_s \beta_s.$$

Thus $G'(h) \leqq H'(h)$ for $h > 0$. Hence $G(h) \leqq H(h)$ for all $h \geqq 0$.

Proof of Theorem 2.1. The proof consists of establishing the following chain of implications: (i) ⇒ (ii) ⇒ (iii) ⇒ (i).

(i) ⇒ (ii): For any $\boldsymbol{p} \in P$, differentiating the equation defining T_p with respect to w, we get

$$(2.14)\qquad T_p'\left[\sum_{s\in S} p_s V_s(f_s(w))\right] = \frac{\sum_{s\in S} p_s U_s'(f_s(w)) f_s'(w)}{\sum_{s\in S} p_s V_s'(f_s(w)) f_s'(w)} = \frac{U_t'(f_t(w))}{V_t'(f_t(w))} > 0$$

for any $t \in S$. Notice that the last equality in Eq. (2.14) follows from equality of the marginal utility of wealth across states of nature on RS. Note also that T_p' is independent of $\boldsymbol{p}$.

Differentiating $ln\ T_p'$ with respect to w, we get [using the last term in Eq. (2.14)]

$$(2.15)\qquad \frac{-T_p''\left[\sum_{s\in S} p_s V_s(f_s(w))\right] \cdot A}{T_p'\left[\sum_{s\in S} p_s V_s(f_s(w))\right]} = \left[-\frac{U_t''(f_t(w))}{U_t'(f_t(w))}\right] - \left[-\frac{V_t''(f_t(w))}{V_t'(f_t(w))}\right],$$

where $A = V_t'(f_t(w))\ \Sigma_{s\in S} p_s f_s'(w) > 0$. From (i), however, the right side of Eq. (2.15) is positive. Hence $T_p'' < 0$.

(ii) ⇒ (iii): For any $\boldsymbol{p} \in P$,

$$\begin{aligned}\sum_{s\in S} p_s U_s(f_s(w-\pi^U)) &\equiv \sum_{s\in S} p_s U_s(f_s(w)+x_s)\\ &= \sum_{s\in S} p_s T_s[V_s(f_s(w)+x_s)] \leqq T_{\boldsymbol{p}}\left[\sum_{s\in S} p_s V_s(f_s(w)+x_s)\right]\\ &= T_{\boldsymbol{p}}\left[\sum_{s\in S} p_s U_s(f_s(w-\pi^V))\right] = \sum_{s\in S} p_s U_s(f_s(w-\pi^V)),\end{aligned}$$

where use has been made of Lemma 2.1. $\Sigma_{s\in S} p_s U_s(f_s(w))$, however, is monotonic increasing in w. Hence $\pi^U(\boldsymbol{f}(w),\boldsymbol{x},\boldsymbol{p}) \geqq \pi^V(\boldsymbol{f}(w),\boldsymbol{x},\boldsymbol{p})$ for all $\boldsymbol{f}(w) \in RS$, $\boldsymbol{x}$ such that $\Sigma_{s\in S} p_s x_s = 0$, and $\boldsymbol{p} \in P$. Since U and V are comparable, this in turn implies that $\pi_U(\boldsymbol{f}(w),\boldsymbol{x},\boldsymbol{p}) \geqq \pi_V(\boldsymbol{f}(w),\boldsymbol{x},\boldsymbol{p})$.

(iii) ⇒ (i): Let $\mathbf{z}$ satisfy $\Sigma_{s\in S} p_s z_s = 0$, and choose $\boldsymbol{x} = h\mathbf{z}$. Differentiating π^U with respect to h and evaluating at $h = 0$ we get

$$\left.\frac{d\pi^U}{dh}\right|_{h=0} = -\frac{\sum_{s\in S} p_s U_s'(f_s(w))z_s}{\sum_{s\in S} p_s U_s'(f_s(w))f_s'(w)} = 0.$$

Differentiating π^U again with respect to h and evaluating at $h = 0$ we obtain

$$\left.\frac{d^2\pi^U}{dh^2}\right|_{h=0} = -\frac{\sum_{s\in S} p_s U_s''(f_s(w))z_s^2}{\sum_{s\in S} p_s U_s'(f_s(w)) \cdot f_s'(w)} = \frac{\sum_{s\in S} p_s\left[-\frac{U_s''(f_s(w))}{U_s'(f_s(w))}\right]z_s^2}{\sum_{s\in S} p_s f_s'(w)}, \tag{2.16}$$

where use has been made of the equality of the marginal utility of wealth across states on RS. Since at $h = 0$, $\pi_U = \pi_V$, and $\pi_U \geqq \pi_V$ if and only if $\pi^U \geqq \pi^V$, for (iii) to hold for all $\boldsymbol{x}$ such that $\Sigma_{s\in S} p_s x_s = 0$ we must have

$$\left.\frac{d^2\pi^U}{dh^2}\right|_{h=0} \geqq \left.\frac{d^2\pi^V}{dh^2}\right|_{h=0}.$$

This implies that

$$-\frac{U_s''(f_s(w))}{U_s'(f_s(w))} \geqq -\frac{V_s''(f_s(w))}{V_s'(f_s(w))}$$

for all $s \in S$. Otherwise we can find $\boldsymbol{p} \in P$ such that Inequality (2.16) is reversed. This establishes (i).

3 Risk Aversion with State-Dependent Preferences: Some Economic Applications

3.1 Introduction

The selection of health or life insurance coverage is an obvious example of a decision where the dependence of the decision maker's preferences on the state of nature is an intrinsic feature of the problem. The critical characteristic that sets these and other decision problems involving state-dependent preferences apart as a subject for analysis is the dependence of the marginal utility of income or wealth on the prevailing state of nature. This difference, however, does not alter the perception that, *ceteris paribus,* a more risk-averse person is expected to buy more comprehensive insurance coverage. If this statement which seems intuitively obvious is to be given a formal meaning, the relations "more risk-averse" and "more comprehensive coverage" must be defined formally. The former relation was defined in Chapter 2. The latter relation is defined below in a natural way for each decision problem, and the assertion about the equivalence of the two relations is formally established. In addition to providing the ultimate justification for the measure of risk aversion defined in the preceding chapter, this discussion illustrates the technical aspects of conducting a comparative statics analysis with respect to this measure.

The present discussion focuses on the problem of the optimal choice of flight insurance coverage, and certain aspects of health insurance, namely permanent injury insurance. The analysis of the relationship between risk aversion and the optimal choice of life insurance in the context of multiperiod consumption saving models is deferred to Chapter 4. A separate treatment is needed because of the added complexity of the life insurance problem, since the utility functions depended on the whole future income stream, rather than a single variable.

3.2 Risk Aversion and Flight Insurance

A passenger about to board a plane considers taking out life insurance for the duration of the flight. Typically, he is offered a schedule of indemnity payments and a corresponding schedule of insurance premiums. The passenger must decide how much insurance to purchase, if any. Of the many factors that influence his decision (the terms of the policy, the decision maker's subjective assessment of the probability of a plane crash, his wealth, the number and age of his dependents, etc.) the discussion will only consider the effect of his attitudes toward risk on his desired coverage. I will compare the desired coverages of two decision makers who are identical in every respect other than their aversion to risk.

The set of states of nature in this instance consists of two states, "life" and "death," which we denote by 0 and 1, respectively. Let the probability of state 0 be p and that of state 1 be $(1-p)$, and suppose that these probabilities are "objective" in the sense that they represent the beliefs of both the decision makers and the insurance company regarding the likely realization of the two states. Denote by I the indemnity payment in case of death and by $l(I)$ the function representing the insurance premium corresponding to each level of I. Thus either I or $l(\cdot)$ is a natural measure of the degree of coverage for this problem.

Consider first the terms of the insurance. We assume that the insurer is risk neutral and that the terms of the policy include a loading factor designed to cover administrative and other costs that are involved in the provision of insurance. In particular we analyze the cases where: (a) the costs are proportional to the indemnity payments and (b) there are set-up costs of writing a policy that are independent of the indemnity payments. In the first case the insurance premium is equal to the actuarial value of the policy $(1-p)I$ plus the loading bI, where $0 \leqq b < p$. The imposition of an upper bound on b ensures that $l < I$, for otherwise the decision maker is better off without insurance. Thus, the terms of the insurance are given by the insurance premium function

$$(3.1) \qquad l(I) = (1 - p + b)I, \qquad b \in [0, p).$$

In the case of fixed costs the insurance premium is

$$(3.2) \qquad l(I) = (1-p)I + c, \qquad c > 0.$$

Next consider the problem from the point of view of a decision maker whose initial (preinsurance) wealth position is $\langle w_0, w_1 \rangle$, where w_i, $i = 0,1$

denotes initial wealth in state *i*. In general, w_0 and w_1 need not be the same, since w_0 may incorporate the present value of the decision maker's future income stream, which is lost in case of his death.

Generally speaking, the purchase of insurance is a method of reallocating wealth across states of nature. In this instance it involves the transfer of wealth from state 0 to state 1. Thus, upon buying insurance, a decision maker whose initial wealth distribution is $\langle w_0, w_1 \rangle$ attains a terminal distribution $\langle y_0, y_1 \rangle$ where, in the case where $l(\cdot)$ is given by (3.1),

$$\text{(3.3)} \quad \begin{aligned} &\text{(a)}\ y_0 = w_0 - l = w_0 - [(1-p)+b]I, \\ &\text{(b)}\ y_1 = w_1 - l + I = w_1 + (p-b)I. \end{aligned}$$

The decision maker's preferences over wealth distributions are represented by the state-dependent expected utility function $\overline{U} = pU_0(y_0) + (1-p)U_1(y_1)$. The function $U_1(\cdot)$ represents the individual's *ex-ante* evaluation of alternative sizes of his estate in case of his death, in the same sense that U_0 represents his evaluation of alternative levels of wealth if he continues to live. The nature of each state is reflected in the properties of the corresponding utility function, but the structure of the objective function itself is not altered by the interpretation of the states.

The optimal level of flight insurance coverage is given by the level of I that maximizes

$$\text{(3.4)} \quad \overline{U}(I) = pU_0(w_0 - [(1-p)+b]I) + (1-p)U_1(w_1 + (p-b)I),$$

subject to $I \geqq 0$. Let I_u^* denote the solution to (3.4), and consider the following question: How would the optimal level of coverage vary with increases in risk aversion? Common sense suggests that, other things being equal, the more risk-averse the decision maker, the more inclined he is to insure himself, and consequently the more comprehensive is his insurance coverage. This intuition is confirmed by the formal analysis, which yields the following theorem.

THEOREM 3.1. *Let U and V be mutually comparable, state-dependent utility functions. If U is more risk averse than V (in the sense of Definition 2.3), then for any initial wealth distribution* $\langle w_0, w_1 \rangle$ *and for all linear insurance terms,* $I_u^* \geqq I_v^*$.

A formal proof of Theorem 3.1 appears in Section 3.5. A simple explanation of the result, however, is possible using Figure 3.1. The reference sets of the two individuals are depicted by *RS*; it is the same for both *U* and *V*

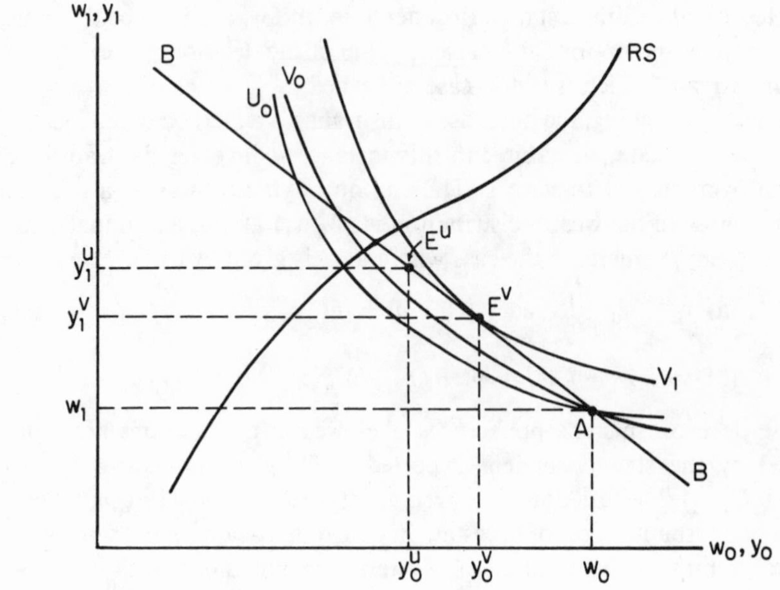

Figure 3.1 Optimal insurance coverage

because of their mutual comparability. The point A denotes the initial wealth distribution. Corresponding to this point are the initial levels of expected utility U_0 and V_0. The slopes of the indifference curves on RS represent the actuarially fair rate of substitution between wealth in the two states. The line BB depicts the insurance policies given by Eq. (3.1), that is, those with proportional loading. Relative to fair insurance BB represents a less favorable rate of substitution, since the compensation in case of death is smaller under the terms of the actual insurance policy than under fair insurance for each and every sacrifice of wealth in state 0. The point E^v depicts the equilibrium of the individual whose preferences are represented by V. This point is to the right of RS. If this individual buys insurance, as is the case in Figure 3.1, then the point E^v is in the interval of the BB curve between A and RS.

Next consider the equilibrium position of the decision maker whose preferences are represented by U. One implication of Theorem 2.1 is that at each and every point to the right of RS the indifference curves of the more risk-averse individual, U, intersect from below those of the less risk-averse individual. At E^v the indifference curve of U intersects that of V from below. Hence the equilibrium point of U must be to the left of E^v. Furthermore, as in the case of V, and by the same logic, the point must be below RS. Hence it is located in the interval of BB between RS and E^v, as in Figure 3.1. The terminal wealth positions of the two individuals are such that $y_0^v > y_0^u$ and $y_1^v < y_1^u$, but by Eq. (3.3a) $y_0^v - y_0^u = -[(1-p)+b](I_v^* - I_u^*)$. Hence $y_0^v > y_0^u$ implies $I_u^* > I_v^*$. In other words, other things being equal, the more risk-averse individual takes out more comprehensive flight insurance coverage.

For an insurance policy whose terms are given by Eq. (3.2), the lump sum loading c does not affect the marginal rate of substitution between w_0 and w_1. It does affect the position of the insurance budget constraint, however, depicted by BB in Figure 3.2. The decision to insure has the nature of "all or nothing." That is, if the decision maker decides to insure he will buy coverage so as to equate the marginal utility of wealth in the two states of nature, and will be at a point on RS such as E^u. Otherwise he will abstain from insuring and remain at A. Since, by Theorem 2.1, $\pi_U \geqq \pi_V$, we have three possible outcomes. If $c < \Pi_v$, then both decision makers buy insurance, and since they are comparable their equilibrium position is represented by the intersection of BB and RS. In this case $y_i^u = y_i^v$, i = 1,2, and $I_u^* = I_v^*$. If $\pi_V < c < \pi_U$, the case depicted in Figure 3.2, then the less risk-averse individ-

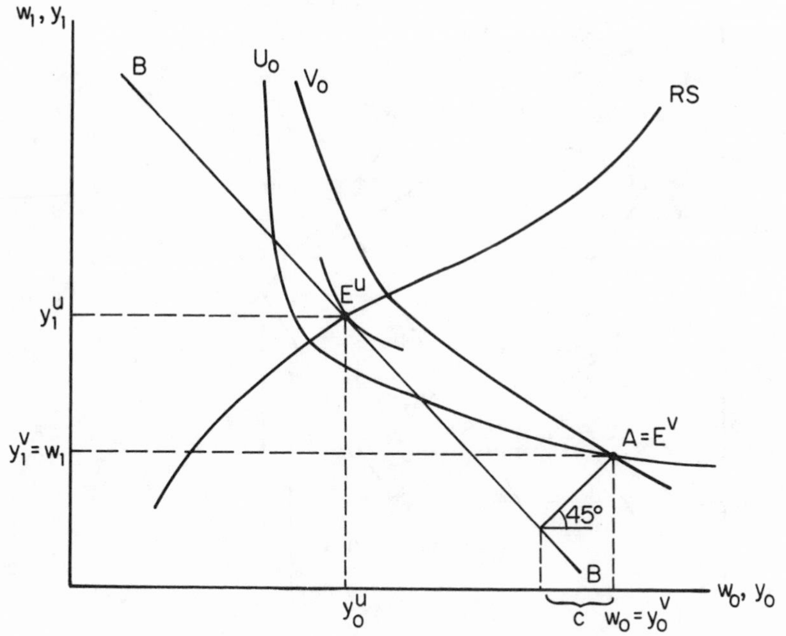

Figure 3.2 Optimal insurance with fixed loading

ual abstains from insurance (the equilibrium position of V is represented by the point A) while the more risk-averse individual chooses the terminal wealth distribution given by the intersection of BB and RS. In this case $I_u^* > I_v^* = 0$. Finally, if $c > \pi_U$, both individuals abstain from insurance—$I_u^* = I_v^* = 0$. Thus, in all cases, $I_u^* \geqq I_v^*$.

The same general principles apply in the analysis of the optimal flight insurance coverage of a given individual at different wealth positions. To see this, consider a decision maker whose preferences are autocomparable and display decreasing absolute risk aversion in the sense of Definition 2.5. A meaningful comparison of his choice of flight insurance coverage at different wealth positions requires that other things, including his exposure to risk, be equal. In the present case risk is defined as the deviation of the actual wealth position from the actuarially equivalent wealth position in the reference set. This is illustrated in Figure 3.3 as the distances between the initial wealth positions A^0, A' and the points K^0 and K' on RS, respectively, where the lines F^0F^0 and $F'F'$ represent actuarially fair insurance.

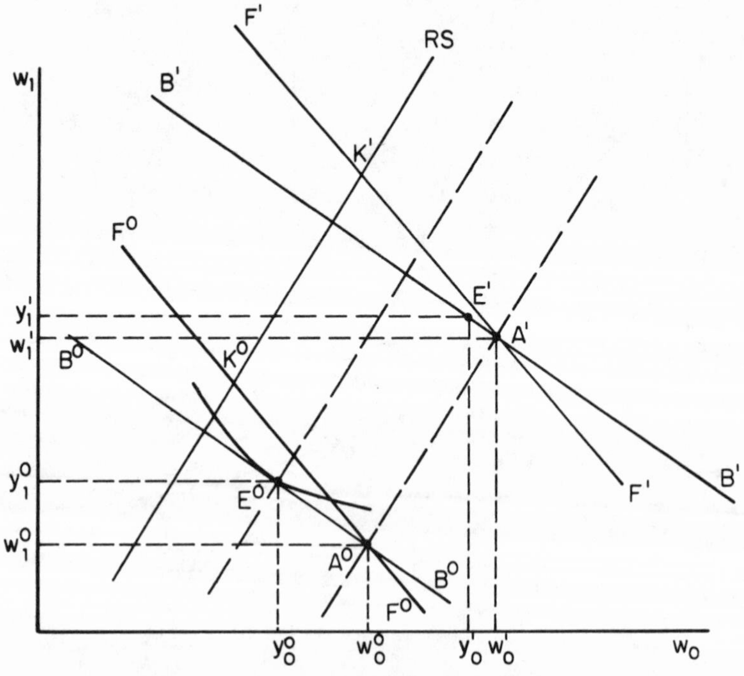

Figure 3.3 Optimal flight insurance with decreasing absolute risk aversion

Clearly, this implies that we consider displacements of the initial wealth position, so that the *changes* in wealth in each state are proportional and the factor of proportionality is the slope of the reference set $w_1' - w_1^0 = \beta(w_0' - w_0^0)$, where β is the slope of RS.

Let B^0B^0 and $B'B'$ in Figure 3.3 denote the constraint imposed by the terms of the insurance policy, and let the optimal position of the individual be E^0 if his initial wealth is A^0 and E' if his initial wealth is A'. Then if the individual displays decreasing absolute risk aversion, E' must be below a line parallel to RS through E^0. (E' will be on this line or above this line if the individual displays constant or increasing absolute risk aversion, respectively.) This conclusion is an immediate implication of Theorem 2.2, as can be easily verified by applying the mapping $M(\mathbf{w} \mid \langle A^0, A' \rangle)$ defined in Chapter 2 to $\mathbf{w} \in R_+^2$, and thus reducing the problem of a given individual at different initial wealth positions to that of comparing two distinct but comparable individuals with the same initial wealth position. The conclusion is that an individual who displays decreasing absolute risk aversion will, for every given risk (measured as an actuarially neutral deviation from the reference set) and all linear insurance terms, purchase more comprehensive coverage, the lower his initial wealth position.

In practice, of course, variations in the initial wealth position are in general independent of the shape of the reference set. A change in the decision maker's wealth position may involve an intrinsic change in his exposure to risk. Observing the actual insurance purchase in such a case does not have a direct bearing on the empirical validity of the above conclusion, since the evidence is contaminated by the inequality of some relevant factors. There is a way of summarizing the analysis that circumvents this problem. Since, given the terms of the policy, the optimal position, say E', is the same for all initial wealth positions on $B'B'$, our conclusion may be stated as follows: If an individual displays decreasing absolute risk aversion, then for any linear insurance terms, the higher is the actuarial value of the initial wealth position, the farther away from the reference set is his terminal wealth position. This statement does not involve the notion of the riskiness of the decision maker's initial position. At the same time, while characterizing the terminal position, it has no immediate implications for the actual purchase of insurance.

Finally, I will illustrate the significance of the condition of autocomparability of the decision maker's preferences for the above result. Suppose that the preferences are not autocomparable, and consider an individual at two alternative initial wealth positions representing the same risk. These posi-

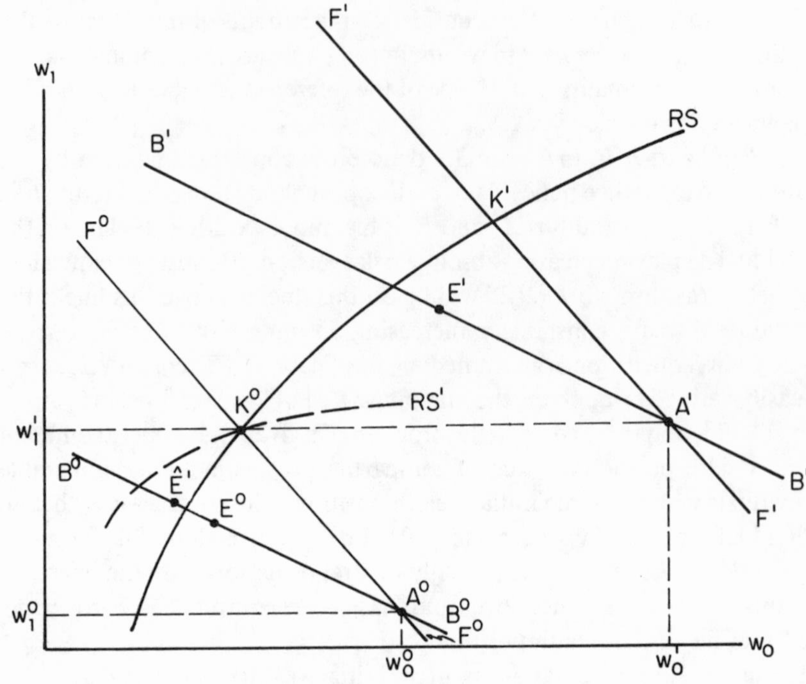

Figure 3.4 Optimal flight insurance with preferences that are not autocomparable

tions are depicted by points A^0 and A' in Figure 3.4. The terminal position E' corresponding to A' is farther away from the reference set than the terminal position E^0, which corresponds to A^0. Yet, even though the insurance terms are the same, the individual buys more insurance when his actuarial wealth is larger. This is due in part to the larger distance, from the initial position, of the reference set along the $B'B'$ line. An illustration of this point is provided by the use of the mapping $M(\mathbf{w}|\langle A^0, A'\rangle)$, which collapses the position A' into A^0 and the position E' into $\hat{E}'$. (RS' in Figure 3.4 depicts the image of a neighborhood of K' under the mapping M.) In this instance proximity to the reference set does not bear a one-to-one relation to the size of the insurance coverage, as in the case of autocomparable preferences.

3.3 Risk Aversion and Health Insurance

It is reasonable to posit that the state of a person's health affects his preferences, and that these effects involve variations not only in his utility of wealth but more importantly in his marginal utility of wealth. The design of an optimal health insurance policy must therefore take into account the state-dependent nature of the insured preferences.

Arrow (1974) analyzed the design of a simple health insurance problem wherein the decision maker must choose among insurance policies specifying a cash payment for each possible state of the insured's health. In Arrow's analysis the choice of insurance policy is constrained in two important ways. First, the insurer is risk neutral, so that insurance premiums depend only on the actuarial value of the benefits and the administrative and other costs of providing the policy. Second, the indemnities are nonnegative, which is the observed practice in health insurance. Nevertheless, this specification of the problem is at variance with the practice of health insurers to offer policies that provide for reimbursement of actual expenses in whole or in part, rather than a cash settlement. To explain the prevalence of the more restrictive reimbursement policies, Arrow appeals to asymmetric information, concerning the actual state of the insured's health, possessed by the parties to the insurance contract, and to the high cost of verification.

It is possible, however, that the appearance of a uniform practice of reimbursement of actual medical expenses is misleading, and that in fact we are facing two types of health hazards that are treated as distinct by insurers and insurees alike: restorable and nonrestorable health conditions. The distinction can be illustrated by comparing two simple examples. In the first situation an individual is infected by a curable disease; in the second he suffers a permanent injury. Clearly, in the case of the curable disease the individual's original state of health and wealth can be restored if he is reimbursed for his medical expenses. If the original position represents an equilibrium, then a policy that reimburses him for his incurred medical expenses is optimal. The case of permanent injury, say loss of a limb, represents a different problem. Even if the injury in itself does not involve loss of income, it permanently changes the decision maker's state of health. A cash settlement is therefore justifiable on welfare grounds. Indeed, such insurance policies are available.

Arrow's model may thus be reinterpreted as a model for the analysis of permanent injury insurance. With this in mind consider the following problem: An expected-utility-maximizing individual faces a choice among health insurance policies. Each policy specifies a nonnegative cash payment contingent upon the individual's state of health. The insurance premium is proportional to the actuarial value of the benefits, and the individual knows the (objective) probabilities of the different states of health and his preinsurance wealth in each state.

For each state of health s in S, let w_s^0 denote the initial (preinsurance) wealth and I_s the indemnity payment. Let h denote the insurance premium, and suppose that

(3.5) $$h = \alpha \sum_{s \in S} p_s I_s,$$

where p_s denotes the probability of s, and $\alpha \geqq 1$ is a parameter representing the loading due to administrative and other costs. Then the individual terminal wealth in state $s \in S$ is given by

(3.6) $$w_s = w_s^0 - h + I_s.$$

The decision maker's problem may be stated as follows: choose a sequence $\{I_s\}_{s \in S}$ so as to maximize

(3.7) $$\sum_{s \in S} p_s U_s(w_s),$$

subject to Eq. (3.5), (3.6), and the nonnegativity constraints $I_s \geqq 0$ for all $s \in S$.

Assuming that, for all s, $U_s(\cdot)$ is concave, the optimal insurance policy for a given h is characterized completely by Eq. (3.5) and

(3.8a) $$U_s'(w_s^0 - h + I_s) \leqq \alpha\lambda;$$

(3.8b) $$U_s'(w_s^0 - h + I_s) < \alpha\lambda \text{ implies } I_s = 0,$$

where λ, the Lagrange multiplier corresponding to Eq. (3.5), is constant across states of health. Thus, for given h the optimal policy is characterized by a critical marginal utility of wealth $\alpha\lambda$ and the following rule: For states of health where the marginal utility of $w_s^0 - h$ falls short of $\alpha\lambda$ the indemnities are zero; for states of health where the marginal utility of $w_s^0 - h$ exceeds $\alpha\lambda$ the benefits are equal to an amount that equates the marginal utility of wealth to $\alpha\lambda$. The value $\hat{w}_s$ given by the equation $U_s'(\hat{w}_s) = \alpha\lambda$ is referred to as the *deductible limit* of state s. Figure 3.5 describes the design of an optimal policy for the case of two states of health. The curves U_1', U_2' depict the marginal utility of wealth in two states. The difference between $w_s^0 - h$ and $\hat{w}_s$ represents the benefits in state s, $s = 1, 2$. In this case the insurance policy provides for 100 percent coverage against losses that reduce wealth in state 2 below the deductible limit $\hat{w}_2$, and no benefits in state 1.

Notice that if the preferences are state independent (or if the marginal utility of wealth is state independent, which is a weaker condition) the marginal utility curves in Figure 3.5 coincide. The deductible limit is the same across states of health, and the optimal insurance policy provides for full coverage of loss of wealth above a minimum deductible. Indeed this case

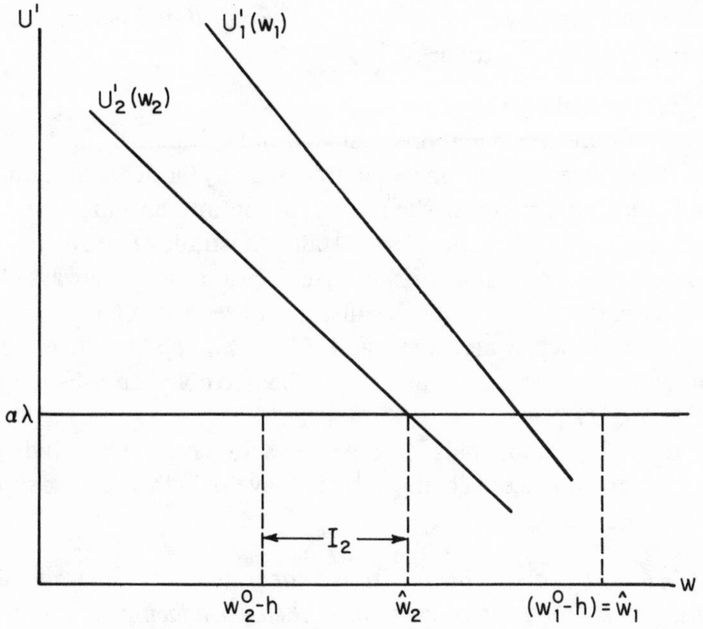

Figure 3.5 The structure of an optimal permanent injury insurance policy

is no different from the usual analysis of property insurance (see Arrow, 1971).

In keeping with the main theme of this analysis I shall focus on how the deductible limits vary with risk aversion. To set the stage I shall present a brief discussion of this question in the context of state-independent preferences. As already mentioned, in this case the optimal insurance policy for risk-averse decision makers provides for full coverage of the loss above a deductible minimum. Intuitively it is to be expected that, *ceteris paribus,* a more risk-averse decision maker, in the sense of Arrow–Pratt, will choose a policy with a larger deductible limit. Notice that under the terms of the insurance policy the only uncertainty about terminal wealth is in regard to the occurrence of losses smaller than the deductible minimum. A reduction of this uncertainty is possible, through an insurance policy that specifies a smaller deductible minimum (a higher deductible limit). Indeed, the following result holds.

PROPOSITION 3.1. *Let $\bar{w}^u$ and $\bar{w}^v$ be the deductible limits corresponding to the state-independent utility functions u(w) and v(w), respectively. Then $\bar{w}^u \geqq \bar{w}^v$*

for every probability distribution of loss of wealth if and only if $-u''(w)/u'(w) \geqslant -v''(w)/v'(w)$ *for all w.*

For proof see Karni (1983b).

The case of state-dependent preferences is not substantially different, except that the number of decision variables—namely the deductible limits—is larger. Under fair insurance, when $\alpha = 1$, the optimal coverage is such that the terminal wealth distribution across states constitutes an element of *RS*. As a consequence, comparable risk-averse decision makers always choose the same coverage. To prove this it suffices to observe that λ in Eqs. (3.8) is equal to $\Sigma_{s\in S} p_s U'_s(w^*_s)$, where $w^*_s \equiv w^0_s + I^*_s - \alpha\Sigma_{s\in S} p_s I^*_s$ and I^*_s is the optimal insurance coverage in *s*. Thus, for Eq. (3.8a) to hold, it must be true that for all $S \in S\ U'_s(w^*_s) = \lambda$.

When $\alpha > 1$ Eq. (3.8b) holds for some states. In these states no indemnity is paid. The consequences of being more risk-averse in this case are summarized in Theorem 3.2.

THEOREM 3.2. *Let U and V be mutually comparable state-dependent utility functions. If U is more risk averse than V, then when facing the same linear insurance terms and the same risk, the deductible limits corresponding to U are at least as large as those of V for each and every state s in S.*

Theorem 3.2 implies that *U* purchases more insurance than *V*, since in each state where both decision makers purchase insurance the minimum deductible chosen by *U* is smaller than that of *V*. In addition there may be states where the indemnities of *V* are zero while those of *U* are positive.

A formal proof of Theorem 3.2 appears in Section 3.5. Here I provide a diagrammatic explanation of this result. To begin with, note that marginal utility of wealth of the more risk-averse individual in each state is given by $T'_s[V_s(w)]V'_s(w)$, where for all $s \in S$, $T_s[\cdot]$ is monotonic increasing and concave. Consider again the equilibrium of *V* in any state *s*, say such that the optimal indemnity is positive. This equilibrium is depicted in Figure 3.6, where w^v_s denotes the terminal wealth and I^v_s represents the indemnity payments in *s*.

The marginal utility of wealth in state *s* of the more risk-averse individual is depicted by $U'_s(w)$. The steeper slope of $U'_s(w)$ reflects that fact that $T'_s[V_s(w)]$ is decreasing in V_s. This last observation is crucial, for it also accounts for the fact that λ^u increases by less than $T'_s[V_s(w^v_s)]$. Note again that λ^u and λ^v are the weighted averages (across states) of the marginal utilities of *U* and *V*, evaluated at the optimal terminal wealths, and that for states where

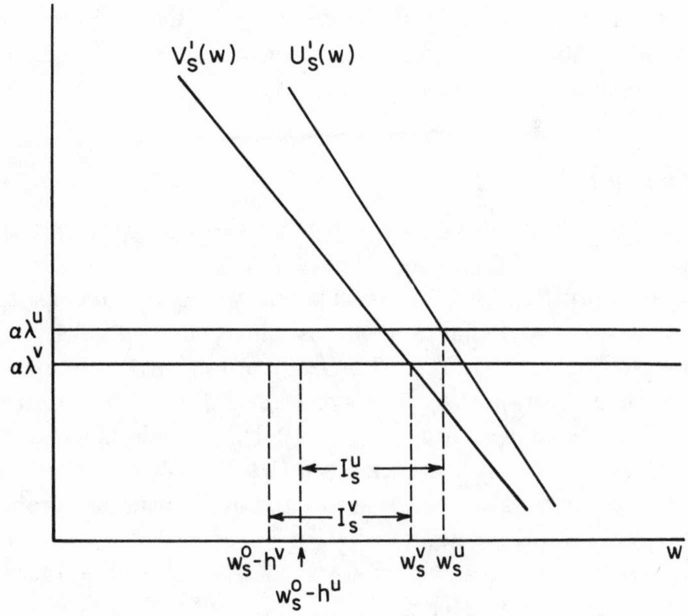

Figure 3.6 Optimal deductible and risk aversion

the marginal utilities of wealth of V are equal to one another the slopes of the transformations T'_s are also equal to one another. Furthermore, for a state t where $I_t^v = 0$, $V'_t[w_t^0 - h^v] < \lambda^v$. Compared to a state s where $I_s > 0$, $T'_t[V_t(w_t^0 - h^v)] < T'_s[V_s(w_s^v)]$, since $V'_t(w_t^0 - h^v) < V'_s(w_s^v)$. Consequently, $\lambda^u < T'_s[V_s(w_s^v)]\lambda^v$. This implies that $\alpha\lambda^u < U'_s(w_s^v)$ as in Figure 3.6, and therefore $w_s^v < w_s^u$. Notice, however, that the increase in the terminal wealth w_s^u relative to w_s^v requires that $I_s^u > I_s^v$. This in turn implies that $h^u > h^v$. However, since an increase of one dollar in I_s contributes one dollar to the terminal wealth in state s and only αp_s dollars to h, and $\alpha p_s < 1$ or insurance is not worth buying, the increase in the insurance premium is smaller than the increase in the terminal wealth in state s. In other words, the net effect on terminal wealth of an increase in one dollar in I_s is $1 - \alpha p_s$, which is positive. Hence $w_s^u > w_s^v$ implies that $I_s^u > I_s^v$.

For states $s \in S$ where $I_s^v = 0$, the same argument applies and leads to the conclusion that $I_s^u \geqq 0$. Applying the same rationale to autocomparable preferences it follows from Theorem 3.2 that an increase in the decision maker's wealth that does not alter his exposure to risk results in an increase (decrease) of the deductible limits if the utility function displays increasing (decreasing) risk aversion for any given linear insurance terms. Here again the restriction to autocomparable preferences is sufficient to assure the comparability of preferences across wealth positions.

3.4 Related Literature

The demand for flight insurance using state-dependent preferences was presented originally by Eisner and Strotz (1961). Their main point, however, was that the implications of the expected utility theory are inconsistent with evidence about the demand for flight insurance.

Analysis of the optimal structure of health insurance policies appeared for the first time in Arrow (1974). Arrow provides a detailed comparative static analysis of the demand for health insurance. His analysis, however, does not include comparative risk aversion. Röell (1983) analyzed the effects of increase in risk aversion on several health and flight insurance problems. In addition to providing an elegant proof of Theorem 3.2, Röell also models situations where full insurance is not available due to moral hazard and nonindependent effects. Her analysis demonstrates the usefulness of extending the measures of risk aversion introduced by Ross (1981) to the case of state-dependent preferences.

3.5 Proofs

3.5.1 Proof of Theorem 3.1

Let y_1^j and y_0^j, $j = u, v$, be the terminal wealth distribution corresponding to I_j^*. Then the first-order optimality condition for U is

$$\frac{\partial E\{U\}}{\partial I} = -p(1-p)[U_0'(y_0^u) - U_1'(y_1^u)] - b[pU_1'(y_1^u) + (1-p)U_0'(y_0^u)] = 0.$$

But $b \geqq 0$, hence $U_1'(y_1^u) \geqq U_0'(y_0^u)$. Thus

$$y_1^u \geqq g(y_0^u), \tag{3.9}$$

where g(·) assigns to each y_0^u the value y_1 such that $\langle y_0^u, y_1 \rangle \in RS_u$. From Theorem 2.1 we have

$$\frac{\partial E\{U\}}{\partial I} = -p(1-p+b)T_1'[V_1(y_1)]V'_1(y_1) + (1-p)(p-b)T_0'[V_0'(y_0)]V_0'(y_0). \tag{3.10}$$

Evaluating Eq. (3.10) at $\langle y_0^u, y_1^u \rangle$ and using Eq. (3.9) we observe that

$$T_1'[V_1(y_1^u)] \leqq T_1'[V_1(g(y_0^u))] = T_0'[V_0(y_0^u)],$$

where the last equality follows from Theorem 2.1. Thus

$$0 = \frac{\partial E\{U\}}{\partial I} \geqq T_0'[V_0(y_0^u)]$$
$$[-p(1-p+b)V_1'(y_1^u) + (1-p)(p-b)V_0'(y_0^u)].$$

Consequently,

$$-p(1-p+b)V_1'(y_1^u) + (1-p)(p-b)V_0'(y_0^u) \leqq 0.$$

By concavity of $E\{V\}$ in I this implies

$$I_u^* \geqq I_v^*.$$

3.5.2 *Proof of Theorem 3.2*

Substituting Eqs. (3.5) and (3.6) in Eq. (3.7) we obtain

(3.11) $$U(\underset{\sim}{I}) \equiv \sum_{s \in S} p_s U_s(w_s^0 + I_s - \alpha \sum_{s \in S} p_s I_s),$$

which is jointly concave in $\underset{\sim}{I}$. Maximizing Eq. (3.11) with respect to $\underset{\sim}{I}$, subject to the nonnegativity constraints $I_s \geqq 0$ for all $s \in S$, the necessary and sufficient conditions are:

(3.12a) $$[U_t'(w_t^u) - \alpha \sum_{s \in S} p_s U_s'(w_s^u)] I_t^u = 0,$$

(3.12b) $$U_t'(w_t^u) - \alpha \sum_{s \in S} p_s U_s'(w_s^u) \leqq 0, \qquad \forall t \in S,$$

where w_s^u and I_s^u are the respective optimal terminal wealth and insurance coverage in state s. Let

$$S^u = \{t \in S \mid U_t'(w_t^u) = \alpha \sum_{s \in S} p_s U_s'(w_s^u)\},$$

$$S^v = \{t \in S \mid V_t'(w_t^v) = \alpha \sum_{s \in S} p_s V_s'(w_s^v)\}.$$

If $\alpha = 1$, then from Eq. (3.12), $U_t'(w_t^u) = U_s'(w_s^u)$ and $V_t'(w_t^v) = V_s'(w_s^v)$ for all s and t in S. Thus $S^u = S^v = S$, and $\{w_s^u\}_{s \in S} \in RS_u$, $\{w_s^v\}_{s \in S} \in RS_v$. Since U and V are mutually comparable, $RS_u = RS_v$, and their optimal insurance and deductible limits are identical.

If $\alpha > 1$, then $S^v \subset S$ and $S^u \subset S$. We shall show that in this case $S^v \subseteq S^u$

and for each $t \in S^v$, $w_t^u \geqq w_t^v$. Denote by $\bar{S}^u$ the complement of S^u in S, and suppose by way of negation that $S^v \cap \bar{S}^u \neq \emptyset$.

For all $s \in S$ and any $t \in S^v$, $T_s'[V_s(w_s^v)] \leqq T_t'[V_t(w_t^v)]$ with strict inequality for some $s \in S$. Thus for all $t \in S^v$,

$$(3.13) \qquad V_t'(w_t^v) > \alpha \sum_{s \in S} p_s V_s'(w_s^v) \frac{T_s'[V_s(w_s^v)]}{T_t'[V_t(w_t^v)]}.$$

Multiplying both sides of Eq. (3.13) by $T_t'[V_t(w_t^v)]$ and using the fact that for all $s \in S$ $U_s'(w_s) = T_s'[V_s(w_s)]V_s'(w_s)$ we get

$$(3.14) \qquad U_t'(w_t^v) > \alpha \sum_{s \in S} p_s U_s'(w_s^v), \qquad \forall t \in S^v.$$

For all $t \in S^v$, however, w_t^v are components of a given element of RS_v. Since U and V are mutually comparable this implies that $T_t'[V_t(w_t^v)] = T_s'[V_s(w_s^v)]$ for all s and t in S^v. Consequently $U_t'(w_t^v) = U_s'(w_s^v)$ for all s and t in S^v.

Next consider the path $\{w_s(\beta)\}_{s \in S}, \beta \in [0,1]$ such that $\{w_s(0)\}_{s \in S} = \{w_s^v\}_{s \in S}$ and as β increases for all $t \in S^v$, $w_t(\beta)$ increases in such a way that $U_t'[w_t(\beta)] = U_s'[w_s(\beta)]$ for all t and s in S^v. Since an increase in w_t requires an increase in I_t, the premium h increases along the path. Consequently, for all $s \notin S^v$, $U_s'[w_s(\beta)]$ increases. Two possible situations may arise: (i) A point is reached where Eq. (3.14) is satisfied by equalities, in which case $S^u = S^v$ but for all $t \in S^v$, $w_t^u \geqslant w_t^v$. (ii) At some point there are $s \notin S^v$ in which $U_s'[w_s(\beta)] = U_t'[w_t(\beta)]$, where $t \in S^v \cap S^u$. In this case, as we move farther along the path we increase $w_s(\beta)$ so as to preserve these equalities as well, until a point is reached where Eq. (3.14) holds with equalities. This will be the case where $S^v \subset S^u$ and for all $s \in S^u$, $w_s^u \geqslant w_s^v$.

4 Risk Aversion and the Demand for Life Insurance

4.1 Introduction

Life insurance provides a means of transferring wealth across states of nature, releasing certain constraints to allow greater flexibility in the formulation of consumption plans. In the absence of life insurance the value of an individual's estate at any point in time depends solely on his initial wealth and past savings. An increase in his bequest at any point in time requires abstention from consumption during a period prior to that point. The availability of life insurance eliminates this restriction and enables the individual to base his bequest plan upon his entire income and consumption streams. By divorcing the bequest from the consumption plan life insurance provides for a richer menu of consumption plans from which to choose.

The bequest motive, while important, is not a *sine qua non* for a theory of demand for life insurance. The essential role of life insurance as a means of separating the size of an individual's bequest from his past savings can be exploited to enlarge the feasible set of consumption plans even in the absence of the bequest motive. Suppose that an individual faces an earnings profile according to which his earnings increase with age. To smooth his consumption stream he needs to resort to borrowing during the early periods of his life. His ability to borrow, however, is impaired by uncertainty about his lifespan. Taking out life insurance in the amount of the loan, with the lender as the beneficiary, provides the necessary collateral. The availability of life insurance enables the individual to secure loans he could not secure otherwise, thereby providing for a larger set of consumption plans to choose from.

The bequest motive and the collateral motive for taking out life insurance policies give rise to distinct models of demand for life insurance. The first to analyze these models was Yaari (1965), who described them as the Marshallian and Fisherian models, respectively. The main difference between the two models is that, whereas the presence of bequest as an argument in the objective function of the Marshallian model imposes an intrinsic penalty on the accumulation of debt, there is nothing in the Fisherian model to inhibit the decision maker from accumulating debt. Consequently, while in the Marshallian model, under reasonable assumptions, decision makers are allowed complete freedom of lending and borrowing, in the Fisherian model this freedom must be restricted.

Our primary concern in this study is the comparative static analysis of demand for life insurance with respect to variations in risk aversion. The analysis is complicated, however, because, in addition to the inherent dependence of the decision maker's preferences over the set of consumption plans on the state of nature (the time of his death), the utility functions that represent the decision maker's preferences in each state depend indirectly on the decision maker's entire income stream. It is the multidimensionality of the utility representation of the individual preferences that sets the life insurance problem apart from the problems analyzed in the preceding chapter and requires a reexamination of the notion of the reference set. Not surprisingly, perhaps, the multidimensionality of the state-dependent utility functions presents the same problem encountered in the analysis of risk aversion with many commodities in the case of state-independent preferences, namely, that comparative risk aversion is only possible among individuals who have identical ordinal preferences on the commodity space (see Chapter 6). The comparative static analysis of demand for life insurance with respect to risk aversion requires that the ordinal preferences, on the space of consumption plans, of the individuals being compared be the same and that their reference sets be identical.

The discussion that follows concentrates exclusively on the effects of uncertain lifetime on the demand for life insurance and draws heavily on Karni and Zilcha (1983), (1985). Uncertainty about future income enters the discussion only insofar as the flow of noninterest earnings stops when the individual dies. That is, as long as the individual is alive there is no uncertainty regarding the size of his income. Similarly, we assume a certain knowledge of all future interest rates. These assumptions simplify the analysis, in that they permit a formulation of optimal consumption and insurance plans at the outset, and since no meaningful new information is acquired as the plans are being executed over time, the plans are not subsequently revised. If either the magnitude of some future noninterest income or the interest rate is uncertain, then the original consumption and insurance plans are contingent on the realization of that income or interest rate.

4.2 The Models

In this section I present the discrete-time versions of both the Marshallian and the Fisherian models, beginning with a survey of elements common to both. Consider a decision maker with uncertain life span. Suppose that time is divided into periods of equal length, say weeks. The decision maker may die during any of these periods, and he dies for certain at the end of period T, if he has not died before, where T is a finite integer. Let s_t denote the event (state of nature) "the decision maker dies during the period t," $t = 1, \ldots, T$, and denote by S the (finite) set $\{s_1, \ldots, s_T\}$ of states of nature. Let p_t denote the probability of the event s_t, and let $\boldsymbol{p} = (p_1, \ldots, p_T)$ be a probability distribution on S. That is, $p_t \geqq 0$ for all t and $\Sigma_{t=1}^{T} p_t = 1$. The set of all $\boldsymbol{p}$ is denoted P.

The decision maker has a noninterest income stream given by the sequence $\boldsymbol{y} = \{y_1, \ldots, y_T\}$, where y_t denotes his noninterest income received at the beginning of the tth period of his life. We assume that the size of each component of the income stream is known with certainty at the beginning of the first period. The number of elements of this stream that will be realized, however, is uncertain. More specifically, in the event s_t the decision maker realizes the truncated sequence that consists of the first t elements of the noninterest incomes $\{y_1, \ldots y_t\}$, to be denoted $\boldsymbol{y}^t$, while the remaining elements $y_{t+1}, \ldots, y_T$ are lost. Finally, let $\boldsymbol{r} = \{r_1, \ldots, r_T\}$ denote the single-period interest rates, all of which are known with certainty at the outset of the first period, prior to the formulation of the consumption plan.

Given his noninterest earnings, the rates of interest, and the probabilities of survival, the decision maker formulates a consumption plan $(c_1, \ldots, c_T)$, where c_t stands for his planned consumption spending during the tth period of his life. The realized consumption agrees with the plan as long as the decision maker is alive. In the event s_t, the realized consumption stream is represented by the truncated sequence $\boldsymbol{c}^t = \{c_1, \ldots, c_t\}$, while the remainder of the plan is not realized. Corresponding to the consumption plan there is a saving or bequest plan represented by the sequence $\{b_1, \ldots, b_T\}$. If s_t occurs, the element b_t of this sequence is realized. Thus, for each state of nature s_t the triplet $(\boldsymbol{y}^t, \boldsymbol{c}^t, b_t)$ describes the realization of noninterest income, consumption spending, and the value of accumulated saving up to the end of period t.

4.2.1 The Marshallian Objective Function

In both the Marshallian and the Fisherian models a decision maker's utility for a given consumption plan depends on the prevailing state of nature. In the Marshallian model the utility of a given plan contingent on the realization of s_t, which we denote U^t, depends on both the consumption up to period t, $\mathbf{c}^t$, and the bequest b_t. Hence $U^t: R^t_+ \times R \rightarrow R$. We assume further that:

ASSUMPTION (A.1). *For each t, $U^t(\mathbf{c}^t;b_t)$ is monotonic increasing, concave, and twice continuously differentiable.*

ASSUMPTION (A.2). *For all values of t, $U^t(0, \ldots, 0;0) = 0$, for $k \leqq t$ $\lim_{c_k \rightarrow 0} U^t_k(\mathbf{c}^t;b_t) = \infty$, $\lim_{c_k \rightarrow \infty} U^t_k(\mathbf{c}^t;b_t) = 0$, and $\lim_{b_t \rightarrow 0} U^t_{t+1}(\mathbf{c}^t;b_t) = \infty$, where U^t_k denotes the partial derivative of U^t with respect to its kth argument.*

The use of a utility index $U^t(\cdot\,,\cdot)$ that depends on the state of nature in (A.1) captures the notion that preferences over consumption–bequest plans are intrinsically state dependent. The concavity of U^t implies risk aversion. Assumption (A.2) is of a more technical nature and is introduced as a sufficient condition for the existence of a solution to the planning problem.

Since the decision maker is an expected-utility-maximizer, given $\mathbf{y}$, $\mathbf{r}$, and $\mathbf{p}$ and the absence of life insurance, his objective is to choose a consumption plan $\mathbf{c}^T$ so as to maximize

$$(4.1) \qquad \sum_{t=1}^{T} p_t U^t(\mathbf{c}^t, b_t)$$

subject to the constraints

$$(4.2) \qquad c_t \geqq 0, \qquad t = 1, \ldots, T$$

and

$$(4.3) \qquad b_t = \sum_{k=1}^{t} (y_k - c_k)\gamma_k(t), \qquad t = 1, \ldots, T,$$

where $\gamma_k(t) = \Pi^t_{\tau=k}(1 + r_\tau)$ for $k \leqq t$, $t = 1, \ldots, T$, and $\gamma_k(k-1) = 1$ by definition. Constraints (4.3) define b_t, the value in period t of past savings, compounded periodically according to the relevant rates of interest.

For a given $\mathbf{y}$ the set of consumption–bequest plans $\mathbf{c}^T \geqq 0$, $\mathbf{b}^T$ that satisfy Constraints (4.3) is not bounded. Assumption (A.2), however, implies that the decision maker will consider only those plans where $b_t \geqq 0$, $t = 1, \ldots, T$. For a given $\mathbf{y}$, $\mathbf{r}$, and $\mathbf{p}$ there exists an optimal consumption–bequest plan $[c^*_1(\mathbf{y},\mathbf{r},\mathbf{p}), \ldots, c^*_T(\mathbf{y},\mathbf{r},\mathbf{p})], [(b^*_1(\mathbf{y},\mathbf{r},\mathbf{p}), \ldots, b^*_T(\mathbf{y},\mathbf{r},\mathbf{p})]$ that maximizes Exp. (4.1) subject to (4.2) and (4.3).

The subsequent exposition is facilitated by the use of indirect utility functions $u^t(\boldsymbol{y},\boldsymbol{r},\boldsymbol{p})$, $t = 1, \ldots, T$, defined for each t as

$$u^t(\boldsymbol{y},\boldsymbol{r},\boldsymbol{p}) = U^t(c_1^*(\boldsymbol{y},\boldsymbol{r},\boldsymbol{p}), \ldots, c_t^*(\boldsymbol{y},\boldsymbol{r},\boldsymbol{p}); b_t^*(\boldsymbol{y},\boldsymbol{r},\boldsymbol{p})). \tag{4.4}$$

We assume that u^t are monotonic increasing, concave, and twice continuously differentiable in $\boldsymbol{y}$.

4.2.2 The Fisherian Objective Function

Whereas in the Marshallian model the state-dependent utility of a consumption plan depends on the realized consumption sequence and the bequest, in the Fisherian model it depends solely on the realized consumption. For each $t = 1, \ldots, T$ the decision maker's preferences over $\boldsymbol{c}^t$ are represented by a real-valued function U^t defined on R^t_+. In addition we assume

ASSUMPTION (A.3). *For each t, $U^t(\boldsymbol{c}^t)$ is monotone increasing, concave, twice continuously differentiable function, and $\lim_{c_i \to 0} U^t_i(\boldsymbol{c}^t) = \infty$, $\lim_{c_i \to \infty} U^t_i(\boldsymbol{c}^t) = 0$, $i = 1, \ldots, t$, $t = 1, \ldots, T$.*

As already mentioned, in the absence of a bequest motive, there is nothing to inhibit the decision maker from incurring debt to finance his consumption. To prevent this behavior external constraints must be imposed on borrowing. These constraints take the form of a requirement that the net saving b_t at the end of each period be nonnegative. Thus given $\boldsymbol{y}$, $\boldsymbol{r}$, and $\boldsymbol{p}$, the decision maker formulates a consumption plan. That is, he chooses $\boldsymbol{c}^T$ so as to maximize

$$\sum_{t=1}^{T} p_t U^t(\boldsymbol{c}^t) \tag{4.5}$$

subject to the constraints

$$c_t \geqq 0, \qquad t = 1, \ldots, T \tag{4.6}$$

and

$$b_t \equiv \sum_{k=1}^{t} (y_k - c_k)\gamma_k(t) \geqq 0, \qquad t = 1, \ldots, T. \tag{4.7}$$

Under Assumption (A.3) an optimal solution exists, and indirect utility functions u^t may be defined for all t as

$$u^t(\boldsymbol{y},\boldsymbol{r},\boldsymbol{p}) = U^t(c_1^*(\boldsymbol{y},\boldsymbol{r},\boldsymbol{p}), \ldots, c_t^*(\boldsymbol{y},\boldsymbol{r},\boldsymbol{p})), \qquad t = 1, \ldots, T.$$

These functions are monotonic increasing, concave, and twice continuously differentiable in $\boldsymbol{y}$.

4.3 Interpersonal Comparison of Risk Aversion—The Marshallian Model

In this section we develop equivalent characterizations of the partial ordering on the set of Marshallian utility functions induced by the relation "more risk-averse than." We begin by considering the issue of comparability.

4.3.1 The Reference Set and Comparability

In Chapter 2 a reference point was defined as the most preferred allocation of wealth across states of nature in the set of actuarially equivalent allocations. This notion applies here as well. A reference point in the Marshallian model represents the most preferred allocation of income over the decision maker's lifetime among all actuarially equivalent allocations. Implicit in this definition is the assumption that, given $\boldsymbol{r}$ and $\boldsymbol{p}$, the individual evaluates any such allocation $\boldsymbol{y}$ in terms of the optimal consumption–bequest plan made attainable by it. In other words, the value of any allocation $\boldsymbol{y}$ is given by $\Sigma_{t=1}^{T} p_t u^t(\boldsymbol{y},\boldsymbol{r},\boldsymbol{p})$.

Second, since incomes are received at different points in time, speaking of actuarially equivalent income streams requires the use of discounting to compare the actuarial value of dollars received at distinct points in time. More specifically, let $\boldsymbol{y}^0$ be the decision maker's initial income stream. The future actuarial value of this stream is given by $\Sigma_{t=1}^{T} \xi_t \gamma_t(T) y_t^0$, where $\xi_t = \Sigma_{\tau=t}^{T} p_t$ is the probability that the decision maker will live to receive y_t^0 and $\gamma_t(T)$ is the compounding factor that represents the value at the end of period T of a dollar received at the start of period t. The set of all income streams that are actuarially equivalent to $\boldsymbol{y}^0$ is given by

$$(4.8)\qquad \sum_{t=1}^{T} \xi_t \gamma_t(T)(y_t - y_t^0) = 0.$$

A reference point $\boldsymbol{y}^*$ is defined as the solution to the following problem. Given $\boldsymbol{r}$ and $\boldsymbol{p}$ choose $\boldsymbol{y}$ so as to maximize

$$(4.9)\qquad \sum_{t=1}^{T} p_t u^t(\boldsymbol{y},\boldsymbol{r},\boldsymbol{p})$$

subject to the constraint given by Eq. (4.8). Letting the actuarial value of the initial income stream take any nonnegative value, we obtain by the procedure described above the set of all the reference points corresponding to the utility function $\{u^t\}_{t=1}^{T}$, which is its reference set. Thus

DEFINITION 4.1 (REFERENCE SET OF A MARSHALLIAN UTILITY). $RS_u(\mathbf{r},\mathbf{p}) = \{\mathbf{y}^* \in R^T_+ | \mathbf{y}^* \text{ maximizes } \Sigma^T_{t=1} p_t u^t(\mathbf{y},\mathbf{r},\mathbf{p}) \text{ subject to } \Sigma^T_{t=1} \xi_t \gamma_t(T) y_t = \theta, \theta \geqq 0\}$.

Consider, for example, a decision maker who lives one or two periods, and denote by p the probability that this decision maker dies during the first period of his life. At the outset of that period the decision maker receives an income y_1^0, and if he survives the first period he receives the noninterest income y_2^0 at the beginning of the second period. Thus the decision maker receives the noninterest income streams $\{y_1^0\}$ and $\{y_1^0, y_2^0\}$ with probabilities 1 and $(1 - p)$, respectively. Given $\mathbf{r}$ and $\mathbf{p}$, one of the decision maker's indifference curves between y_1 and y_2—that is, the set of sequences $\{y_1, y_2\}$ such that $pu^1(\mathbf{y},\mathbf{r},\mathbf{p}) + (1 - p)u^2(\mathbf{y},\mathbf{r},\mathbf{p})$ is constant—is depicted by $\bar{\mathbf{u}}$ in Figure 4.1. Implicit in the construction of $\bar{\mathbf{u}}$ is the assumption that the decision maker selects the optimal consumption plan corresponding to each sequence $\{y_1, y_2\}$.

The set of actuarially equivalent income streams corresponding to $\mathbf{y}^0$—the set of sequences $\{y_1, y_2\}$ such that

$$y_1 + (1 - \mathrm{p})\frac{y_2}{1 + \mathrm{r}} = y_1^0 + (1 - \mathrm{p})\frac{y_2^0}{1 + \mathrm{r}}$$

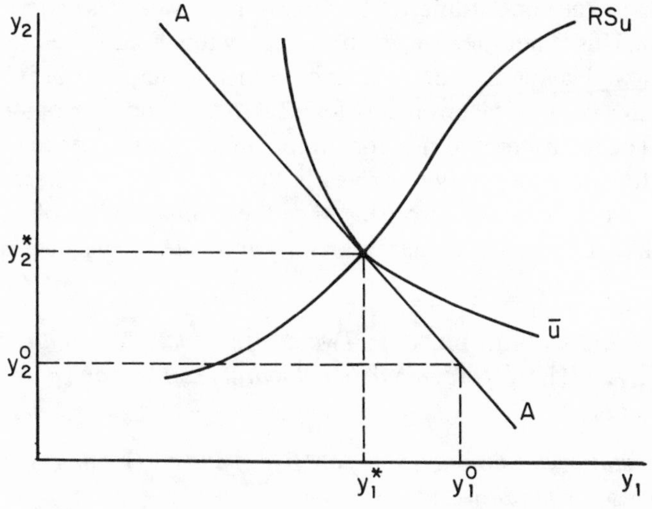

Figure 4.1 The reference set of a Marshallian utility

is depicted by the line AA. The reference point $\langle y_1^*, y_2^* \rangle$ is the tangency point between $\bar{\mathbf{u}}$ and AA. RS_u depicts the reference set.

Returning to Definition (4.1) it is easy to verify that on the reference set the following must hold:

$$(4.10) \qquad \sum_{t=1}^{T} p_t u_k^t(\mathbf{y}^*) = \frac{\xi_k}{p_T} \gamma_k(T-1) \, \Sigma_{t=1}^{T} p_t u_T^t(\mathbf{y}^*),$$

$$k = 1, \ldots, T-1, \mathbf{y}^* \in RS.$$

Thus, given $\boldsymbol{r}$ and $\boldsymbol{p}$ we see that for each $y_1 = y_1^*$, the $T-1$ equations in (4.10) uniquely determine the sequence $y_2^*, \ldots, y_T^*$ such that $\mathbf{y}^* \in RS$. Hence we can define $T-1$ scalar-valued functions $f_2, \ldots, f_T$ such that if $f_1(z) \equiv z$, we have

$$(4.11) \qquad RS_u(\boldsymbol{r},\boldsymbol{p}) = \{f_1(y), f_2(y), \ldots, f_T(y) | y \in R_+\}.$$

It can be verified from the definition that f_t, $t = 1, \ldots, T$ are monotonic increasing, continuous, and differentiable functions on R_+.

Next consider the issue of comparability. When the utility function has a single argument, say wealth as was the case in Chapter 2, the comparability of attitudes toward risk required only that the individuals being compared have identical reference sets. In that instance the problem of comparability was considerably simplified because, in each state of nature, all the utility functions represent the same ordinal preferences—more wealth is preferred over less wealth. This is not the case when the utility functions have more than one argument. Having the same reference set neither implies nor is implied by the holding of identical ordinal preferences over the domain of the utility function. The requisite condition for comparability of attitudes toward risk of utility functions of many variables is that the ordinal preferences be identical. Hence it is not surprising that the comparability of attitudes toward risk in the presence of many variables and state dependence has both requisites.

DEFINITION 4.2 (COMPARABILITY). *Two decision makers with utility functions $\{U^t\}_{t=1}^T$ and $\{V^t\}_{t=1}^T$ are said to be comparable under* $\mathbf{r}$ *and* $\mathbf{p}$ *if and only if, given* $\mathbf{r}$ *and* $\mathbf{p}$,

(a) their optimal consumption plans $\mathbf{c}^{*u}(\mathbf{y},\mathbf{r},\mathbf{p})$ and $\mathbf{c}^{*v}(\mathbf{y},\mathbf{r},\mathbf{p})$, respectively, are the same for all $\mathbf{y} \in R_+^T$;

(b) their reference sets $RS_u(\mathbf{r},\mathbf{p})$ and $RS_v(\mathbf{r},\mathbf{p})$, respectively, are identical.

Part (a) of Definition 4.2 also implies the existence, for the given $\boldsymbol{r}$ and $\boldsymbol{p}$, of monotonic increasing functions F_t: $R \to R$, $t = 1, \ldots, T$, such that $u^t(\boldsymbol{y},\boldsymbol{r},\boldsymbol{p}) = F_t[v^t(\boldsymbol{y},\boldsymbol{r},\boldsymbol{p})]$ for all $\boldsymbol{y} \in R^T_+$. It will be seen later that the implication of condition (b) of Definition 4.2 is that the functions F_t all have the same slope when $\boldsymbol{y} \in RS$.

Later I shall fix $\boldsymbol{r}$ and $\boldsymbol{p}$, to simplify the notation from here on the dependence of u^t and v^t on $\boldsymbol{r}$ and $\boldsymbol{p}$ will be suppressed.

4.3.2 Risk Premium and Risk Aversion in the Small

In principle, the measurement of risk aversion by the risk premium (the maximum actuarial value the decision maker would forgo rather than bear a given risk) applies to models of life insurance. The main difference between the problem at hand and the measurement of risk aversion in the problem of flight insurance in Chapter 3 is that the risks, as well as the risk premiums, are spread over time. Hence the scalar measure of risk aversion is the largest discounted actuarial value that a decision maker would forgo rather than bear a given risk. The premium is calculated in two stages: First we find the element of RS that represents the same level of expected utility as the risky position. This gives rise to a vector risk premium function. Second, we take the present actuarial value of this vector, which is the desired scalar measure of risk aversion. Let $\boldsymbol{f}(y - \pi)$ be the *reference equivalent* of the risk given by $\boldsymbol{f}(y) + \boldsymbol{x}$, where $\boldsymbol{x}$ satisfies $\Sigma_{k=1}^{T} \xi_k \gamma_k(T) x_k = 0$. Formally, the reference equivalent is the element of the reference set (the analogue of certainty equivalent in the case of state-independent preferences) defined by

$$(4.12) \qquad \sum_{t=1}^{T} p_t u^t(\boldsymbol{f}(y - \pi)) = \sum_{t=1}^{T} p_t u^t(\boldsymbol{f}(y) + \boldsymbol{x}),$$

where the expression on the right side is assumed to exist. The vector risk premium function is $[\boldsymbol{f}(y) - \boldsymbol{f}(y - \pi)]$, and the scalar measure of risk aversion Q is defined by

$$(4.13) \qquad Q[\boldsymbol{f}(y),\boldsymbol{x}] = \sum_{t=1}^{T} \frac{\xi_t}{\gamma_1(t-1)} [f_t(y) - f_t(y - \pi)].$$

Using these notions we define the relation "more risk averse."

DEFINITION 4.3 ("MORE RISK AVERSE THAN"). *Let U and V be two state-dependent utility functions that are comparable under* $\boldsymbol{r}$ *and* $\boldsymbol{p}$ *with indirect utility functions* $\{u^t\}_{t=1}^{T}$, $\{v^t\}_{t=1}^{T}$ *and risk premium functions* Q_U *and* Q_V, *respectively. Then U is said to be more risk averse than V if and only if* $Q_U[\boldsymbol{f}(y),\boldsymbol{x}] \geqq Q_V[\boldsymbol{f}(y),\boldsymbol{x}]$ *for all y and* $\boldsymbol{x}$ *that satisfy* $\Sigma_{t=1}^{T} \xi_t \gamma_t(T) x_t = 0$.

Clearly, $Q_U \geqq Q_V$ is equivalent to $\pi_U[f(y),x] \geqq \pi_V[f(y),x]$, where π_U and π_V are the first entries in the vector risk premium functions of U and V, respectively.

For small risks—that is, small deviations x from $f(y)$—the magnitude of π_U can be approximated by taking the Taylor expansion of both sides of (4.12) around $f(y)$ and solving for π_U. Taking a linear approximation of the expression on the left side of Eq. (4.12) and using Eq. (4.10) we get

$$\begin{aligned}\sum_{t=1}^{T} p_t u^t(f(y-\pi_u)) &\approx \sum_{t=1}^{T} p_t u^t(f(y)) - \pi_u \sum_{t=1}^{T} p_t \sum_{k=1}^{T} u_k^t(f(y)) f_k'(y)\\ &= \sum_{t=1}^{T} p_t u^t(f(y)) - \pi_u \sum_{t=1}^{T} p_t u_1^t(f(y)) \times \sum_{k=1}^{T} f_k'(y)\xi_k[\gamma_1(k-1)]^{-1}.\end{aligned} \tag{4.14}$$

Taking a Taylor expansion of the expression on the right side of Eq. (4.12) we obtain

$$\begin{aligned}\sum_{t=1}^{T} p_t u^t(f(y)+x) \approx \sum_{t=1}^{T} p_t u^t(f(y)) &+ \sum_{t=1}^{T} p_t \sum_{k=1}^{T} u_k^t(f(y))x_k\\ &+ \frac{1}{2}\sum_{t=1}^{T} p_t \sum_{k=1}^{T}\sum_{j=1}^{T} u_{kj}^t(f(y))x_k x_j.\end{aligned} \tag{4.15}$$

Since $\Sigma_{k=1}^{T}\xi_k\gamma_k(T)x_k = 0$, we have, using Eq. (4.10),

$$\sum_{t=1}^{T} p_t \sum_{k=1}^{T} u_k^t(f(y))x_k = \left[\sum_{t=1}^{T} p_t u_1^t(f(y))\right] \sum_{k=1}^{T} \frac{\xi_k x_k}{\gamma_1(k-1)} = 0.$$

Let

$$R_U(y) = \left[-\frac{\sum_{t=1}^{T} p_t u_{kj}^t(y)}{\sum_{t=1}^{T} p_t u_1^t(y)} \right]_{\substack{1\leq k\leq T\\ 1\leq j\leq T}}.$$

Then, equating Eqs. (4.14) and (4.15) as required by Eq. (4.12), we obtain the following expression for π:

(4.16) $$\pi_u[f(y),x] \approx \frac{1}{2}\left[\sum_{k=1}^{T} \frac{\xi_k f_k'(y)}{\gamma_1(k-1)}\right]^{-1} x\, R_U[f(y)]x'.$$

where x' is the transpose of x.

Taking a linear approximation of $Q_U(\,\cdot\,,\,\cdot\,)$ around $f(y)$ we get

(4.17) $$Q_U[f(y),x] \approx \pi_u \sum_{t=1}^{T} \frac{\xi_t}{\gamma_1(t-1)} f_t'(y).$$

From Expressions (4.16) and (4.17) we obtain

(4.18) $$Q_U[f(y),x] = \tfrac{1}{2} x\, R_U[f(y)]x'.$$

Thus $R_U[f(y)]$ is a matrix measure of local risk aversion. Furthermore, $Q_U \geqq Q_V$ implies that for small risks $x[R_U[f(y)] - R_V[f(y)]]x' \geqq 0$ for all actuarialy neutral x.

For small risks the difference between the quadratic forms above is another way of presenting the relation "more risk-averse than." This measure reveals the properties of the utility functions that make one person more risk-averse than another. In the next subsection, I shall compare the attitudes of individuals toward large risks. Ranking individuals by their risk premiums produces a partial order on the set of comparable decision makers. For small risks the ranking of individuals according to this criterion produces a complete ordering on the set of comparable decision makers.

4.3.3 Comparative Risk Aversion

Since they include monetary outcomes that may be far apart in the domain of the utility functions, the comparison of attitudes toward large risks involves properties of the utility functions everywhere in the domain. However, if the local measures of absolute risk aversion of two individuals satisfy the conditions described above everywhere in the domain, then comparison of global attitudes toward risk is possible. Three equivalent characterizations of the relation "more risk-averse" in the large appear in Theorem 4.1.

THEOREM 4.1. *Let $U \equiv \{u^k\}_{k=1}^T$ and $V \equiv \{v^k\}_{k=1}^T$ be state-dependent utility functions (where u^k and v^k, $k = 1, \ldots, T$, are the indirect utility functions). If U and V are comparable under $\mathbf{r}$ and $\mathbf{p}$, then the following three conditions are equivalent.*

(i) The quadratic form $x[R_U(y^*) - R_V(y^*)]\, x'$ is positive for all y^* in RS and x such that $\Sigma_{k=1}^T \xi_k \gamma_k(T) x_k = 0$.

(ii) There exists a transformation $F: R^1 \to R^1$ such that $F[\Sigma_{t=1}^T p_t v^t(y^*)] =$

$\Sigma_{t=1}^{T} p_t u^t(\mathbf{y}^*)$ for all $\mathbf{y}^* \in RS$, $F' \geqq 0$, $F'' \leqq 0$, and $F'[\Sigma_{t=1}^{T} p_t v^t(\mathbf{y}^*)] = F_k'[v^k(\mathbf{y}^*)]$ for all $\mathbf{y}^* \in RS$, $k = 1,2, \ldots, T$.
(iii) $\pi_U(\mathbf{y}^*,\mathbf{x}) \geqq \pi_V(\mathbf{y}^*,\mathbf{x})$ for all $\mathbf{y}^* \in RS$ and all $\mathbf{x}$ that satisfy $\Sigma_{k=1}^{T} \xi_k \gamma_k(T) x_k = 0$.

Theorem 4.1 is the analogue of Theorem 2.1, and it provides us with the measures of risk aversion necessary to conduct comparative static analysis in the Marshallian model.

4.4 Interpersonal Comparison of Risk Aversion— The Fisherian Model

The difference between the Marshallian and the Fisherian models lies in the absence of the bequest motive among Fisherian decision makers. In view of the intimate relations between the structure of the reference set and the measures of risk aversion on one hand and the structure of the objective functional on the other, it is interesting to compare the measurement of risk aversion in the Marshallian and Fisherian models.

As in the Marshallian model, the reference set in the Fisherian model is the set of optimal allocations of income across states of nature that would obtain if actuarially fair transfers across states were allowed. The difference between the two models is that in the Fisherian model, allocations $\mathbf{y}^*$ in RS satisfy $y_t^* = c_t^*(\mathbf{y}^*,\mathbf{r},\mathbf{p})$, $t = 1, \ldots, T$ where $\mathbf{c}^*(\mathbf{y}^*,\mathbf{r},\mathbf{p})$ is the optimal consumption plan given by the solution to Eqs. (4.5)–(4.7). In other words, the optimal allocation of incomes across states is such that the optimal bequest at each and every period is zero. To see this, we observe that $\mathbf{y}^* \in RS$ is obtained from the solution of the following problem:

Choose a consumption plan $\mathbf{c}$ and an allocation $\mathbf{y}$ so as to maximize

$$(4.19)\qquad \sum_{t=1}^{T} p_t U^t(c_1, \ldots, c_T)$$

subject to the constraints

$$(4.20)\qquad c_t \geqq 0, \qquad t = 1, \ldots, T,$$

$$(4.21)\qquad b_t = \sum_{k=1}^{t} \gamma_k(t)(y_k - c_k) \geqq 0, \qquad t = 1, \ldots, T, \text{ and}$$

$$(4.22)\qquad \sum_{t=1}^{T} \frac{\xi_t}{\gamma_1(t-1)}(y_t - y_t^0) = 0.$$

The Lagrangian function for this model is

$$(4.23)\qquad L(\mathbf{c},\mathbf{y},\lambda_1, \ldots, \lambda_T,\mu) = \sum_{t=1}^{T} p_t U^t(c_1, \ldots, c_T) + \sum_{t=1}^{T} \lambda_t \sum_{k=1}^{t} \gamma_k(t)(y_k - c_k) + \mu\left[\sum_{t=1}^{T} \frac{\xi_t}{\gamma_1(t-1)}(y_t - y_t^0)\right].$$

The first-order optimality conditions are

$$(4.24)\qquad \frac{\partial L}{\partial c_j} = \sum_{t=j}^{T} p_t U_j^t(\mathbf{c}^*) - \sum_{t=j}^{T} \lambda_t^* \gamma_j(t) = 0, \qquad j = 1, \ldots, T,$$

$$(4.25)\qquad \frac{\partial L}{\partial y_i} = \sum_{t=i}^{T} \lambda_t^* \gamma_i(t) - \mu \frac{\xi_i}{\gamma_1(i-1)} = 0, \qquad i = 1, \ldots, T.$$

From (4.24) and (4.25) we obtain that $\mu = \gamma_1(T-1)U_T^T(\mathbf{c}^*)$ and

$$(4.26)\qquad \sum_{t=j}^{T} p_j U_j^t(\mathbf{c}^*) = \xi_j \gamma_j(T-1) U_T^T(\mathbf{c}^*), \qquad j = 1, \ldots, T.$$

Next we prove the claim that $\lambda_j^* > 0, j = 1, \ldots, T-1$. Suppose by way of negation that for some k, $1 \leqq k \leqq T-1$, $\lambda_k^* = 0$. Then from Eq. (4.25) we have

$$\mu \frac{\xi_k}{\gamma_1(k-1)} = \sum_{t=k}^{T} \lambda_t^* \gamma_k(t) = \sum_{t=k+1}^{T} \lambda_t^* \gamma_k(t)$$
$$= (1 + r_k) \sum_{t=k+1}^{T} \lambda_t^* \gamma_{k+1}(t)$$
$$= (1 + r_k)\mu \frac{\xi_{k+1}}{\gamma_1(k)} = \mu \frac{\xi_{k+1}}{\gamma_1(k-1)}.$$

The first and the last expressions in this chain of equalities imply, however, that $\xi_k = \xi_{k+1}$, a contradiction. Thus $\lambda_k^* > 0$ for $k = 1, \ldots, T$. Hence $b_k^*(\mathbf{y}^*) = 0$ for $k = 1, \ldots, T$, $\mathbf{y}^* \in RS$. In other words, $y_t^* = c_t^*(\mathbf{y}^*,\mathbf{r},\mathbf{p})$. We have proved that $RS_U(\mathbf{r},\mathbf{p}) = \{\mathbf{y}^* \in R_+^T \mid \text{for all } t, y_t^* = c_t^*(\mathbf{y}^*,\mathbf{r},\mathbf{p})$, where $\mathbf{c}^*(\mathbf{y}^*,\mathbf{r},\mathbf{p})$ is the optimal consumption plan given $\mathbf{y}^*,\mathbf{r}$ and $\mathbf{p}\}$.

The above discussion may be illustrated diagrammatically. Consider a decision maker who lives one or two periods, and let p denote the probability that he dies during the first period. At the outset of the first period he receives noninterest income y_1, and if he survives the first period he receives noninterest income y_2 at the start of the second period.

One of the decision maker's indifference curves between first-period and second-period consumption is depicted by $\overline{U}$ in Figure 4.2. An indifference curve between first-period and second-period noninterest income is depicted by $\overline{u}$. $\overline{u}$ and $\overline{U}$ coincide above point B. The overall convexity of $\overline{u}$ is an implication of risk aversion. The linear section of $\overline{u}$ corresponds to the situation where saving is positive in the first period, in which case the subjective rate of substitution between income in the first and the second period is determined by the market rate of interest.

The line AA depicts actuarially equivalent sequences of noninterest income streams. The actuarially fair rate of substitution between income in the first and the second period is determined by the market rate of interest and the probability of survival, and is equal to $-(1+r)/(1-p)$, which is smaller than $-(1+r)$, the slope of the bottom part of $\overline{u}$. The tangency point B is the point on RS_U.

Finally, notice that the definition of RS_U in conjunction with Eqs. (4.26) permits us to choose arbitrarily a level of y_1^*, and $y_2^*, \ldots, y_T^*$ are uniquely determined, so that $\boldsymbol{y}^* \in RS_U(\boldsymbol{r},\boldsymbol{p})$. Thus, as in the Marshallian model, we can define T monotonic increasing and differentiable scalar-valued func-

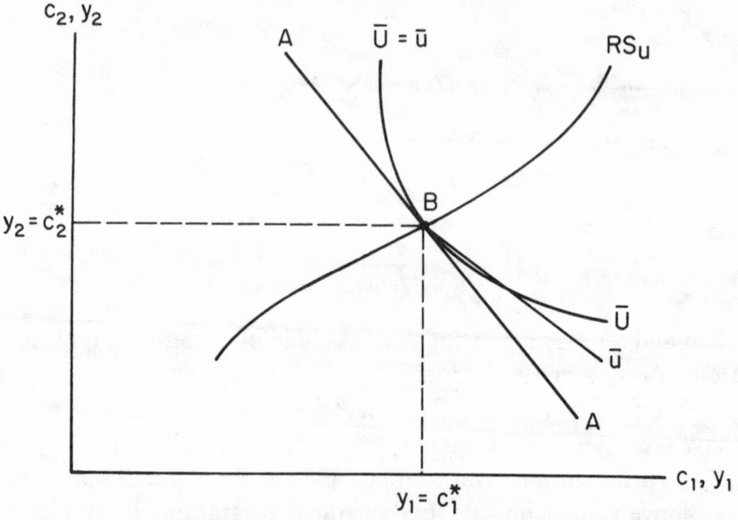

Figure 4.2 The reference set in the Fisherian model

tions $f_1, \ldots, f_T$ on R, where $f_1(y) \equiv y$ and $RS_U(\mathbf{r},\mathbf{p}) = \{f_1(y), \ldots, f_T(y) | y \in R_+\}$.

The issues of comparability and of the measurement of risk aversion of comparable decision makers in the Fisherian model are not substantially different from those in the Marshallian model. Comparability requires that, given $\mathbf{r}$ and $\mathbf{p}$, decision makers have identical optimal consumption plans for all $\mathbf{y}$ and the same reference sets. The measurement of risk aversion of comparable individuals has the same three characterizations as in Theorem 4.1. Thus the only essential difference between the models is the characterization of the reference set, which in the Fisherian model takes the form of income streams such that the corresponding optimal consumption plans yield zero saving in each period.

4.5 Risk Aversion and the Demand for Life Insurance

The availability of life insurance permits a greater freedom of choice among consumption–bequest plans. Presently our main concern is the effect of risk aversion on the choice of optimal life insurance plans. In particular we are interested in whether, *ceteris paribus,* a more risk-averse decision maker buys more life insurance than a comparable but less risk-averse decision maker. We begin by introducing life insurance into our models in a formal manner.

4.5.1 Actuarial Notes and Life Insurance

In practice life insurance is a contingent contract that specifies the transfer of a sum of money called the insurance premium from the insured to the insurer in the event that the insured is alive, in exchange for an indemnity payment to the insured's beneficiaries in the event of his death. It is convenient to model this practice using the notion of actuarial notes. Unlike a regular note an actuarial note represents an obligation that is automatically canceled if the individual who issued or purchased such a note dies before the note's redemption date. If, for example, an individual issues a one-period actuarial note, the note stays on the books and must be redeemed at the end of the period if the individual is still alive. If, however, the decision maker dies during the period his estate is held free of any obligation arising from the note. Because of the risk involved, were anyone to buy such notes he would need to be paid interest in excess of the interest paid on regular notes.

The analogy between taking out a life insurance policy and holding a portfolio of actuarial and regular notes is made clear if we consider a decision maker whose initial noninterest income stream is given by the sequence $\{y_1, \ldots, y_T\}$. Suppose that at the outset of the first period the decision maker issues z_1 dollars worth of one-period actuarial notes and uses the proceeds to purchase the same value in regular notes. In effect the combined transaction amounts to taking out a life insurance policy for z_1 dollars. To verify this claim, note that at the start of the second period one of two possible situations will arise. (a) If the decision maker dies during the first period his estate is held free of any obligation arising from the issue of the actuarial notes, while it includes the value of the regular notes. Consequently the decision maker bequeaths to his beneficiaries the value z_1 of the regular notes. This is the indemnity to which the beneficiaries would be entitled according to the terms of the life insurance policy. (b) If the decision maker is alive at the start of the second period he must redeem the actuarial notes, which he does by selling the regular notes and paying the difference in interest out of his second-period income. This is analogous to paying the insurance premium specified by the life insurance policy.

From the viewpoint of the insurer the holding of actuarial notes entails an opportunity cost of the interest foregone on regular notes and the risk of losing the investment if the issuer of the actuarial notes dies before their redemption date. Suppose that the insurer is risk neutral and that he requires a proportional loading, denoted by m, to cover the cost of providing insurance. The interest rate on one-period actuarial notes issued at the start of the jth period of the decision maker's lifetime, i_j, is given by the equation

$$(1 - m)(\xi_{j+1}/\xi_j)(1 + i_j) = 1 + r_j, \qquad j = 1, \ldots, T - 1. \tag{4.27}$$

Notice that ξ_{j+1}/ξ_j, $j = 1, \ldots, T$, is the conditional probability that the decision maker does not die during the jth period of his lifetime, given that he didn't die before the start of the jth period. Thus the expression on the left side of Eq. (4.27) is the expected net return on a one-period actuarial note purchased by the insurer at the outset of the jth period. The expression on the right side of the same equation is the opportunity cost of this transaction. Solving for i_j we get

$$1 + i_j = \left(\frac{1 + r_j}{1 - m}\right)\xi_j/\xi_{j+1}, \qquad j = 1, \ldots, T - 1. \tag{4.28}$$

Since by definition $\xi_{T+1} = 0$, i_T is not defined. The decision maker will not live to redeem the notes issued at the beginning of the last period of his lifetime.

The insurance premium n_j is the difference between the interest on actuarial and regular notes. Thus

$$(4.29)\qquad n_j \equiv i_j - r_j = \frac{1+r_j}{1-m}\left[\frac{p_j}{\xi_{j+1}} - m\right], \qquad j = 1, \ldots, T-1.$$

An actuarial note is said to be *fair* if $m = 0$. The premium on one dollar's worth of a fair one-period term life insurance policy is $(1 + r_j)p_j/\xi_{j+1}$.

Finally, notice that in the same sense that the selling of actuarial notes amounts to the purchase of life insurance, the purchase of actuarial notes redeemable only if the purchaser is alive at the redemption date amounts to the purchase of annuities. Because of this symmetry the market for annuities does not represent a distinct analytical problem. I shall later exploit this analogy to draw some comparative static results about the effect of risk aversion on the demand for annuities.

Choices of an optimal life insurance plan and an optimal consumption–bequest plan must be made simultaneously. It is convenient to present the problem of formulating an optimal life insurance plan using the indirect utility functions, thus bringing to the fore those aspects of the problem which are directly relevant to the choice of life insurance. Consider, therefore, an individual who chooses a life insurance plan $\{z_1, \ldots, z_{t-1}\}$ so as to maximize

$$(4.30)\qquad \sum_{t=1}^{T} p_t v^t(y_1 + z_1, y_2 - (1 + i_1)z_1 + z_2, \ldots, y_T - (1 + i_{T-1})z_{T-1})$$

subject to

$$(4.31)\qquad 1 + i_j = \left(\frac{1+r_j}{1-m}\right)(\xi_j/\xi_{j+1}), \qquad j = 1, \ldots, T-1.$$

Notice that by setting $z_T = 0$ we imposed the constraint that the decision maker must settle his account with the insurer at the start of the last period of his lifetime.

Since $\Sigma_{t=1}^{T} p^t v^t$ is concave, the optimality conditions are

$$(4.32)\qquad \sum_{t=1}^{T} p_t[v_j^t - v_{j+1}^t(1 + i_j)] = 0, \qquad j = 1, \ldots, T-1.$$

Let $\hat{z}_j = z_j^* - (1 + i_{j-1})z_{j-1}^*, j = 1, \ldots, T$, where $\mathbf{z}^*$ is the solution to Eq. (4.32) and $z_0^* = 0$. Then $\hat{z}_j$ is the net transfer of income to state j. For fair actuarial notes we have the result given in Proposition 4.1.

PROPOSITION 4.1. *If fair actuarial notes are available, then the solution to Eq. (4.32) is such that* $\mathbf{y} + \mathbf{z} \in RS_V$.

In other words, under fair insurance terms, taking out an optimal life insurance plan is equivalent to rearranging the initial income stream so as to attain a point on the reference set. Consequently, all comparable decision makers with the same initial noninterest income stream take out identical fair life insurance policies.

4.5.2 Comparative Statics Analysis of a Two-Period Model with Unfair Insurance

Because the provision of life insurance involves a cost which, in general, is not fixed, insurance terms are usually unfair. In that case the comparative statics analysis of a two-period model differs from that of models with more than two periods. The difference is because in a two-period model there is a single decision variable, namely how much insurance to take out during the first period. (The second-period insurance is necessarily zero.) With more than two periods we have multiple decision variables, and the interactions among these variables render the results ambiguous. (The nature of the interaction among the variables and their consequences is explained in the following subsection.) In the two-period model we obtain the intuitive result that, *ceteris paribus,* a more risk-averse decision maker buys more life insurance or annuities than a comparable less risk-averse decision maker with the same initial noninterest income stream. This conclusion is the essence of Theorem 4.2 and its corollary.

THEOREM 4.2. *Let* $U = \{u^1, u^2\}$ *and* $V = \{v^1, v^2\}$ *be the utility functions of comparable decision makers. Suppose that U is more risk averse than V. Let* $m \geqq 0$ *and denote by* z_1^{*u} *and* z_1^{*v} *the optimal insurance coverage of U and V, respectively. Then* $|z_1^{*u}| \geqq |z_1^{*v}|$.

COROLLARY 4.1. *(a) If the initial* $\mathbf{y}$ *is such that a risk-averse decision maker buys life insurance, then a comparable more risk-averse decision maker with the same initial noninterest income will buy more life insurance.*
(b) If the initial $\mathbf{y}$ *is such that a risk-averse decision maker buys annuities, then a comparable more risk-averse decision maker with the same initial noninterest income will buy more annuities.*

We turn next to the case where the planning horizon exceeds two periods.

4.5.3 Limitations of the Theory

Comparisons of the extent of coverage in a life insurance model with planning horizons of more than two periods require a measure of the level of coverage. A simple but rather strong measure defines an insurance plan as more comprehensive if it provides for larger coverage period-by-period. Another natural and weaker measure is the compounded actuarial loss of income associated with the plan as a whole. This is equivalent to the compounded actuarial value of the insurance loading, which measures the value of the economic resources required for the insurance plan. Unfortunately, even under this weak measure it is impossible to conclude that, *ceteris paribus,* a more risk-averse decision maker takes out a more comprehensive insurance policy. Consider two comparable risk-averse decision makers with utility functions $U = \{u^k\}_{k=1}^T$ and $V = \{v^k\}_{k=1}^T$, where $T \geqq 3$, and suppose that U is more risk averse than V. Denote by $\mathbf{z}^u = (z_1^{*u}, \ldots, z_{T-1}^{*u})$ and $\mathbf{z}^v = (z_1^{*v}, \ldots, z_{T-1}^{*v})$ the optimal insurance plans of U and V, respectively, and let $\mathbf{y} = (y_1, \ldots, y_T)$ be the initial income stream. When V purchases an insurance plan $\mathbf{z}^v$ in a way that maximizes his lifetime expected utility, his income distribution becomes $[y_1 + z_1^{*v}, y_2 + z_2^{*v} - (1 + i_1)z_1^{*v}, \ldots, y_T - (1 + i_{T-1})z_{T-1}^{*v}]$. The compounded actuarial value of his lifetime income declines by θ^v, where (let $z_0 = z_T = 0$)

$$\theta^v = \sum_{k=1}^{T} \xi_k \gamma_k (T-1)\{y_k - [y_k + z_k^{*v} - (1 + i_{k-1})z_{k-1}^{*v}]\}, \tag{4.33}$$

which can be reduced to

$$\theta^v = \frac{m}{1-m} \sum_{k=1}^{T-1} \xi_k \gamma_k (T-1) z_k^{*v}. \tag{4.34}$$

Defining θ^u in a similar manner, the result concerning the relative magnitudes of θ^u and θ^v is stated in Proposition 4.2.

PROPOSITION 4.2. *Let $T \geqq 3$ and $\mathbf{z}^u, \mathbf{z}^v$ be the optimal life insurance–annuity plans for comparable risk-averse decision makers U and V under unfair insurance. That U is more risk averse than V does not imply that $\theta^u \geqq \theta^v$.*

This rather surprising conclusion has to do with the multidimensionality of the objective function and not its state-dependent nature. Suppose that the more risk-averse decision maker U buys more life insurance coverage in period one than the comparable less risk-averse decision maker V. If both decision makers survive the first period, then at the outset of the second period, since $y_2 - (1 + i_1)z_1^{*u} < y_2 - (1 + i_1)z_1^{*v}$, U has a lower income than V. The "income effect" on U's subsequent demand for insurance is ambiguous and may offset the difference in the premium resulting from the first-period insurance. An example given later will illustrate this point and constitute a proof of Proposition 4.2. The claim that it is the multivariate nature of the objective function rather than its state-dependent nature that is responsible for this result is easily verified by comparing Proposition 4.2 with Theorem 3.2, where the state-dependent nature of the utility function did not result in any ambiguity regarding which individual buys more health insurance in each state.

4.6 Decreasing Absolute Risk Aversion and the Demand for Life Insurance

Generally speaking, variations in income produce corresponding variations in individual attitudes toward risk. Consequently, a comparative statics analysis of individual demand for life insurance with respect to changes in the income stream requires a measure of the corresponding variations in attitudes toward risk. Our discussion thus far indicates that a prerequisite for defining such a measure is that individual preferences over income streams be self-comparable (see Chapter 2). The exact sense in which preferences are self-comparable is provided in the Definition 4.4.

DEFINITION 4.4 (AUTOCOMPARABILITY). *A utility function* $\{U^t\}_{t=1}^T$ *is said to be autocomparable under* $\mathbf{r}$ *and* $\mathbf{p}$ *if and only if, given* $\mathbf{r}$ *and* $\mathbf{p}$,

(a) *the corresponding indirect utility functions* u^t, $t = 1, \ldots, T$, *are homothetic;*

(b) *the reference set* RS_U *is linear—*$\mathbf{y}^* \in RS_U \Rightarrow \lambda \mathbf{y}^* \in RS_U$ *for all* $\lambda > 0$.

The linearity of the reference set was discussed in Chapter 2 and needs no further elaboration. The restriction on preferences in part (a) of Definition 4.4 reflects the multivariate nature of the problem at hand and is analogous to the restriction imposed by Kihlstrom and Mirman (1981) to obtain measures of decreasing risk aversion with many commodities.

Assuming risk aversion, then given $\mathbf{r}$ and $\mathbf{p}$ the indirect utility functions u^t, $t = 1, \ldots, T$, are concave representations of a convex ordinal preference relation on the set of nonnegative income streams. They have least concave representations (see Debreu, 1976). Lemma 4.1 asserts that the least concave representations are linear homogeneous functions on R_+^T.

LEMMA 4.1. *Let $\{u^t\}_{t=1}^T$ be the indirect utility functions corresponding to the autocomparable utility functions $\{U^t\}_{t=1}^T$. Then there exist linear homogeneous utilities $\{v^t\}_{t=1}^T$ such that, given* $\mathbf{r}$ *and* $\mathbf{p}$, *v^t is the least concave representation of the preferences represented by u^t, $t = 1, \ldots, T$.*

Lemma 4.1 implies the existence of a monotonically increasing and concave transformation $F_t: R^1 \rightarrow R^1$ such that $u^t = F_t[v^t]$ for all $\mathbf{y} \in R_+^T$ and $t = 1, \ldots, T$. In addition we can define a monotonically increasing transformation F such that $\Sigma_{t=1}^T p_t u^t(\mathbf{y}^*) = F[\Sigma_{t=1}^T p_t v^t(\mathbf{y}^*)]$ for all $\mathbf{y}^* \in RS_U$. By the linearity of RS_U, F is defined for proportional variations in $\mathbf{y}^*$, and since $\Sigma_{t=1}^T p_t u^t(\mathbf{y})$ is concave in $\mathbf{y}$, while the argument of F is linear homogeneous in $\mathbf{y}$ it follows that F must be concave. We use F to define the notion of decreasing (increasing, constant) risk aversion.

DEFINITION 4.5. *The utility function $\{U\}_{t=1}^T$ is said to display decreasing (increasing, constant) risk aversion if it is autocomparable and if F defined by $\Sigma_{t=1}^T p_t u^t(\mathbf{y}^*) = F[\Sigma_{t=1}^T p_t v^t(\mathbf{y}^*)]$ displays decreasing (increasing, constant) risk aversion in the sense that the Arrow–Pratt measure of absolute risk aversion for F declines (increases, stays the same) with the argument of F.*

Interestingly enough, this definition implies that each F_t, $t = 1, \ldots, T$, displays the same attitude toward risk as F.

LEMMA 4.2. *If $\{U\}_{t=1}^T$ displays decreasing (increasing, constant) risk aversion, then F_t, $t = 1, \ldots, T$, displays decreasing (increasing, constant) risk aversion in the sense of Arrow–Pratt.*

The following are immediate implications of Definition 4.5 and Theorems 4.1 and 4.2, respectively.

COROLLARY 4.2. *If $\{U^t\}_{t=1}^T$ displays decreasing absolute risk aversion in the sense of Definition 4.5, then given* $\mathbf{r}$ *and* $\mathbf{p}$, *$\pi(\mathbf{y}^*, \mathbf{x}) > \pi(\alpha\mathbf{y}^*, \mathbf{x})$ for all $\mathbf{y}^* \in RS_U$, $\alpha > 1$, and $\mathbf{x}$ satisfying $\Sigma_{k=1}^T \xi_k \gamma_k(T) x_k = 0$, where π is the risk premium defined in Eq. (4.12).*

COROLLARY 4.3. *Let $\mathbf{x}$ satisfy $\Sigma_{k=1}^2 \xi_k \gamma_k(2) x_k = 0$ and let $\mathbf{y}(\alpha) = \alpha\mathbf{y}^* + \mathbf{x}$. Then a risk-averse decision maker displaying decreasing (increasing, constant) absolute risk aversion buys less (more, the same) life insurance coverage, the larger is α. The same result holds if the decision maker buys annuities.*

Notice that the variations in the income stream in Corollary 4.3 are such that the risk, defined in terms of deviations of the actual income stream from the reference set, remains unchanged. Other variations in y involve changes in the risk as perceived by the individual under consideration, hence their effect on the level of insurance cannot be attributed solely to changes in individual attitudes toward risk.

4.7 Related Work

A formal analysis of individual demand for life insurance appears in Yaari (1965). Yaari formulated the Marshallian and Fisherian models in continuous time and introduced the device of actuarial notes to represent life insurance and annuities. Yaari's main concern was the effect of the availability of life insurance on the allocation of consumption spending over time. Moffet (1978) extended Yaari's analysis to include death benefits. Neither of these authors nor those who applied Yaari's framework to the study of annuities attempted to analyze the effect of risk aversion on the demand for life insurance or annuities. The first such analysis appears in Karni and Zilcha (1983, 1985).

4.8 Proofs

4.8.1 Proof of Theorem 4.1. (i) ⇒ (ii). Since $y^* = f(y)$, differentiating the first equality in (ii) with respect to y and using Eq. (4.10), we get

$$F'\left[\sum_{t=1}^{T} p_t v^t(f(y))\right] = \frac{\sum_{t=1}^{T} p_t u_k^t(f(y))}{\sum_{t=1}^{T} p_t v_k^t(f(y))} \quad \text{for } k = 1, \ldots, T.$$

Given $y > 0$, let us choose

$$\lambda = (\lambda_1, \ldots, \lambda_T) \in R^T \text{ and } \delta = (\delta_1, \ldots, \delta_T) \in R^T$$

that satisfy the following $T + 2$ conditions:

(a) $$\sum_{k=1}^{T} \xi_k \gamma_k(T) \delta_k = 0,$$

(b) $$\sum_{k=1}^{T} \lambda_k > 0,$$

(c)
$$\frac{\lambda_k \gamma_1(k-1)}{\xi_k} \times \left\{ \frac{\sum_{t=1}^{T} p_t \sum_{j=1}^{T} u_{kj}^t(f(y)) f_j'(y)}{\sum_{t=1}^{T} p_t u_k^t(f(y))} - \frac{\sum_{t=1}^{T} p_t \sum_{j=1}^{T} v_{kj}^t(f(y)) f_j'(y)}{\sum_{t=1}^{T} p_t v_k^t(f(y))} \right\}$$
$$\leqq \left\{ \frac{\sum_{t=1}^{T} p_t \sum_{j=1}^{T} u_{kj}^t(f(y)) \delta_j \delta_k}{u_1^t(f(y))} - \frac{\sum_{t=1}^{T} p_t \sum_{j=1}^{T} v_{kj}^t(f(y)) \delta_j \delta_k}{v_1^t(f(y))} \right\}$$

for $k = 1,2,3, \ldots, T$. We have enough degrees of freedom to choose such $\boldsymbol{\lambda}$ and $\boldsymbol{\delta}$.

Now taking the logarithm of both sides in

$$(F'[\ ])^{\sum_{k=1}^{T} \lambda_k} = \prod_{k=1}^{T} \left\{ \frac{\sum_{t=1}^{T} p_t u_k^t(f(y))}{\sum_{t=1}^{T} p_t v_k^t(f(y))} \right\}^{\lambda_k}$$

and differentiating with respect to y, we obtain that the sign of $(F''/F')[\sum_{t=1}^{T} p_t v^t(f(y))]$ is nonpositive, since by (i) and the choice of $\boldsymbol{\delta}$,

$$\sum_{k=1}^{T} \sum_{j=1}^{T} \left\{ \frac{\sum_{t=1}^{T} p_t u_{kj}^t(f(y))}{\sum_{t=1}^{T} p_t u_1^t(f(y))} - \frac{\sum_{t=1}^{T} p_t v_{kj}^t(f(y))}{\sum_{t=1}^{T} p_t v_1^t(f(y))} \right\} \delta_j \delta_k \leqq 0.$$

Thus for each given $y > 0$, $F''[\sum_{t=1}^{T} p_t v^t(f(y))] \leqq 0$.

State Lemma 4.3 to prove that (ii) ⇒ (iii).

LEMMA 4.3. *For any* $\boldsymbol{x}$ *that satisfies* $\sum_{k=1}^{T} \xi_k \gamma_k(T) x_k = 0$, *the following inequality holds:*

$$\sum_{k=1}^{T} p_k F_k[v^k(f(y) + \boldsymbol{x})] \leqq F\left[\sum_{k=1}^{T} p_k v^k(f(y) + \boldsymbol{x}) \right].$$

Let $\boldsymbol{x}$ satisfy $\Sigma_{k=1}^{T}\xi_k\gamma_k(T)x_k = 0$. Then

$$\begin{aligned}\sum_{t=1}^{T} p_t u^t(\boldsymbol{f}(y-\pi_U)) &= \sum_{t=1}^{T} p_t u^t(\boldsymbol{f}(y)+\boldsymbol{x})\\ &= \sum_{t=1}^{T} p_t F_t[v^t(\boldsymbol{f}(y)+\boldsymbol{x})]\\ &\leqq F\left[\sum_{t=1}^{T} p_t v^t(\boldsymbol{f}(y)+\boldsymbol{x})\right]\\ &= F\left[\sum_{t=1}^{T} p_t v^t(\boldsymbol{f}(y-\pi_V))\right]\\ &= \sum_{t=1}^{T} p_t u^t(\boldsymbol{f}(y-\pi_V)),\end{aligned}$$

where the inequality follows from Lemma 4.3, the second equality is a consequence of the comparability of U and V, and the last equality is hypothesized in (ii). Thus, by the monotonicity of $u^t(\boldsymbol{f}(y))$ in y for $t = 1, \ldots, T$, it follows that $\pi_V \leqq \pi_U$.

(iii) ⇒ (i): Let $\boldsymbol{z}$ satisfy $\Sigma_{k=1}^{T}\xi_k\gamma_k(T)z_k = 0$ and choose $\boldsymbol{x} = h\boldsymbol{z}$. Differentiating π_V with respect to h, evaluating at $h = 0$, and using Eq. (4.10), we get

$$\left.\frac{d\pi_V}{dh}\right|_{h=0} = -\frac{\sum_{t=1}^{T} p_t \sum_{k=1}^{T} v_k^t(\boldsymbol{f}(y))z_k}{\sum_{t=1}^{T} p_t \sum_{k=1}^{T} v_k^t(\boldsymbol{f}(y))f_k'(y)} = 0.$$

Differentiating π_V once again and evaluating at $h = 0$ we get

$$\begin{aligned}\left.\frac{d^2\pi_V}{dh^2}\right|_{h=0} &= -\frac{\sum_{t=1}^{T} p_t \sum_{k=1}^{T}\sum_{j=1}^{T} v_{kj}^t(\boldsymbol{f}(y))z_k z_j}{\sum_{t=1}^{T} p_t \sum_{k=1}^{T} v_k^t(\boldsymbol{f}(y))f_k'(y)}\\ &= -\frac{\sum_{k=1}^{T}\sum_{j=1}^{T}\left[\sum_{t=1}^{T} p_t v_{kj}^t(\boldsymbol{f}(y))\right] z_k z_j}{\sum_{t=1}^{T} p_t u_1^t(\boldsymbol{f}(y)) \sum_{k=1}^{T}\left(\dfrac{\xi_k f_k'(y)}{\gamma_1(k-1)}\right)},\end{aligned}$$

where use has been made of Eq. (4.10). For (iii) to hold for all $\boldsymbol{x}$ we must have

$$\left.\frac{d^2\pi_U}{dh^2}\right|_{h=0} \geqq \left.\frac{d^2\pi_V}{dh^2}\right|_{h=0}$$

for all $\boldsymbol{z}$ satisfying the condition above. This implies (i).

To complete the proof of the theorem we prove Lemma 4.3. Given $\boldsymbol{x}$ that satisfies $\Sigma_{k=1}^{T}\xi_k\gamma_k(T)x_k = 0$ and $\boldsymbol{y}^*$ in RS, let us define the following two functions:

$$G(h) = \sum_{k=1}^{T} p_k F_k[v^k(\boldsymbol{y}^* + h\boldsymbol{x})],$$

$$H(h) = F\left[\sum_{k=1}^{T} p_k v^k(\boldsymbol{y}^* + h\boldsymbol{x})\right].$$

Then, clearly, $G(0) = H(0)$. From the concavity of v^k we obtain, for $k = 1, \ldots, T$,

$$v^k(\boldsymbol{y}^* + h\boldsymbol{x}) - v^k(\boldsymbol{y}^*) \geqq h \sum_{j=1}^{T} v_j^k(\boldsymbol{y}^* + h\boldsymbol{x})x_j \equiv h\beta_k. \tag{4.35}$$

On the other hand we have

$$v^k(\boldsymbol{y}^* + h\boldsymbol{x}) - v^k(\boldsymbol{y}^*) \leqq h \sum_{j=1}^{T} v_j^k(\boldsymbol{y}^*)x_j \equiv h\alpha_k. \tag{4.36}$$

From (4.35) and (4.36) we obtain that, for $k = 1, \ldots, T$,

$$v^k(\boldsymbol{y}^* + h\boldsymbol{x}) > v^k(\boldsymbol{y}^*) \Rightarrow \alpha_k > 0,$$
$$v^k(\boldsymbol{y}^* + h\boldsymbol{x}) < v^k(\boldsymbol{y}^*) \Rightarrow \beta_k < 0.$$

We can show now that $\beta_k \leqq \alpha_k$ for all k.

$$\beta_k = \sum_{j=1}^{T} v_j^k(\boldsymbol{y}^* + h\boldsymbol{x})x_j = \sum_{j=1}^{T}\left[v_j^k(\boldsymbol{y}^*)x_j + \sum_{i=1}^{T} v_{ji}^k(\boldsymbol{y}^* + \bar{\theta}\boldsymbol{x})x_j x_i\right]$$
$$\leqq \sum_{j=1}^{T} v_j^k(\boldsymbol{y}^*)x_j \equiv \alpha_k,$$

where $0 \leqq \bar{\theta} \leqq h$ and the concavity of v^k was used. One can easily show from Eq. (4.35) that

$$\beta_k > 0 \Rightarrow F_k'[v^k(\boldsymbol{y}^* + h\boldsymbol{x})] < F_k'[v^k(\boldsymbol{y}^*)].$$

Thus

$$F_k'[v^k(\boldsymbol{y}^* + h\boldsymbol{x})]\beta_k \leqq F_k'[v^k(\boldsymbol{y}^*)]\beta_k \text{ for } k = 1, \ldots, T. \tag{4.37}$$

Now, differentiating $G(h)$ with respect to h and using Eq. (4.35), we get

$$\begin{aligned} G'(h) &= \sum_{k=1}^{T} p_k F'_k[v^k(\mathbf{y}^* + h\mathbf{x})] \sum_{j=1}^{T} v_j^k(\mathbf{y}^* + h\mathbf{x})x_j \\ &= \sum_{k=1}^{T} p_k F'_k[v^k(\mathbf{y}^* + h\mathbf{x})]\beta_k \leqq \sum_{k=1}^{T} p_k F'_k[v^k(\mathbf{y}^*)]\beta_k \\ &= \sum_{k=1}^{T} p_k F'\left[\sum_{l=1}^{T} p_l v^l(\mathbf{y}^*)\right]\beta_k \\ &\leqq \sum_{k=1}^{T} p_k F'\left[\sum_{l=1}^{T} p_l v^l(\mathbf{y}^* + h\mathbf{x})\right]\beta_k. \end{aligned}$$

Since $\mathbf{y}^*$ in RS, $\sum_{l=1}^{T} p_l v^l(\mathbf{y}^*) \geqq \sum_{l=1}^{T} p_l v^l(\mathbf{y}^* + h\mathbf{x})$.

Now, differentiating $H(h)$, we have

$$\begin{aligned} H'(h) &= F'\left[\sum_{k=1}^{T} p_k v^k(\mathbf{y}^* + h\mathbf{x})\right] \sum_{k=1}^{T} p_k \sum_{l=1}^{T} v_l^k(\mathbf{y}^* + h\mathbf{x})x_l \\ &= F'\left[\sum_{k=1}^{T} p_k v^k(\mathbf{y}^* + h\mathbf{x})\right] \sum_{k=1}^{T} p_k\beta_k. \end{aligned}$$

Hence $G'(h) \leqq H'(h)$ for $h > 0$. Thus $G(h) \leqq H(h)$ for all $h > 0$.

4.8.2 Proof of Proposition 4.1: On the reference set we have, from Eq. (4.10),

$$\xi_{j+1} \sum_{t=1}^{T} p_t v_j^t = \xi_j(1 + r_j) \sum_{t=1}^{T} p_t v_{j+1}^t, \qquad j = 1, \ldots, T-1.$$

For $m = 0$ these conditions follow immediately from Eq. (4.32).

4.8.3 Proof of Theorem 4.2: Let $\mathbf{y} = (y_1, y_2)$ be given, $\mathbf{y} \notin RS$. Consider the line through $\mathbf{y}$ $\mathscr{A} = \{[y_1 + z, y_2 - (1 + i_1)z] | z \in R^1\}$. It intersects RS at $\mathbf{y}^* = (y_1^*, y_2^*)$. Since $m > 0$ the optimum of U and V is not on RS. Let us assume that $z_1^{*u} > 0$, $z_1^{*v} > 0$ (the case where z_1^{*u}, $z_1^{*v} < 0$ can be treated similarly). Denote by $\hat{\mathbf{y}}^u = [y_1 + z_1^{*u}, y_2 - (1 + i_1)z_1^{*u}]$ and $\hat{\mathbf{y}}^v = [y_1 + z_1^{*v}, y_2 - (1 + i_1)z_1^{*v}]$ the optimal income distributions for U and V, correspondingly. Then $\hat{\mathbf{y}}^u$ and $\hat{\mathbf{y}}^v$ are on $\mathscr{A}$ between $\mathbf{y}$ and $\mathbf{y}^*$ (note that for very small m they are close to RS, while for large m they are both $\mathbf{y}$, since $z_1^{*u} = z_1^{*v} = 0$). Now show that $\hat{\mathbf{y}}^u$ is closer to RS than $\hat{\mathbf{y}}^v$. Consider the following maximization problems for V and U:

$$\max_q \sum_{t=1}^{2} p_t v^t(y_1^* + q, y_2^* - (1 + i_1)q),$$

$$\max_q \sum_{t=1}^{2} p_t F_t[v^t(y_1^* + q, y_2^* - (1 + i_1)q)].$$

The first-order conditions are

(4.38) $$0 = \sum_{t=1}^{2} p_t[v_1^t(y_1^* + q^v, y_2^* - (1 + i_1)q^v) - (1 + i_1)v_2^t(y_1^* + q^v, y_2^* - (1 + i_1)q^v)],$$

(4.39) $$0 = \sum_{t=1}^{2} p_t F_t'[\ ][v_1^t(y_1^* + q^u, y_2^* - (1 + i_1)q^u) - (1 + i_1)v_2^t(y_1^* + q^u, y_2^* - (1 + i_1)q^u)].$$

When $m > 0$, $(1 + i_1) > (1 + r_1)$, hence from Eq. (4.10) we obtain

$$\sum_{t=1}^{2} p_t v_1^t(y^*) < (1 + i_1)\sum_{t=1}^{2} p_t v_2^t(y^*) \text{ on } RS.$$

This implies that $p_1[v_1^1(y^*) - (1 + i_1)v_2^1(y^*)] < - p_2[v_1^2(y^*) - (1 + i_1) v_2^2(y^*)]$. Since as q increases the first-period consumption or bequest, or both, must increase

$$\left.\frac{dv^1}{dq}\right|_{q=0} > 0$$

we obtain that

$$\left.\frac{dv^2}{dq}\right|_{q=0} < 0.$$

Thus $v^1(y_1^* + q^u, y_2^* - (1 + i_1)q^u) > v^1(y^*)$ and $v^2(y_1^* + q^u, y_2^* - (1 + i_1)q^u) < v^2(y^*)$. Therefore

$$\begin{aligned} &F_1'[v^1(y_1^* + q^u, y_2^* - (1 + i_1)q^u)] \\ &\quad < F_1'[v^1(y^*)] = F_2'[v^2(y^*)] \\ &\quad < F_2'[v^2(y_1^* + q^u, y_2^* - (1 + i_1)q^u)]. \end{aligned}$$

From Eq. (4.39) we obtain

$$(4.40) \qquad \sum_{t=1}^{2} p_t[v_1^t(y_1^* + q^u, y_2^* - (1+i_1)q^u) - (1+i_1)v_2^t(y_1^* + q^u, y_2^* - (1+i_1)q^u)] > 0.$$

But since $\Sigma_{t=1}^{2} p_t v^t$ is a strictly concave function of q, Eqs. (4.40) and (4.38) imply that $q^u < q^v$. Therefore $z_1^{*u} > z_1^{*v}$.

*4.8.4 **Proof of Proposition 4.2:*** The following example shows that $\theta^u < \theta^v$. Let $T = 3$ and consider the utility function V defined as follows: For some strictly concave functions $w_1, w_2, w_3, \psi_1, \psi_2, \psi_3$ defined on R_{+}^1,

$$V^\tau(c_1, \ldots, c_\tau; b_\tau) = \sum_{t=1}^{\tau} w_t(c_t) + \psi_\tau(b_\tau) \quad \text{for } \tau = 1,2,3.$$

Thus V chooses $\mathbf{c}$, z_1, and z_2 so as to maximize

$$(4.41) \qquad \sum_{t=1}^{3} [\xi_t w_t(c_t) + p_t \psi_t(b_t)]$$

Such that $c_t \geqq 0$, $t = 1,2,3$.

$$b_1 = \gamma_1(1)[y_1 - c_1 + z_1],$$
$$b_2 = \gamma_2(2)[y_2 - c_2 + z_2 - (1+i_1)z_1] + \gamma_2(2)b_1,$$
$$b_3 = \gamma_3(3)[y_3 - c_3 - (1+i_2)z_2] + \gamma_3(3)b_2.$$

Denote by z_1^{*v}, z_2^{*v} the optimal levels of actuarial notes purchased by V. We make the following assumptions:

ASSUMPTION (a.1). $-[\psi_1''(x)]/[\psi_1'(x)] \geqq 1$ and $\psi'''(x) \leqq 0$ *for all* $x \geqq 1$.

ASSUMPTION (a.2). $-[\psi_2''(x)]/[\psi_2'(x)] \geqq 4$ *and* $\psi_2'''(x) \leqq 0$ *for all* $x \geqq 1$.

ASSUMPTION (a.3). $-[\psi_3''(x)]/[\psi_3'(x)] \leqq (1/2)[p_3(1-m)]/[\gamma_2(3)]$ *and* $\psi_3'''(x) \geqq 0$ *for all* $x \geqq 1$.

ASSUMPTION (a.4). $-[w_1''(x)]/[w_1'(x)] \geqq \gamma_1(1)$ *and* $w_1'''(x) \leqq 0$ *for all* $x \geqq 1$.

ASSUMPTION (a.5). $r_k \geqq 0$ *for* $k = 1,2,3$.

ASSUMPTION (a.6). *The incomes* $\mathbf{y} = (\bar{y}_1, \bar{y}_2, \bar{y}_3)$ *are chosen large enough that* $c_k^{*v} \geqq 1, b_k^{*v} \geqq 1$ *for* $k = 1,2,3$.

Now let us choose U, comparable to V and more risk-averse than V, as follows. Given the income stream $\bar{\mathbf{y}} = (\bar{y}_1, \bar{y}_2, \bar{y}_3)$, which satisfies Assumption (a.6), the direct utility functions of U are

$$U^1 = F_1[w_1(c_1) + \psi_1[\gamma_1(1)(\bar{y}_1 - c_1)]],$$
$$U^2 = F_2[w_1(c_1) + w_2(c_2) + \psi_2[\gamma_1(2)(\bar{y}_1 - c_1) + \gamma_2(2)(\bar{y}_2 - c_2)]],$$
$$U^3 = F_3[w_1(c_1) + w_2(c_2) + w_3(c_3) + \psi_3[\gamma_1(3)(\bar{y}_1 - c_1) + \gamma_2(3)(\bar{y}_2 - c_2) + \gamma_3(3)(\bar{y}_3 - c_3)]],$$

Where F_1, F_2, F_3 are increasing concave and are chosen such that U is comparable to V and the following conditions hold.

ASSUMPTION (a.7). *F_2 and F_3 satisfy $1/2 \leqq F_2'(x) \leqq 2$, $1/2 \leqq F_3'(x) \leqq 2$ for all $x > 0$.*

ASSUMPTION (a.8). *At the optimum of U we have $F_1' \leqq F_3'$ and $F_2' \leqq F_3'$.*

It is straightforward to see that Assumptions (a.1)–(a.8) can coexist without violating any of the earlier assumptions of the model. These assumptions guarantee that $\theta^u = (m/1 - m)\gamma_2(2)[\gamma_1(1)z_1^{*u} + \xi_2 z_2^{*u}]$ is *smaller* than $\theta^v = (m/1 - m)\gamma_2(2)[\gamma_1(1)z_1^{*v} + \xi_2 z_2^{*v}]$, establishing Proposition 4.2. This can be stated formally as Lemma 4.4.

LEMMA 4.4. *Let U be more risk-averse than V and assume that Assumptions (a.1)–(a.8) hold. Then $\theta^u < \theta^v$.*

Proof of Lemma 4.4. The first-order conditions for the maximum of Exp. (4.41) are

$$w_1'(c_1^{*v}) - p_1\gamma_1(1)\psi_1'(b_1^{*v}) - p_2\gamma_1(2)\psi_2'(b_2^{*v}) - p_3\gamma_1(3)\psi_3'(b_3^{*v}) = 0, \tag{4.42}$$

$$\xi_2 w_2'(c_2^{*v}) - p_2\gamma_2(2)\psi_2'(b_2^{*v}) - p_3\gamma_2(3)\psi_3'(b_3^{*v}) = 0, \tag{4.43}$$

$$p_3 w_3'(c_3^{*v}) = p_3\gamma_3(3)\psi_3'(b_3^{*v}) = 0, \tag{4.44}$$

$$p_1\gamma_1(1)\psi_1'(b_1^{*v}) + p_2[-(1 + i_1)\gamma_2(2) + \gamma_1(2)]\psi_2'(b_2^{*v}) + p_3[-(1 + i_1)\gamma_2(3) + \gamma_1(3)]\psi_3'(b_3^{*v}) = 0, \tag{4.45}$$

$$p_2\gamma_2(2)\psi_2'(b_2^{*v}) + p_3\psi_3'(b_3^{*v})[-(1 + i_2)\gamma_3(3) + \gamma_2(3)] = 0. \tag{4.46}$$

The following relationships between the marginal utilities at the optimum are easily derived from (4.42)–(4.46).

$$w_3'(c_3^{*v}) = \gamma_3(3)\psi_3'(b_3^{*v}) \tag{4.47}$$

$$w_2'(c_2^{*v}) = \frac{\gamma_2(2)}{1 - m} w_3'(c_3^{*v}) \tag{4.48}$$

$$(4.49)\qquad w_1'(c_1^{*v}) = \frac{\gamma_1(2)}{(1-m)^2}\, w_3'(c_3^{*v})$$

$$(4.50)\qquad p_1\psi_1'(b_1^{*v}) = \frac{\gamma_2(3)}{(1-m)^2}(p_1 + m\xi_2)\psi_3'(b_3^{*v})$$

$$(4.51)\qquad p_2\psi_2'(b_2^{*v}) = \frac{\gamma_3(3)}{1-m}(p_2 + mp_3)\psi_3'(b_3^{*v})$$

The optimization problem for U, given $\bar{y}$, is: Choose $\mathbf{c}$, z_1, and z_2 so as to maximize

$$(4.52)\qquad p_1F_1[w_1(c_1) + \psi_1(b_1)] + p_2F_2[w_1(c_1) + w_2(c_2) + \psi_2(b_2)] + p_3F_3[w_1(c_1) + w_2(c_2) + w_3(c_3) + \psi_3(b_3)]$$

such that $c_i \geqq 0$ for $i = 1,2,3$. The elements b_1, b_2, b_3 are defined by Eq. (4.3) for the given $(\bar{y}_1, \bar{y}_2, \bar{y}_3)$. Rearranging the first-order conditions for this problem, we obtain

$$(4.53)\qquad w_3'(c_3^{*u}) = \gamma_3(3)\psi_3'(b_3^{*u}),$$

$$(4.54)\qquad w_2'(c_2^{*u}) = \frac{\gamma_2(2)}{1-m}\left(\frac{\xi_2 F_3'}{p_2F_2' + p_3F_3'}\right) w_3'(c_3^{*u}),$$

$$(4.55)\qquad w_1'(c_1^{*u}) = \frac{\gamma_1(2)}{(1-m)^2}\left(\frac{F_3'}{p_1F_1' + p_2F_2' + p_3F_3'}\right) w_3'(c_3^{*u}),$$

$$(4.56)\qquad p_1\psi_1'(b_1^{*u}) = \frac{\gamma_2(3)(p_1 + m\xi_2)}{(1-m)^2}\left[\frac{\xi_2 + (1-m)(p_1+p_2)}{\xi_2}\right] \times \frac{F_3'}{F_1'}\psi_3'(b_3^{*u}),$$

$$(4.57)\qquad p_2\psi_2'(b_2^{*u}) = \frac{\gamma_3(3)(p_2 + mp_3)}{1-m}\,\frac{F_3'}{F_2'}\,\psi_3'(b_3^{*u}),$$

where F_1', F_2', F_3' are evaluated at the optimum of U. Denote by z_1^{*u} and z_2^{*u} the optimal levels of actuarial notes purchased by U. From Eqs. (4.47)–(4.57) we have

$$(4.58)\qquad \frac{w_3'(c_3^{*u})}{w_3'(c_3^{*v})} = \frac{\psi_3'(b_3^{*u})}{\psi_3'(b_3^{*v})},$$

$$(4.59)\qquad \frac{w_1'(c_1^{*u})}{w_3'(c_3^{*u})} \geqq \frac{w_1'(c_1^{*v})}{w_3'(c_3^{*v})} \quad\text{and}\quad \frac{w_2'(c_2^{*u})}{w_3'(c_3^{*v})} \geqq \frac{w_2'(c_2^{*v})}{w_3'(c_3^{*v})},$$

(4.60) $$\frac{\psi_1'(b_1^{*u})}{\psi_3'(b_3^{*u})} \geqq \frac{\psi_1'(b_1^{*v})}{\psi_3'(b_3^{*v})} \quad \text{and} \quad \frac{\psi_2'(b_2^{*u})}{\psi_3'(b_3^{*u})} \geqq \frac{\psi_2'(b_2^{*v})}{\psi_3'(b_3^{*v})}.$$

Since these functions are concave we draw the following conclusions:

(4.61) $$c_3^{*u} \geqq c_3^{*v} \Leftrightarrow b_3^{*u} \geqq b_3^{*v} \quad \text{and} \quad c_2^{*u} > c_2^{*v} \Rightarrow c_3^{*u} > c_3^{*v},$$

(4.62) $$c_3^{*u} < c_3^{*v} \Rightarrow c_1^{*u} < c_1^{*v} \quad \text{and} \quad c_1^{*u} > c_1^{*v} \Rightarrow c_3^{*u} > c_3^{*v},$$

(4.63) $$b_3^{*u} < b_3^{*v} \Rightarrow b_2^{*u} < b_2^{*v} \quad \text{and} \quad b_2^{*u} > b_2^{*v} \Rightarrow b_3^{*u} > b_3^{*v},$$

(4.64) $$b_1^{*u} > b_1^{*v} \Rightarrow b_3^{*u} > b_3^{*v} \quad \text{and} \quad c_1^{*u} < c_1^{*v}.$$

Note that the second part of (4.64) follows from the implications $c_1^{*u} > c_1^{*v} \Rightarrow c_2^{*u} > c_2^{*v}$ and $c_3^{*u} > c_3^{*v} \Rightarrow b_2^{*u} > b_2^{*v}$ and $b_3^{*u} > b_3^{*v}$. Thus $b_1^{*u} > b_1^{*v}$ is impossible by the optimality assumption.

Now assume that $b_3^{*u} < b_3^{*v}$. Then $b_2^{*u} < b_2^{*v}$ and $b_1^{*u} < b_1^{*v}$. By Exp. (4.61) $c_3^{*u} < c_3^{*v}$. Hence $c_1^{*u} < c_1^{*v}$ and $c_2^{*u} < c_2^{*v}$. The optimal consumption–bequest plan for U is strictly *smaller* at each date than that for V. Since the optimal consumption–bequest plan for V is feasible for U this is a contradiction. Therefore, we must have $b_3^{*u} > b_3^{*v}$ and $c_3^{*u} > c_3^{*v}$.

To prove the Lemma we have to show that

(4.65) $$\gamma_1(1)(z_1^{*u} - z_1^{*v}) + \xi_2(z_2^{*u} - z_2^{*v}) < 0.$$

From the constraints of (4.41) it is easy to derive that

$$\gamma_1(1)z_1 + \xi_2 z_2 = b_1 + \gamma_1(1)c_1 - \gamma_1(1)y_1 + (1-m)p_3\left[-\frac{b_3}{1+r_3} + y_3 - c_3 + b_2\right].$$

To simplify the writing let us take $\gamma_1(1) = \gamma_2(2) = \gamma_3(3) = 1$. Then to prove (4.65) we show that

(4.66) $$(b_1^{*u} - b_1^{*v}) + (c_1^{*u} - c_1^{*v}) + (1-m)p_3[(b_3^{*v} - b_3^{*u}) + (c_3^{*v} - c_3^{*u}) + (b_2^{*u} - b_2^{*v}) < 0.$$

From (4.64) we see that if $b_1^{*u} - b_1^{*v} > 0$ then $c_1^{*u} - c_1^{*v} \leqq 0$, and if $c_1{}^{*u} - c_1^{*v} > 0$ then $b_1^{*u} - b_1^{*v} \leqq 0$. Let us first consider the case where $b_1^{*u} - b_1^{*v} > 0$. From Exps. (4.50) and (4.56) we have

$$\frac{\psi_1'(b_1^{*u})}{\psi_1'(b_1^{*v})} \geqq \left[\frac{\xi_2 + (1-m)(p_1 + p_2)}{\xi_2}\right] \frac{\psi_3'(b_3^{*u})}{\psi_3'(b_3^{*v})}.$$

Hence

$$\left[-\frac{\psi_1''(\hat{b}_1)}{\psi_1'(b_1^{*v})}\right](b_1^{*v}-b_1^{*u}) > \frac{(p_1+p_2)(1-m)}{\xi_2}\frac{\psi_3'(b_3^{*u})}{\psi_3'(b_3^{*v})} + \left[\frac{\psi_3''(\hat{b}_3)}{\psi_3'(b_3^{*v})}\right](b_3^{*v}-b_3^{*u}), \tag{4.67}$$

where $b_1^{*v} \leqq \hat{b}_1 \leqq b_1^{*u}$ and $b_3^{*v} \leqq \hat{b}_3 \leqq b_3^{*u}$. Inequality (4.67) implies that

$$\left[-\frac{\psi_1''(b_1^{*v})}{\psi_1'(b_1^{*v})}\right](b_1^{*u}-b_1^{*v}) + \left[\frac{\psi_3''(\hat{b}_3)}{\psi_3'(\hat{b}_3)}\right](b_3^{*v}-b_3^{*u}) < 0. \tag{4.68}$$

Hence, by Assumptions (a.1), (a.3), and (a.6) we obtain from (4.68) that

$$(b_1^{*u}-b_1^{*v}) + \tfrac{1}{2}(1-m)p_3(b_3^{*v}-b_3^{*u}) < 0. \tag{4.69}$$

Now assume that $c_1^{*u} - c_1^{*v} > 0$. From (4.49) and (4.55) we have

$$\frac{w_1'(c_1^{*u})}{w_1'(c_1^{*v})} = \sigma\frac{w_3'(c_3^{*u})}{w_3'(c_3^{*v})},$$

where $\sigma > 1$. Using (4.58)

$$\frac{w_1'(c_1^{*u})}{w_1'(c_1^{*v})} - 1 = (\sigma-1)\frac{\psi_3'(b_3^{*u})}{\psi_3'(b_3^{*v})} + \left[\frac{\psi_3'(b_3^{*u})}{\psi_3'(b_3^{*v})} - 1\right]. \tag{4.70}$$

Using the mean value theorem, Assumption (a.3), and Assumption (a.4), we obtain from (4.70)

$$\left[-\frac{w_1''(c_1^{*v})}{w_1'(c_1^{*v})}\right](c_1^{*u}-c_1^{*v}) + \left[-\frac{\psi_3''(b_3^{*v})}{\psi_3'(b_3^{*v})}\right](b_3^{*v}-b_3^{*u}) < 0,$$

which implies that

$$(c_1^{*u}-c_1^{*v}) + \tfrac{1}{2}(1-m)p_3(b_3^{*v}-b_3^{*u}) < 0. \tag{4.71}$$

Now from Exp. (4.51) and (4.57) we have

$$\frac{F_2'}{F_3'}\left[\frac{\psi_2'(b_2^{*u})}{\psi_2'(b_2^{*v})} - 1\right] > \frac{\psi_3'(b_3^{*u})}{\psi_3'(b_3^{*v})} - 1. \tag{4.72}$$

Now using the mean value theorem and Assumptions (a.2), (a.3), (a.5), and (a.7), we obtain from Exp. (4.72)

$$\frac{F_2'}{F_3'}\left[-\frac{\psi_2''(b_2^{*v})}{\psi_2'(b_2^{*v})}\right](b_2^{*u}-b_2^{*v}) + \left[-\frac{\psi_3''(\hat{b}_3)}{\psi_3'(\hat{b}_3)}\right](b_3^{*v}-b_3^{*u}) < 0.$$

Hence

(4.73) $$b_2^{*u} - b_2^{*v} + \tfrac{1}{2}(b_3^{*v} - b_3^{*u}) < 0.$$

But Exps. (4.69), (4.71), and (4.73) imply (4.66). This proves Lemma 4.4.

4.8.5 Proof of Lemma 4.1: Since u^t is homothetic there exist F_t such that for $t = 1, \ldots, T$, $u^t = F_t[v^t]$ where v^t is homogeneous of degree one on R_+^T. The proof that if u^t is concave then F_t is concave is the same as in Kihlstrom and Mirman (1981). If $\bar{v}^t$ and $\bar{\bar{v}}^t \in v^t(R_+^T)$, there exist $\mathbf{y} \in R_+^T$ and λ such that $v^t(\mathbf{y}) = \bar{v}^t$ and $v^t(\lambda \mathbf{y}) = \bar{\bar{v}}^t$. For $\mu \in (0,1)$,

$$\begin{aligned} F_t[\mu\bar{v}^t + (1-\mu)\bar{\bar{v}}^t] &= F_t[\mu v^t(\mathbf{y}) + (1-\mu)v^t(\lambda\mathbf{y})] \\ &= F_t[(\mu + (1-\mu)\lambda)v^t(\mathbf{y})] = F_t[v^t((\mu + (1-\mu)\lambda)\mathbf{y})] \\ &= F_t[v^t(\mu\mathbf{y} + (1-\mu)\lambda\mathbf{y})] = u^t(\mu\mathbf{y} + (1-\mu)\lambda\mathbf{y}) \\ &\geqq \mu u^t(\mathbf{y}) + (1-\mu)u^t(\lambda\mathbf{y}) = \mu F_t[v^t(\mathbf{y})] + (1-\mu)F_t[v^t(\lambda\mathbf{y})] \\ &= \mu F_t[\bar{v}^t] + (1-\mu)F_t[\bar{\bar{v}}^t], \qquad t = 1, \ldots, T, \end{aligned}$$

where the inequality follows from the concavity of u^t.

4.8.6 Proof of Lemma 4.2: Given $\mathbf{y}^0$ let $\mathbf{y}^* \in RS_V$ be the solution to

$$\max_{\mathbf{y}} \sum_{t=1}^{T} p_t u^t(\mathbf{y}) = \max_{\mathbf{y}} \sum_{t=1}^{T} p_t F_t[v^t(\mathbf{y})]$$

subject to $\Sigma_{t=1}^T \xi_t \gamma_t(T)(y_t - y_t^0) = 0$.

By part (b) of Definition 4.4 the solution to the same problem, given $\lambda\mathbf{y}^0$, $\lambda > 0$, is $\lambda\mathbf{y}^*$. The first-order optimality conditions are

(4.74) $$\sum_{t=1}^{T} p_t F_t'[\lambda v^t(\mathbf{y}^*)]v_k^t(\mathbf{y}^*) = \mu(\lambda)\xi_k\gamma_k(T), \qquad k = 1, \ldots, T,$$

where use has been made of the fact that v^t are linear homogeneous and v_k^t are homogeneous of degree zero in $\mathbf{y}$, $k, t = 1, \ldots, T$. Consequently, for all real $\lambda > 0$,

$$\frac{F_t'[v^t(\mathbf{y}^*)]}{\mu(1)} = \frac{F_t'[\lambda v^t(\mathbf{y}^*)]}{\mu(\lambda)}, \qquad t = 1, \ldots, T.$$

Thus for all $\lambda > 0$,

(4.75) $$-\log\frac{F_t'[\lambda v^t(\mathbf{y}^*)]}{F_t'[v^t(\mathbf{y}^*)]} = -\log\frac{F_k'[\lambda v^k(\mathbf{y}^*)]}{F_k'[v^k(\mathbf{y}^*)]}, \qquad k,t = 1, \ldots, T.$$

The left and right sides of Eq. (4.75), however, are the integrals from $v^j(\mathbf{y}^*)$

to $\lambda v^j(y^*), j = k,t$, of $-[F_t''(x)]/[F_t'(x)]$ and $-[F_k''(x)]/[F_k'(x)]$, respectively. Hence Eq. (4.75) implies that

$$(4.76)\qquad -\frac{F_t''(x)}{F_t'(x)} = -\frac{F_k''(x)}{F_k'(x)} \quad \text{for all } x \text{ and } t,k = 1, \ldots, T.$$

By definition for every $\lambda > 0$, $y^* \in RS_U$,

$$(4.77)\qquad \sum_{t=1}^{T} p_t F_t[\lambda v^t(y^*)] = F\left[\lambda \sum_{t=1}^{T} p_t v^t(y^*)\right].$$

Differentiating both sides of (4.77) with respect to λ, we obtain

$$(4.78)\qquad \sum_{t=1}^{T} p_t v^t(y^*)\left\{F_t'[\lambda v^t(y^*)] - F'\left[\lambda \sum_{t=1}^{T} p_t v^t(y^*)\right]\right\} = 0.$$

Dividing (4.78) by $F'\ [\lambda \Sigma_{t=1}^{T} p_t v^t(y^*)]$, we get

$$(4.79)\qquad \sum_{t=1}^{T} p_t v^t(y^*) \frac{F_t'[\lambda v^t(y^*)]}{F'\left[\lambda \sum_{t=1}^{T} p_t v^t(y^*)\right]} = \sum_{t=1}^{T} p_t v^t(y^*)$$

for all $\lambda > 0$, but Eq. (4.75) implies that changes in λ change F_t', $t = 1, \ldots,$ T equiproportionately. Hence Eq. (4.79) implies that for all $\lambda > 0$

$$(4.80)\qquad \frac{F_1'[\lambda v^t(y^*)]}{F'\left[\lambda \sum_{t=1}^{T} p_t v^t(y^*)\right]} = \frac{F_1'[v^t(y^*)]}{F'\left[\sum_{t=1}^{T} p_t v^t(y^*)\right]}.$$

By the same argument as above this implies

$$-\frac{F_1''(x)}{F_1'(x)} = -\frac{F''(x)}{F'(x)}$$

for all x, which together with Eq. (4.76) completes the proof.

5 Increasing Risk with State-Dependent Preferences: Measurement and Economic Consequences

5.1 Introduction

The responses of decision makers to variations in the risks facing them constitute an important aspect of the theory of individual behavior under uncertainty. Analysis of these responses requires a definition of the notion of increasing risk. Since all risk-averse individuals seek to avoid increases in risk, it is natural to define one prospect as more risky than another if all risk-averse individuals prefer the latter to the former.

According to the expected utility theory this definition involves a comparison between the mathematical expectation of all real-valued concave functions defined over the sample space. While intuitively appealing, this definition is not easy to apply. Fortunately, however, there are two other equivalent characterizations of the notion of increasing risk that do lend themselves to comparative statics analysis of the responses of decision makers to variations in risk. Let Y and X be two random variables with the same mean. Then, loosely speaking, Y is considered riskier than X if (a) it is distributed as X plus noise, or (b) it has more weight in the tails than X (that is, compared to X, the random variable Y has a wider spread).

This definition is useful for the analysis of decision problems that involve state-independent preferences. The sample space in such problems represents possible levels of wealth or income. Our main concern, however, is the study of the responses of decision makers to variations in risk when the preferences are state-dependent. Uncertainty in this case is expressed as a joint probability distribution over the product space of states of nature and wealth. We need to extend the definition of increasing risk accordingly. A straightforward extension is obtained by applying the definition of increasing risk to the conditional probability distribution over wealth in each state of nature. According to our previous analysis (see Chapter 2), a state-dependent utility function is said to display risk aversion if and only if in every state of nature it is a concave function of wealth, so an increase in risk defined as a mean-preserving increase in spread of the conditional (on the state) distribution on wealth reduces the expected utility of every risk-averse decision maker. From a theoretical point of view such an extension is rather trivial. A more interesting approach, which would allow for more general mean-wealth-preserving shifts of the probability distribution can be obtained at the cost of restricting its applicability to specific classes of decision makers. In particular, we shall pursue a definition of increasing risk that applies to all decision makers with the same reference set. In addition to being a natural outgrowth of our definition of the relation "more risk-averse" to state-dependent preferences, this restriction brings to the fore the correspondence between the notion of comparability of decision makers relative to the relation "more risk-averse" and their views regarding the ranking of probability distributions according to their riskiness. It also leads to another, equivalent characterization of the relation "more risk-averse" that would not be apparent otherwise. Finally, extending the definition of increasing risk in this manner will permit comparative statics analysis of certain shifts in the probability distribution not included in the usual definition.

5.2 The Measurement of Risk

In this section we present a definition of increasing risk for state-dependent preferences. The definition can be stated in three equivalent ways that are analogous to those obtained in the case of state-independent preferences. The definition applies to a class of decision makers that have the same reference set, that is, decision makers who are comparable in the sense of Definition 2.2.

5.2.1 Preferences and Riskiness

As before, we denote by S the finite set of states of nature. For each $s \in S$ let $[a,b]$ be an interval denoting the domain of the random variable wealth. Let M be the set of real-valued functions on the product space $B = \{(w,s) | w \in [a,b],\ s \in S\}$ such that for all $s \in S$, $u \in M$ is concave in w. Let m be any function in M such that m is strictly concave in w for all s. Let $V(m) = \{v \in M | RS_m \subset RS_v\}$. Thus m is globally comparable to every element of $V(m)$ in the sense of Definition 2.2. Let $u^0 \equiv w$. That is, u^0 is the state-independent linear utility function on R_+. Then $u^0 = \cap_{m \in M} V(m)$. To see this notice that for all $s \in S$, $[a,b] \in RS_{u^0}$. Hence by definition, $RS_u \subset RS_{u^0}$ for all $u \in M$.

Our first definition of the relation "riskier than" captures the intuitive notion that one distribution is more risky than another relative to $V(m)$ if all the decision makers whose utility functions are in $V(m)$ prefer the latter to the former. To state this idea formally we introduce the following additional notation. Let h_p denote the joint probability distribution on B defined as $h_p(w,s) = p(s)h(w|s)$, where for all $s \in S$, $p(s)$ is the probability of s and $h(w|s)$ denotes the conditional probability distribution of w given s. Denote by $D(B)$ the set of all joint probability distributions on B. Then, assuming expected-utility-maximizing behavior, we define the relation R^m-riskier.

DEFINITION 5.1 *Given $\mathbf{p} \in P$ and h_p, $g_p \in D(B)$, g_p is said to to be R^m-riskier than h_p if and only if, for all $u \in V(m)$,*

$$\sum_{s \in S} p(s) \int_a^b u(w,s)[g(w|s) - h(w|s)]dw \leq 0.$$

The binary relation on the set $D(B)$ induced by Definition 5.1 is denoted R^m.

LEMMA 5.1. *R^m is a preordering (that is, it is reflexive and transitive).*

The proof is straightforward. R^m is not antisymmetric. This is an immediate consequence of Lemma 5.2 and Theorem 5.1 below.

Definition 5.1 states that a pair of probability distributions belong to R^m if all decision makers whose utility functions are in $V(m)$ agree on the relative riskiness of the two distributions and if the probability distribution over S implicit in the elements of R^m is the same. Thus, if h_p and $g_{p'}$ are in R^m (if one of them is R^m-riskier than the other), then $p(s) = p'(s)$ for all $s \in S$. Hence the relation "riskier than" pertains to probability distributions on wealth.

Finally, note that for every given level of unconditional mean wealth the most preferred and thus the least risky distribution according to R^m is given by the element of the reference set RS_m with that level of actuarial wealth. This observation follows directly from the observation that a reference point represents the distribution with the highest expected utility of all the distributions in $D(B)$ that have the same unconditional mean wealth.

This discussion can be illustrated diagrammatically for the case where there are two states of nature, say s and t. The line AA in Figure 5.1 depicts random variables in B with constant unconditional mean wealth, and in each state of nature the conditional distribution of w is degenerate. For a strictly concave state-dependent utility function $u \in V(m)$ the indifference curves $\bar{u}_0$ and $\bar{u}_1$ represent given levels of expected utility. Clearly K is the most preferred distribution in AA. L and M are equally preferred, yet they are not the same distribution, which is a demonstration that R^m is not antisymmetric. A shift from K to M is a mean-wealth-preserving increase in risk as far

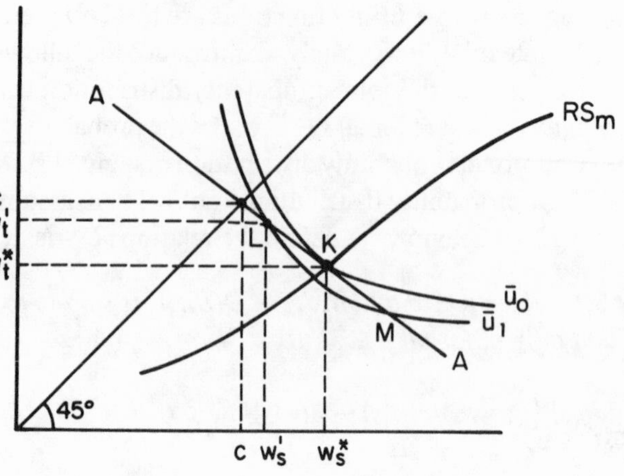

Figure 5.1 Increasing risk according to $V(m)$

as *all* the individuals whose utility functions are in $V(m)$ are concerned. Yet this shift is not a mean-preserving increase in spread in the sense defined for the case of state-independent preferences. Finally, by Jensen's inequality it is clear that any other distribution in B such that the conditional expectation is a point in AA is inferior to the distribution represented by the same point in AA.

5.2.2 The Integral Conditions

When preferences are state independent the notion of mean-preserving increase in spread is captured by the following conditions: Let H and J be two cumulative distribution functions on the interval $[a,b]$; H is said to be more risky or to represent a mean-preserving increase in spread over J if and only if

$$\int_a^b [H(x) - J(x)]dx = 0, \tag{5.1}$$

$$\int_a^y [H(x) - J(x)]dx \geqq 0, \qquad y \in [a,b). \tag{5.2}$$

Equation (5.1) asserts the equality of the means, and Inequality (5.2) asserts that H has a wider spread than J.

To extend the integral conditions (5.1) and (5.2) to the case of state-dependent preferences in a manner consistent with Definition 5.1 we recall (see Section 2.2) that RS_m may be described by a vector of the monotonic increasing and continuous function $f^m(w)$ where for an arbitrary state, say t, in S, $f_t^m(w) = w$. Suppose that for all $s \in S$, $f_s^m(a) = a$, $f_s^m(b) = b$ (this is a matter of definition which entails no essential loss of generality) and consider again Figure 5.1. The point L represents a discrete random variable that has the same unconditional mean wealth but is more risky than the discrete random variable represented by K. The conditional cumulative distribution functions corresponding to these random variables are represented by the solid and broken lines, respectively, in Figure 5.2. Consider the following procedure for integrating the difference between the two cumulative probability distributions over the interval $[a,b]$. When we integrate the difference between two conditional cumulative distribution functions up to any point $y \in [a,b]$ in state t we integrate the difference between the conditional cumulative distribution functions in state s up to $f_s^m(y)$. Thus in each state we "accumulate" the area representing the difference between the conditional cumulative distribution functions to the left of w_s^* before proceeding to the areas to the right of it. We can take a weighted averge of these areas using the probability distribution on S. As illustrated in Figure 5.2 this weighted average is nonnegative for every $y \in [a,b)$, which is analogous to Condition (5.2), and for $y = b$ the weighted average is zero, which is the analogue of Eq. (5.1). Thus, by analogy, L should be considered more risky than K relative to $V(m)$. This agrees with Definition 5.1.

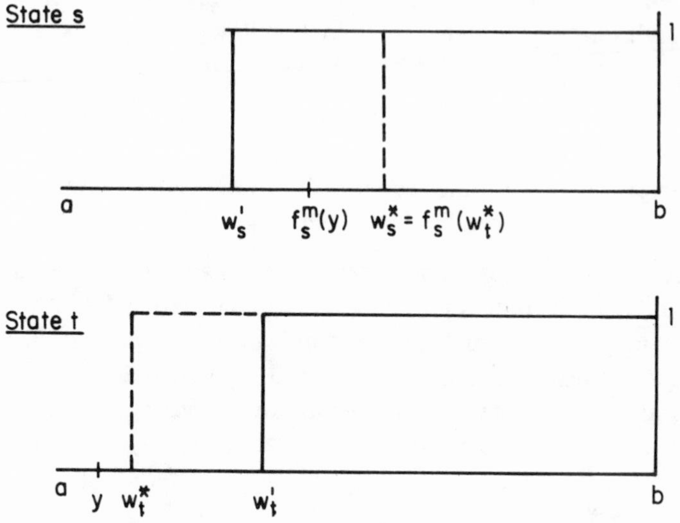

Figure 5.2 The cumulative distribution functions corresponding to L and K

DEFINITION 5.2. *Given $\mathbf{p} \in P$ and h_p, $g_p \in D(B)$, for each $s \in S$ let $H(\cdot|s)$ and $G(\cdot|s)$ be the conditional cumulative distribution functions corresponding to h_p and g_p, respectively. Then g_p is said to be I^m-riskier than h_p if and only if:*

(a) $$T^m(b) = \sum_{s\in S} p(s) \int_a^b [G(w|s) - H(w|s)]dw = 0,$$

(b) $$T^m(y) = \sum_{s\in S} p(s) \int_a^{f_s^m(y)} [G(w|s) - H(w|s)]dw \geqq 0, \qquad y \in [a,b).$$

As in the case of state-independent preferences, condition (a) implies equality of unconditional mean wealth and condition (b) gives a formal meaning to the notion that g_p has a larger spread than h_p.

The binary relation on $D(B)$ induced by Definition 5.2 is denoted I^m.

LEMMA 5.2. *I^m is not antisymmetric.*

The preceding discussion provides the intuition for Theorem 5.1.

THEOREM 5.1. *The binary relations R^m-riskier and I^m-riskier are equivalent.*

5.2.3 A Third Definition

When preferences are state independent a random variable Y that takes values in some close interval, say $[a,b]$, is considered more risky than another variable X defined on the same domain if Y is distributed as X plus noise. This condition may be stated formally as follows:

(5.3) $$Y =_d X + Z,$$

(5.4) $$E\{Z|X\} = 0 \quad \text{for all } X,$$

where $=_d$ means "distributed as" and Z, the noise, is a random variable that takes values in the interval $[a-b, b-a]$.

When the preferences are state dependent an analogous definition, for a class $V(m)$ of utility functions, that agrees with our earlier definitions may be stated as follows: Let Y and X be random variables defined on B, and let Z be a random variable that takes values in $\hat{B} \equiv \{(w,s)|w \in [a-b, b-a], s \in S\}$. For all $s \in S$ denote the conditional random variable by a subscript s. Then Y is said to be more risky than X relative to $V(w)$ if, for all $s \in S$,

(5.5) $$Y_s =_d X_s + Z_s,$$

(5.6) $$E\{Z_s|X_s\}(X_s - x_s^*) \geqq 0 \quad \text{for all } X_s,$$

where x_s^* is the s coordinate of the vector $\mathbf{x}^* \in RS_m$ and $\Sigma_{s \in S} p(s)(x_s^* - E\{X_s\}) = 0$,

(5.7) $\qquad E\{Z\} = 0.$

With that in mind we define the relation N^m-riskier.

DEFINITION 5.3. *A random variable Y defined on B is said to be N^m-riskier than a random variable X defined on B if and only if there exists a random variable Z that takes values in $\hat{B}$ such that Exps. (5.5), (5.6), and (5.7) are satisfied.*

Note that if conditions analogous to Eqs. (5.3) and (5.4) defined on the conditional random variable X_s, Y_s, and Z_s hold for all $s \in S$, then Exps. (5.5)–(5.7) hold. Thus, the addition of noise to a conditional random variable in some states of nature constitutes a special case of our definition.

The relation N^m-riskier may be stated in terms of probability distributions rather than random variables. A joint probability distribution $g_{\mathbf{p}}$ in $D(B)$ is N^m-riskier than a joint probability distribution $h_{\mathbf{p}}$ in $D(B)$ (that is, $g_{\mathbf{p}} N^m h_{\mathbf{p}}$) if and only if for all $s \in S$ there exists a joint cumulative distribution function M^s on $[a,b] \times [a-b, b-a]$ such that, if for all $s \in S$

(5.8) $\qquad J^s(y) = \Pr\{X_s + Z_s \leqq y\},$

then

(5.9) $\qquad H(x|s) = M^s(x, b-a), \qquad x \in [a,b],$

(5.10) $\qquad G(y|s) = J^s(y), \qquad y \in [a,b],$

for all $s \in S$

(5.11) $\qquad E\{Z_s|X_s\}(X_s - x_s^*) \geqq 0 \quad \text{for all } X_s,$

and

(5.12) $\qquad E\{Z\} = 0.$

Unlike the definition for state-independent preferences, when preferences are state dependent the noise added to the conditional (on states) distributions of wealth need not have zero mean in each state. As indicated by condition (5.11) or equivalently (5.6), for values of wealth larger (smaller) than x_s^*, the coordinate of the reference distribution for the given state, the conditional mean of Z_s may be positive (negative). Condition (5.12) requires that the unconditional mean of Z be zero.

5.2.4 Equivalence

Definition 5.3 is in agreement with Definitions 5.1 and 5.2. This result can be stated as a theorem

THEOREM 5.2. *The binary relations R^m, I^m, and N^m are equivalent.*

If the decision maker's preferences are state independent—if $u(w,s) = u(w)$ for all $s \in S$—then Theorem 5.2 implies the well-known result of Rothschild and Stiglitz (1970). Let $D[a,b]$ be the set of cumulative distribution functions on the closed interval $[a,b]$, and define the following binary relations: (a) For each H and J in $D[a,b]$, H is R-riskier than J if and only if $\int_a^b u(w)[dH(w) - dJ(w)] \leqq 0$ for all concave functions u on $[a,b]$. (b) H is I-riskier than J if and only if they satisfy Conditions (5.1)–(5.2). (c) A random variable Y defined on $[a,b]$ is said to be N-riskier than a random variable X defined on the same domain if and only if they satisfy Conditions (5.3)–(5.4).

Theorem 5.2 implies a corollary.

COROLLARY 5.1. (Rothschild and Stiglitz, 1970) *The relations R-riskier, I-riskier, and N-riskier are equivalent.*

5.3 Economic Consequences

Definitions, by their very nature, are arbitrary; their merit lies in their usefulness for analysis of a particular class of concrete problems. Mindful of the comparative statics results of Rothschild and Stiglitz (1971), which involve the effect of increasing risk on the optimal portfolio composition with state-independent preferences, I chose to analyze an analogous problem with state-dependent preferences. In addition to illustrating the usefulness of the definition proposed in the preceding section, this analysis demonstrates the analogy between the economic consequences of increasing risk with state-independent and state-dependent preferences.

The effect of an increase in the riskiness of a risky asset on the allocation of a portfolio between a risky and a risk-free asset is, in general, ambiguous. A sufficient condition for such an increase in risk to reduce the investment in the risky asset, however, is that the partial derivative of the utility function with respect to the share of the risky asset in the portfolio be a concave function of the rate of return on the risky asset. Essentially the same result is obtained for the case of state-dependent preferences, provided the reference set is linear. When considering the portfolio selection problem with state-dependent preferences we must recognize that the analogue of the risk-free asset mentioned above is the least risky asset, namely the asset that yields a distribution of wealth corresponding to a point on the reference set.

5.3.1 A Portfolio Selection Problem

Consider an individual who is employed by a firm to which he claims part ownership. For the sake of concreteness, think of the individual as a partner in a law firm or a part owner of a restaurant. Let S be the set of the individual's states of health and suppose that, in addition to affecting his well-being, the state of health of the individual affects his productivity. As an employee our individual receives a salary, and in his capacity as an owner he draws a share of the profits, say α. The productivity of the individual bears a direct relation to the profits of the establishment and may also affect his salary.

Suppose that fair health insurance is available so that if he was only an employee (if $\alpha = 0$) the decision maker's insured income would constitute an element of his reference set. As a part owner, however, the decision maker forgoes part of his salary for a share in the profits, which depend *inter alia* on his health.

For each $s \in S$ let $\tilde{z}_s$ be a random variable defined on $[a,b]$, representing the return in state s. The decision maker's terminal wealth position in each state is given by $w_s = w_s^* + \alpha\tilde{z}_s$, where w_s^* denotes his "full salary" (his wealth if $\alpha = 0$) and $\mathbf{w}^*$ is an element of the reference set of the decision maker under consideration. Let $u \in V(m)$ be the decision maker's utility function. Then the optimal value of α, to be denoted α^*, is obtained by solving the problem: Choose $\alpha \in [0,1]$ so as to maximize

$$(5.13) \qquad \sum_{s \in S} p(s) \int_a^b u(w_s^* + \alpha z_s, s) dG(z|s),$$

where $G(z|s)$ is the conditional cumulative distribution function of z. Assuming an internal solution, the optimality condition is

$$(5.14) \qquad \sum_{s \in S} p(s) \int_a^b u'(w_s^* + \alpha z_s, s) z_s dG(z|s) = 0.$$

To anlayze the effect of increasing risk on α^* consider a family of distributions $\{g_{\mathbf{p}}(\cdot, \mathbf{r})\} \subset D(B)$, where $\mathbf{r}$ is an element of $|S|$-dimensional Euclidean space identifying a member of this family. We use the convention that when $r^s \geqq \hat{r}^s$ for all $s \in S$, then $\mathbf{r}$ represents a riskier distribution than $\hat{\mathbf{r}}$. Increasing risk may take many forms. We define a *directional increase in risk* as follows: For $t \geqq 0$, $\mathbf{r}(t) = \mathbf{r} + t \cdot \boldsymbol{\beta}$ where for each $s \in S$, $\beta_s \geqq 0$. The integral conditions in Definition 5.2 may be written as

$$T^m(b) = \sum_{s \in S} p(s) \int_a^b G_r(x, r^s|s)\beta_s dx = 0, \tag{5.15}$$

$$T^m(y) = \sum_{s \in S} p(s) \int_a^{f_s^m(y)} G_r(x, r^s|s)\beta_s dx \geqq 0, \qquad y \in [a,b), \tag{5.16}$$

where G_r denotes the partial derivative of G with respect to r^s.

Differentiating the first-order optimality condition (5.14) with respect to α^* and t we obtain

$$\frac{d\alpha^*}{dt} = \frac{\sum_{s \in S} p(s) \int_a^b u'(w_s^* + \alpha^* z_s, s) z_s G_{zr}(z_s, r^s)\beta_s dz_s}{-\sum_{s \in S} p(s) \int_a^b u''(w_s^* + \alpha^* z_s, s) z_s^2 G_z(z_s, r^w) dz_s}. \tag{5.17}$$

The sign of (5.17) determines the effect of increasing risk on the optimal portfolio position of the decision maker, between holding the least risky and the risky asset. This effect, as in the case of state-independent preferences, is ambiguous. A sufficient condition for increasing risk to have an unambiguous effect is given in Proposition 5.1.

PROPOSITION 5.1. *If the reference set RS_m is linear, then a sufficient condition for α^* to decrease (increase) with increase in risk is that $\partial u(f_s^m(w^* + \alpha z_t), s)/\partial\alpha$ is a concave (convex) function of z_t.*

Comparing Proposition 5.1 with the effect of increasing risk on the allocation of a portfolio between a risky and a risk-free asset in the case of state-independent preferences, we observe that: (a) In the case of state-independent preferences the linearity of the reference set is implied, since it is implicit in the structure of the preferences. (b) Essentially the same condition on the marginal utility of the share of the risky asset in the portfolio is required to eliminate the ambiguity concerning the effect of increasing risk. In view of these observations we conclude that portfolio selection analysis with state-dependent preferences and using our definition of increasing risk is analogous to that with state-independent preferences.

That increasing risk does not necessarily make risk-averse decision makers reduce their exposure to risk by reducing their demand for the risky asset may seem at variance with common sense. Careful reflection, however, reveals the error in this intuition. An increase in risk, by definition, reduces the expected utility of risk-averse decision makers. Portfolio allocation decisions are "marginal decisions," in the sense that they involve the properties of the marginal utility. A mean-preserving increase in spread increases the probability of higher as well as lower marginal utilities. Consequently, its effect on the expected marginal utility is ambiguous. One exception to this general observation involves the allocation between a risk-free asset and a bet.

5.3.2 Bets with State-Dependent Preferences

A bet on an event θ, a subset of S, is an asset that pays $r + \gamma$ if some $s \in \theta$ prevails and $r - \lambda$ otherwise. A decision to participate in a bet is therefore a portfolio allocation decision. When the decision maker's preferences are independent of the event on which the bet is placed—when the decision maker does not care whether a flip of a coin results in heads up or tails up except insofar as it determines his reward—an increase in the riskiness of the bet will have the effect of reducing the optimal investment in that bet of all risk-averse individuals. This result, which was origninated by Rothschild and Stiglitz (1971), has its counterpart in the case where the bet is placed on an event of direct concern to the decision maker's well-being.

Bets on events that matter to the decision maker are quite common. A simple example of such a bet involves the outcome of a sporting event. When an avid fan bets on the outcome of a match involving his favorite team, the outcome may affect his utility directly and, more importantly, it may affect the marginal utility of his wealth. Hence the analysis of the effect of increasing risk on the level of investment in such bets must be modified to take account of the nature of the decision maker's preferences. In particular, the definition of increasing risk relevant to this problem is the one introduced in the preceding section. Utilizing this definition we shall see that an increase in the riskiness of a bet will have the effect of reducing investments in that bet by all decision makers whose utility functions are in $V(m)$.

Let $S = \{\theta,\bar{\theta}\}$ be the set of events. As before, given the actuarial value, the least risky distribution of wealth across events is given by the ordered pair $\langle w^*_\theta, w^*_{\bar{\theta}} \rangle \in RS_m$. Since the monetary outcome of a bet in each event is certain, the integral conditions in Definition 5.2 assume a simple form. Let B and C denote two bets on θ paying $r + \gamma_k$ if θ and $r - \lambda_k$ if $\bar{\theta}$, $k = B,C$, where r denotes the expected monetary gain and λ_k, $\gamma_k > 0$. Let

$$e_1 = r - \lambda_C \qquad e_2 = r - \lambda_B$$
$$e_3 = r + \gamma_B \qquad e_4 = r + \gamma_C$$

According to Definition 5.2, C is more risky than B if

$$(5.18)\qquad [1-p(\theta)](e_2-e_1)+p(\theta)(e_3-e_4)=0$$

$$(5.19)\qquad \begin{cases}[1-p(\theta)](y-e_1)\geqq 0, & y\in[e_1,e_2],\\ [1-p(\theta)](e_2-e_1)+p(\theta)(e_3-y)\geqq 0, & y\in[e_3,e_4],\end{cases}$$

where $p(\theta)$ denotes the probability of θ. A risk-averse decision maker refrains from participating in fair bets; if he is to participate in a bet the expected return r must be positive. Also, if the solution is nontrivial we must assume that $r-\lambda_k<0$, $k=C,B$. In conjunction with (5.18) and (5.19) this implies that $e_1<e_2<0<e_3<e_4$.

Consider a decision maker whose initial wealth distribution $\langle w_\theta^*, w_{\bar\theta}^*\rangle$ is a reference point. Denote by α_k his investment in bet k. The decision maker's terminal wealth is given by

$$w_\theta(\alpha)=w_\theta^*+\alpha_k(r+\gamma_k)\quad\text{if }\theta\text{ prevails and}$$
$$w_{\bar\theta}(\alpha)=w_{\bar\theta}^*+\alpha_k(r-\lambda_k)\quad\text{if }\bar\theta\text{ prevails}$$

Given the bet k, the decision maker chooses α_k so as to maximize the expected utility of his terminal wealth, namely

$$(5.20)\qquad p(\theta)u(w_\theta^*+\alpha_k(r+\gamma_k),\theta)+(1-p(\theta))u(w_{\bar\theta}^*+\alpha_k(r-\lambda_k),\bar\theta),$$

subject to $\alpha_k(r-\lambda_k)+w_{\bar\theta}^*\geqq 0$.

The constraint assures that the decision maker is always able to pay all bet-associated debts out of his initial wealth. Assuming an internal solution and denoting the optimal level of α_k by α_k^*, the first order conditions are

$$(5.21)\qquad p(\theta)u'(w_\theta(\alpha_k^*),\theta)(r+\gamma_k)+(1-p(\theta))u'(w_{\bar\theta}(\alpha_k^*),\bar\theta)(r-\lambda_k)=0.$$

Consequently, $\alpha_B^*\gtreqless\alpha_C^*$ as

$$(5.22)\qquad p(\theta)u'(w_\theta(\alpha_B^*),\theta)(r+\gamma_C) + (1-p(\theta))u'(w_{\bar\theta}(\alpha_B^*),\bar\theta)(r-\lambda_C)\gtreqless 0.$$

Subtracting (5.21) for $k=B$ from (5.22), we obtain

$$(5.23)\qquad u'(w_\theta(\alpha_B^*),\theta)p(\theta)(e_4-e_3) + u'(w_{\bar\theta}(\alpha_B^*),\bar\theta)(1-p(\theta))(e_1-e_2)\gtreqless 0,$$

and the sign of (5.23) is the same as that of (5.22).

Since $u'(w_\theta^*,\theta)=u'(w_{\bar\theta}^*,\bar\theta)$, multiplying Condition (5.18) by $-u'(w_\theta^*,\theta)$ we get

$$(5.24)\qquad u'(w_\theta^*,\theta)p(\theta)(e_4-e_3)+u'(w_{\bar\theta}^*,\bar\theta)[1-p(\theta)](e_1-e_2)=0.$$

Subtracting Eq. (5.24) from (5.23) we obtain

$$(5.25) \quad [u'(w_\theta(\alpha_B^*),\theta) - u'(w_\theta^*,\theta)]p(\theta)(e_4 - e_3) + [u'(w_{\bar\theta}(\alpha_B^*),\bar\theta) - u'(w_{\bar\theta}^*,\bar\theta)](1 - p(\theta))(e_1 - e_2) < 0,$$

where the inequality follows from $w_\theta(\alpha_B^*) > w_\theta^*$ and $w_{\bar\theta}(\alpha_B^*) < w_{\bar\theta}^*$ and u being strictly concave in each state. Consequently, Exp. (5.22) is negative and $\alpha_C^* < \alpha_B^*$. This discussion may be summarized in a proposition.

PROPOSITION 5.2 *When choosing a portfolio allocation between a least-risk asset and a bet on an event, a risk-averse decision maker whose preferences are event dependent always reduces his investment in the bet when the bet becomes more risky.*

Proposition 5.2 is an obvious state-dependent analogue of the result concerning participation in bets when the preferences are state independent. Unlike Proposition 5.1, Proposition 5.2 does not require that the reference set be linear. Together these propositions illustrate the applicability of our definition of the relation "more risky" to state-dependent preferences.

The restriction of the applicability of our definition to classes of individuals with the same reference set and that of Proposition 5.2 to individuals whose preferences are autocomparable are indeed significant from a practical (empirical) point of view. It is important to recognize that the theoretical underpinnings of this definition are the same as those for state-independent preferences. In the latter case these restrictions are naturally satisifed. Ours, however, is the more general definition, in that it implies the other and also permits the extension of the analysis to problems that cannot be satisfactorily formulated without taking into account the state-dependent nature of the decision maker's preferences.

5.4 The Relation "More Risk-Averse" Revisited

An alternative definition of the notion of increasing risk for state-independent preferences that preserve the expectation of the utility function rather than the mean of the random variable itself was examined by Diamond and Stiglitz (1974). Since the utility function is a function of control variables as well as the exogenous random variables, the definition applies to a given level of controls. One distribution is considered to be more risky than another if and only if both yield the same expected utility, but the former induces a wider spread of the utility than the latter.

This definition of increasing risk—mean-utility-preserving increase in spread—suggests another natural definition of the relation "more risk-averse" for state-independent preferences, which is equivalent to the definition of Pratt (1964) (see Chapter 2). Consider a mean-utility-preserving increase in spread for one individual. If another individual facing the same variation in the distribution of the random variable experiences a decline in his expected utility, then the latter individual is said to be more risk averse than the former.

Essentially the same kind of relationship exists between the notion of mean-utility-preserving increase in risk (to be defined below) and the characterization of the relation "more risk-averse" in the case of state-dependent preferences. The formal definition of the notion of mean-utility-preserving increase in risk for state-dependent utility functions requires introduction of the following additional notations: For each $s \in S$ let ξ_s be a random variable defined by $\xi_s = u(w,\alpha,s)$, where α denotes the control variable, and let $\xi_s^a \equiv u(a,\alpha,s)$, $\xi_s^b \equiv u(b,\alpha,s)$. Let $\hat{g}_p(\xi_s,s) = p(s)\hat{g}(\xi_s|s)$, where $\hat{g}(\cdot|s)$ denotes the conditional distribution function of ξ_s given s, induced by $g(w|s)$. Denoting by $\hat{G}(\xi_s|s)$ the cumulative probability distribution function corresponding to $\hat{g}(\xi_s|s)$, we introduce a definition.

DEFINITION 5.4 *Given $u \in V(m)$, the joint probability distribution $\hat{g}_p$ induced by $g_p \in D(B)$ is said to be riskier than the joint probability distribution $\hat{h}_p$ induced by $h_p \in D(B)$ if and only if*

(a) $$\hat{T}(b) = \sum_{s \in S} p(s) \int_{\xi_s^a}^{\xi_s^b} [\hat{G}(\xi_s|s) - \hat{H}(\xi_s|s)]\, d\xi_s = 0,$$

(b) $$\hat{T}(y) = \sum_{s \in S} p(s) \int_{\xi_s^a}^{u(f_{g_p}(y),\alpha,s]} [\hat{G}(\xi_s|s) - \hat{H}(\xi_s|s)]\, d\xi_s \geqq 0$$

for all $y \in [a,b)$.

It can be shown (see Demers, 1983) that if u and v are in $V(m)$ then any increase in risk that is mean-utility-preserving for u according to Definition 5.4 is mean-utility-reducing for v if and only if v is more risk-averse than u in the sense of Definition 2.3. This result can be explained diagramatically as in Figure 5.3. Let there be two states of nature. As we already know (see Chapter 2), if v is more risk-averse than u according to Definition 2.3, then the indifference curves of v intersect those of u as indicated in Figure 5.3. Point A is a least risky distribution for both u and v. Consider the distribution represented by point B. Relative to A, point B represents a mean-utility-preserving

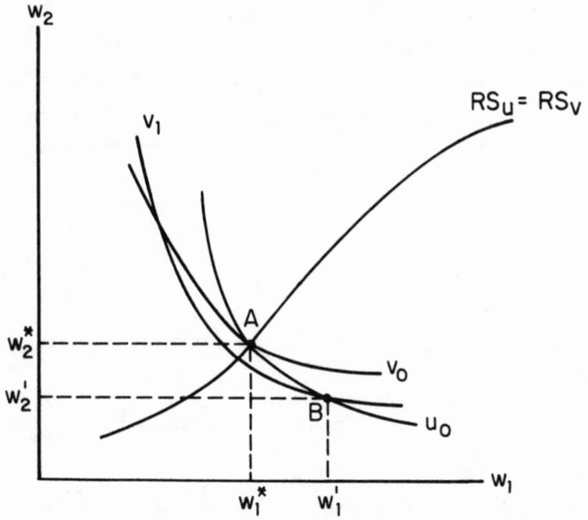

Figure 5.3 Mean-utility-preserving increase in risk

increase in risk for u. [The expected utility is the same at A and B, but $u(w_1',1) > u(w_1^*,1)$ and $u(w_2',2) < u(w_2^*,2)$.] From the viewpoint of v, however, the shift from A to B involves a decline in the expected utility from v_0 to v_1. Thus v is more risk averse according to the present definition, and the two definitions of the relation "more risk-averse" are consistent.

5.5 Related Work

The question of the relative riskiness of different random variables has been studied by mathematicians and statisticians and was brought to the attention of economists through the work of Rothschild and Stiglitz (1970). A discussion and references to the mathematical literature appear in Schmeidler (1979) and references to the statistical literature appear in Rothschild and Stiglitz (1972).

The notion of mean-utility-preserving increase in risk for state-independent preferences originated in the work of Diamond and Stiglitz (1974). The extension of this definition to state-dependent preferences and the result showing the relationship between mean-utility-preserving increase in risk and the definition of the relation "more risk-averse" appeared originally in Demers (1983).

Comparative statics analysis of increasing risk of several decision problems involving state-independent preferences appeared in Rothschild and Stiglitz (1971) and in Diamond and Stiglitz (1974). In particular, Rothschild and Stiglitz analyze the portfolio selection problems that appear in Section 5.3 for the case of state-independent utility functions. Some of the results of this chapter appear in Karni (1984).

5.6 Proofs

5.6.1 Proof of Lemma 5.2

Given $\mathbf{p} \in P$, let $h_{\mathbf{p}}$ and $g_{\mathbf{p}}$ in $D(B)$ satisfy $g_{\mathbf{p}} I^m h_{\mathbf{p}}$ and $h_{\mathbf{p}} I^m g_{\mathbf{p}}$. For all $s \in S$ define

$$Q_1(w|s) = G(w|s) - H(w|s), \qquad Q_2 = H(w|s) - G(w|s).$$

Hence, for all $s \in S$, $Q_1(w|s) + Q_2(w|s) = 0$. By Definition 5.2,

$$T_k^m(y) = \sum_{s \in S} p(s) \int_a^{f_s^m(y)} Q_k(w|s)dw \geqq 0, \qquad y \in [a,b),\ k = 1,2.$$

But

$$T_1^m(y) + T_2^m(y) = \sum_{s \in S} p(s) \int_a^{f_s^m(y)} [Q_1(w|s) + Q_2(w|s)]dw = 0,$$
$$y \in [a,b).$$

Hence $T_k^m(y) = 0$, $k = 1,2$, $y \in [a,b)$.

For each $s \in S$, $Q_1(w|s)$ is a difference between two monotonic functions. Thus it is a function of bounded variations, and its discontinuity points form a set of measure zero. For each $s \in S$ denote this set $N(s)$. Define

$$\hat{Q}_1(w|s) = \begin{cases} 0 & \text{for } w \in N(s) \\ Q_1(w|s) & \text{otherwise.} \end{cases}$$

Then

$$T_1^m(y) = \sum_{s \in S} p(s) \int_a^{f_s^m(y)} \hat{Q}_1(w|s)dw.$$

Suppose that there exists a point $(\hat{w},\hat{s}) \in B$ such that $\hat{Q}_1(\hat{w}|\hat{s}) \neq 0$. For the sake of concreteness let $\hat{s} = t$ and $\hat{Q}_1(\hat{w}|\hat{s}) > 0$. Then $\hat{Q}_1(\hat{w}|\hat{s}) > 0$ on $[\hat{w} - \epsilon, \hat{w} + \epsilon]$ for some $\epsilon > 0$. It is possible that for some $s' \in S$ and an interval $[f_{s'}^m(\hat{w} - \epsilon), f_{s'}^m(\hat{w} + \epsilon)]$, $\hat{Q}_1(w'|s')p(s') = -\hat{Q}_1(w|\hat{s})p(\hat{s})$, where $w' = f_{s'}^m(w)$,

$w \in [\hat{w} - \epsilon, \hat{w} + \epsilon]$, and $Q_1(w|s) \equiv 0$ otherwise. Thus the integral conditions in Definition 5.2 are satisfied, while $g_{\mathbf{p}}$ and $h_{\mathbf{p}}$ are not identical on a set of measure larger than zero.

5.6.2 Proof of Theorem 5.1

Given $\mathbf{p} \in P$ and for all $u \in V(m)$, by Definition 5.1, $g_{\mathbf{p}} R^m h_{\mathbf{p}}$ if and only if

$$\sum_{s \in S} p(s) \int_a^b u(w,s)[g(w|s) - h(w|s)]dw \leqq 0. \tag{5.26}$$

Integrating by parts and using $G(a|s) = H(a|s) = 0$, $G(b|s) = H(b|s) = 1$, we obtain

$$\sum_{s \in S} p(s) \int_a^b u_w(w,s)[G(w|s) - H(w|s)]dw \geqq 0, \tag{5.27}$$

where $u_w(\cdot\,,\cdot)$ denotes the partial derivative of $u(\cdot\,,\cdot)$ with respect to w. Since for all $s \in S$, $u_w(f_s^m(w), s) = u_w(w,t)$ we can rewrite Exp. (5.27) to obtain

$$\sum_{s \in S} p(s) \int_a^b u_w(w,t)[G(f_s^m(w)|s) - H(f_s^m(w)|s)]dw \geqq 0.$$

Integrating by parts we get

$$\sum_{s \in S} p(s)\left[\frac{d}{dw} f_s^m(w)\right] \{u_w(w,t)T^m(w)\Big|_a^b - \int_a^b u_{ww}(w,t)T^m(w)dw\} \geqq 0, \tag{5.28}$$

where $u_{ww}(\cdot\,,t)$ is the second partial derivative of $u(\cdot\,,t)$ with respect to w.

To prove that $R^m \Rightarrow I^m$ recall that u^0, the state-independent linear utility function, is in $V(m)$. Thus for all $s \in S$, $u^0(w,s) = w$. Substituting in Exp. (5.27) and by definition of $T^m(b)$, we get $T^m(b) \geqq 0$.

Let $\hat{u}^0(w,s) = -w$ for all $s \in S$. Clearly, $\hat{u}^0 \in V(m)$. By the same argument as above, this implies $T^m(b) \leqq 0$. Hence $T^m(b) = 0$, which is condition (a) in Definition 5.1.

To establish condition (b) in that definition consider the function which for all $s \in S$ is given by $b_s^m(w,y) = \max[f_s^m(y) - w, 0]$. Then $-b_s^m(\cdot\,,\cdot)$ is concave in w for all s. Furthermore, differentiating with respect to w we get, for all $s \in S$, $y \in [a,b]$, and all m,

$$\frac{d}{dw}[-b_s^m(w,y)] = \begin{cases} 1 & w \leqq f_s^m(y) \\ 0 & \text{otherwise.} \end{cases}$$

Hence, for all $s, s' \in S$,

$$\frac{d}{dw}[-b_s^m(w,y)] = \frac{d}{dw}[-b_{s'}^m(w,y)], \qquad y \in [a,b].$$

Consequently, by definition, $-b_s^m(w,y) \in V(m)$. Given any $y \in [a,b)$ let $u(w,s) = -b_s^m(w,y)$. Then, substituting for u_w in Exp. (5.27) we get

$$T^m(y) = \sum_{s \in S} p(s) \int_a^{f_s^m(y)} [G(w|s) - H(w|s)]dw \geqq 0, \qquad y \in [a,b).$$

This completes the proof that $R^m \Rightarrow I^m$.

To show that $I^m \Rightarrow R^m$ notice that since $T^m(a) = T^m(b) = 0$, the first term in Exp. (5.28) is zero. Since $T^m(w) \geqq 0$ for all $w \in [a,b)$, if there is a $u \in V(m)$ that is convex in any open interval in $[a,b]$, then we choose $T^m(w) > 0$ where u is convex and $T^m(w) = 0$ otherwise, to obtain a contradiction of Exp. (5.28). Thus all $u \in V(m)$ are concave.

5.6.3 Introduction to the Proof of Theorem 5.2

Since, by Theorem 5.1, $R^m \Leftrightarrow I^m$, we need to show that $I^m \Rightarrow N^m \Rightarrow R^m$. The proof of the implication $I^m \Rightarrow N^m$ is particularly long. We shall establish this implication for discrete random variables and indicate briefly how this can be extended to $D(B)$.

To begin with we note that if Y and X in Definition 5.3 are discrete random variables defined over the set $\{a_1, \ldots, a_n\}$ and $h_j^s = \Pr\{x_s = a_j^s\}$, $l_j^s = \Pr\{y_s = a_j^s\}$, then YN^mX if and only if for all $s \in S$ there exist numbers $c_{jk}^s \geqq 0$ such that

$$\text{(5.29)} \qquad \sum_{k=1}^{n} c_{jk}^s = 1, \qquad j = 1, \ldots, n,$$

$$\text{(5.30)} \qquad \sum_{k=1}^{n} c_{jk}^s (a_k^s - a_j^s)(a_j^s - x_s^*) \geqq 0, \qquad j = 1, \ldots, n,$$

$$\text{(5.31)} \qquad \sum_{s \in S} p(s) \sum_{k}^{n} \sum_{j}^{n} c_{jk}^s h_j^s (a_k^s - a_j^s) = 0,$$

$$\text{(5.32)} \qquad l_k^s = \sum_{j=1}^{n} c_{jk}^s h_j^s, \qquad k = 1, \ldots, n.$$

Using matrix notation and denoting the column unit vector by $\boldsymbol{e}$ we have, for all $s \in S$,

(5.29′) $\quad C^s\boldsymbol{e} = \boldsymbol{e}$,

(5.32′) $\quad \boldsymbol{l}^s = \boldsymbol{h}^s C^s$,

(5.30′) $\quad (a_j^s - x_s^*)C_j^s\boldsymbol{a}^s \geqq (a_j^s - x_s^*)a_j^s, \qquad j = 1, \ldots, n,$

where C_j^s denotes the jth row of C^s and $\boldsymbol{a}^s$ is the transpose of $(a_1^s, \ldots, a_n^s)$.

Next we prove the claim that for discrete random variables with finite numbers of points the relation N^m is transitive.

LEMMA 5.3: *Let X^i, $i = 1,2,3$, be random variables taking values in B and for each $s \in S$ let X_s^i be the corresponding conditional (on the state of nature) random variables on $[a,b]$. If for each $s \in S$, X_s^i, $i = 1,2,3$, are concentrated at a finite number of points, then $X^3N^mX^2$ and $X^2N^mX^1$ imply $X^3N^mX^1$.*

Proof of Lemma 5.3: For all $s \in S$ let J_s^i, $i = 1,2,3$, be vectors defining the cumulative distribution functions of the conditional random variables X_s^i, respectively. If $X^3N^mX^2$ and $X^2N^mX^1$, then there exist nonnegative matrices C_1^s and C_2^s such that for all $s \in S$

$$C_1^s\boldsymbol{e} = C_2^s\boldsymbol{e} = \boldsymbol{e},$$
$$AC_i^s\boldsymbol{a}^s \geqq A\boldsymbol{a}^s, \qquad i = 1,2,$$

where A in an $n \times n$ diagonal matrix with diagonal elements $(a_j^s - x_s^*)$, $j = 1, \ldots, n$, and $J_s^2 = J_s^1C_1^s$, $J_s^3 = J_s^2C_2^s$. For all $s \in S$ let $C_s^* = C_1^s \cdot C_2^s$. Then $J_s^3 = J_s^1C_s^*$, $C_s^*\boldsymbol{e} = C_1^s \cdot C_2^s\boldsymbol{e} = \boldsymbol{e}$, and $AC_s^*\boldsymbol{a}^s = AC_1^sC_2^s\boldsymbol{a}^s = AC_1^sA^{-1}AC_2^s\boldsymbol{a}^s \geqq AC_1^sA^{-1}A\boldsymbol{a}^s = AC_1^s\boldsymbol{a}^s \geqq A\boldsymbol{a}^s$.

Define the operation of unconditional mean-preserving spread for discrete random variables as follows: For each $s \in S$ let $\Pr\{X = a_j|s\} = x_{sa_j}$ and $\Pr\{Y = a_j|s\} = y_{sa_j}$ where $\Sigma_j x_{sa_j} = \Sigma_j y_{sa_j} = 1$ and for each $s \in S$, $\{a_j\}$ is an increasing sequence of real numbers in $[a,b]$. Suppose that $x_{sa_j} = y_{sa_j}$ for all but four points in the sample space (a_1,t), (a_2,t), (a_3,s) and (a_4,s), where s may be equal to t. Define

$$\gamma_{kj} = x_{ka_j} - y_{ka_j}, \qquad k = s,t, \quad j = 1, \ldots, 4.$$

If $a_3 \geqq f_s^m(a_2)$, $\gamma_{t1} = -\gamma_{t2} \geqq 0$ and $\gamma_{s4} = -\gamma_{s3} \geqq 0$,

$$p(t)\left[\sum_{j=1}^{2} \gamma_{sj}a_j\right] + p(s)\left[\sum_{j=3}^{4} \gamma_{tj}a_j\right] = 0,$$

and g_p and h_p are the probability distributions of the random variables whose monetary realizations are denoted X and Y, respectively, then g_p is said to be different from h_p by a single unconditional mean-preserving spread.

LEMMA 5.4. *Let g_p and h_p in $D[B]$ be such that $g_p I^m h_p$ and for each $s \in S$ the conditional cumulative distribution functions of g_p and h_p have a finite number of points of increase. Then there exists a sequence of distributions $\{l_p^n\}$ in $D[B]$ such that $l_p^0 = h_p$ and $l_p^n = g_p$ and l_p^k differs from l_p^{k-1} by a single unconditional mean-preserving spread for $k = 1, \ldots, n$.*

Proof of Lemma 5.4: For all $s \in S$ let $D(x|s) \equiv G(x|s) - H(x|s)$. Thus for all $s \in S$, $D(\cdot|s)$ is a step function with a finite number of steps. If $D(x|s) \equiv 0$ for all $s \in S$, then $h_p = g_p$ and the lemma is trivially true. Suppose that for some $S' \subset S$ and subintervals of $[a,b]$, $D(x|s) \neq 0$. If for all $s \in S'$, $D(x|s)$ satisfies the integral conditions

$$\text{(i)} \quad \int_a^b D(x|s)dx = 0, \qquad \text{(ii)} \int_a^y D(x|s)dx \geqq 0, \qquad y \in [a,b),$$

then, by Rothschild and Stiglitz (1970) Lemma 1, $G(x|s)$ can be obtained from $H(x|s)$ by a finite number of mean-preserving spreads. Since S' is finite, the lemma is true. Suppose, therefore, that for some $s \in S$ the above integral conditions do not hold, and instead conditions (a) and (b) in Definition 5.2 hold. Then, for each state of nature separately we follow the procedure outlined in the proof of Lemma 1 in Rothschild and Stiglitz (1970). After a finite number of mean-preserving spread operations, the difference function $D(\cdot|s)$ will be either nonnegative or nonpositive for each s. Denote by S' and S'' the subsets of S such that for all $s \in S'$, $D(\cdot|s)$ is nonnegative and for all $s \in S''$, $D(\cdot|s)$ is nonpositive. For each $s \in S' \cup S''$ let $I_1(s)$ be the first step and let $\hat{I}_1(s) = (f_s^m)^{-1}[I_1(s)] = [\hat{a}_1(s), \hat{b}_1(s)]$.

Of all $s \in S'$ choose s' such that $\hat{a}_1(s') = \min_{s \in S'} \hat{a}_1(s)$ and of all $s \in S''$ select s'' such that $a_1(s'') = \min_{s \in S''} \hat{a}_1(s)$. Then, by condition (b) of Definition 5.2, $\hat{a}_1(s') < \hat{a}_1(s'')$. (If the minimum is not unique, select s' or s'' arbitrarily from among the states that satisfy the condition.) Let $\gamma_{s_1'}$ be the value of $D(\cdot|s')$ on $I_1(s')$ and $\gamma_{s_1''}$ be the value of $D(\cdot|s'')$ on $I_1(s'')$. Then, either

$$p(s')\gamma_{s_1'} I_1(s') \geqq p(s'')\gamma_{s_1''} I_1(s'') \quad \text{or}$$
$$p(s')\gamma_{s_1'} I_1(s') < p(s'')\gamma_{s_1''} I_1(s'').$$

If the first inequality holds, let $I_1'(s')$ be such that $I_1'(s') \subset I_1(s')$ where the lower end-point of the two intervals is the same, and

$$p(s')\gamma_{s'_1}I'_1(s') = p(s'')\gamma_{s''_1}I''_1(s'')$$

where $I''_1(s'') = I_1(s'')$. If the second inequality holds, let $I''_1(s'')$ be such that $I''_1(s'') \subset I_1(s'')$ where the lower end-points of the two intervals are the same. Let $I'_1(s') = I_1(s)$ and

$$p(s')\gamma_{s'_1}I'_1(s') = p(s'')\gamma_{s''_1}I''_1(s'').$$

Define

$$L_1(x,s) = \begin{cases} \gamma_{s'_1} & \text{for } x \in I'_1(s'),\ s = s', \\ \gamma_{s''_1} & \text{for } x \in I''_1(s''),\ s = s'', \\ 0 & \text{otherwise.} \end{cases}$$

Denote by H^0 the cumulative distribution function corresponding to h_p, and let $H^1 = H^0 + L_1(x,s)$. Then H^1 differs from H^0 by a single unconditional mean-preserving spread and G, the cumulative distribution function of g_p, satisfies GI^mH^1.

By repeating this procedure we define L_2 and $H^2 = H^1 + L_2$. Since S is finite and for each $s \in S$, $[G(\cdot|s) - H(\cdot|s)]$ is a step function with a finite number of steps, the process terminates after a finite number of iterations.

5.6.4 *A Proof of Theorem 5.2 for Discrete Random Variables with Finite Number of Values*

(a) $I^m \Rightarrow N^m$. Let g_p and h_p in $D[B]$ be discrete joint probability distributions corresponding to the random variables Y and X, respectively. Suppose that the corresponding cumulative distribution functions have finite numbers of points of increase. Let $g_pI^mh_p$ and assume that g_p and h_p assign the same probability to all but four points a^s_1, a^s_2, a^t_1, a^t_2 such that $a^s_1 < a^s_2 < x^*_s$ and $x^*_t < a^t_2 < a^t_1$. Let $\Pr\{x_s = a^r_k\} = l_{kr}$ and $\Pr\{Y_s = a^r_k\} = h_{kr}$, $k = 1,2$, $r = s,t$. If $\gamma_{kr} = h_{kr} - l_{kr}$, $k = 1,2$, $r = s,t$, then

$$\gamma_{1s} = -\gamma_{2s} \geqq 0, \quad \gamma_{1t} = -\gamma_{2t} \geqq 0 \quad \text{and} \tag{5.33}$$

$$\sum_{s \in S} p(s) \sum_{k=1}^{2} \gamma_{ks}a^s_k = 0 \tag{5.34}$$

are the implications of conditions (b) and (a) of Definition 5.2, respectively. We need to demonstrate the existence of C^r, $r = 1,2$, satisfying Eqs. (5.29)–

(5.32). Let

$$\{c_{kj}^s\} = \begin{pmatrix} 1 & 0 \\ -\frac{\gamma_{2s}}{l_{2s}} & \frac{h_{2s}}{l_{2s}} \end{pmatrix}, \quad \{c_{kj}^t\} = \begin{pmatrix} 1 & 0 \\ -\frac{\gamma_{2t}}{l_{2t}} & \frac{h_{2t}}{l_{2t}} \end{pmatrix}.$$

Clearly $\Sigma_{j=1}^2 c_{kj}^r = 1$, $r = s,t$, $k = 1,2$, hence Eq. (5.29) holds. Next consider the sums (5.30). Let $r = s$,

$$\sum_{j=1}^{2} c_{1j}^s(a_j^s - a_1^s)(a_1^s - x_s^*) = 0,$$

$$\sum_{j=1}^{2} c_{2j}^s(a_j^s - a_2^s)(a_2^s - x_s^*) = -\frac{\gamma_{2s}}{l_{2s}}(a_1^s - a_2^s)(a_2^s - x_s^*) \geqq 0,$$

where use has been made of the fact that $a_1^s < a_2^s < x_s^*$ and $-\gamma_{2s} \geqq 0$. Similarly for $r = t$. Thus Eq. (5.30) holds. To show that Eq. (5.31) holds we calculate

$$\begin{aligned}
&\sum_{s\in S} p(s) \sum_{k=1}^{2} l_{ks} \sum_{j=1}^{2} c_{kj}^s(a_j^s - a_k^s) \\
&\quad = p(s)\left\{l_{1s}[1\cdot 0 + 0\cdot(\ )] + l_{2s}\left[-\frac{\gamma_{2s}}{l_{2s}}(a_1^s - a_2^s) + \frac{h_{2s}}{l_{2s}}\cdot 0\right]\right\} \\
&\quad\quad + p(t)\left\{l_{1t}[1\cdot 0 + 0\cdot(\ )] + l_{2t}\left[-\frac{\gamma_{2t}}{l_{2t}}(a_1^t - a_2^t) + \frac{h_{2t}}{l_{2t}}\cdot 0\right]\right\} \\
&\quad = p(s)[-\gamma_{2s}(a_1^s - a_2^s)] + p(t)[-\gamma_{2t}(a_1^t - a_2^t)] \\
&\quad = p(s)[\gamma_{1s}a_1^s + \gamma_{2s}^s a_2^s] + p(t)[\gamma_{1t}a_1^t + \gamma_{2t}a_2^t] = 0,
\end{aligned}$$

where the last two equalities follow from Eqs. (5.33) and (5.34), respectively.

Finally, to establish that Eq. (5.32) holds we define the conditional random variable Z_s as follows. For all $s \in S$,

$$c_{kj}^s = \Pr\{Z_s = a_j^s - a_k^s | X_s = a_k^s\}.$$

Then Z_s is a random variable conditional on s and X_s and satisfies Eqs. (5.29), (5.30), and (5.31). The condition given in Eq. (5.32) can be stated as $Y_s = {}_dX_s + Z_s$, $s \in S$. Consider the random variable defined for all $s \in S$ as

$$Y_1^s = X_s + Z_s.$$

Then, by Eq. (5.31), Y_1^s is a random variable with the same mean as X_s. It differs from Y_s only if it attributes different probability weights to a_k^r, $k = 1,2$, $r = s,t$. But

$$\begin{aligned}\Pr\{Y_1^s = a_2^s\} &= \Pr\{X_s = a_2^s\}\Pr\{Z_s = 0|X_s = a_2^s\} \\ &\quad + \Pr\{X_s = a_1^s\}\Pr\{Z_s = a_2^s - a_1^s|X_s = a_1^s\} \\ &= l_{2s} \cdot \frac{h_{2s}}{l_{2s}} + 0 = h_{2s} = \Pr\{Y_s = a_2^s\}.\end{aligned}$$

Similarly, $\Pr\{Y_1^t = a_2^t\} = \Pr\{Y_t = a_2^t\}$.

$$\begin{aligned}\Pr\{Y_1^s = a_1^s\} &= \Pr\{X_s = a_1^s\}\Pr\{Z_s = 0|X_s = a_1^s\} \\ &\quad + \Pr\{X_s = a_2^s\}\Pr\{Z_s = a_1^s - a_2^s|X_s = a_2^s\} \\ &= l_{1s} \cdot 1 + l_{2s}\frac{\gamma_{1s}}{l_{2s}} = h_{1s} = \Pr\{Y_s = a_1^s\}.\end{aligned}$$

By a similar argument, $\Pr\{Y_1^t = a_1^t\} = \Pr\{Y_t = a_1^t\}$. Consequently, $Y_1^s = {}_dY_s = {}_dX_s + Z_s$ for all $s \in S$, and YN^mX.

To extend this result to all joint probability distributions in $D[B]$ whose cumulative distribution functions have finite numbers of points of increase we note that by Lemma 5.4 and Lemma 5.3, $g_pI^mh_p$ implies $g_pN^mh_p$.

To extend the result to all $D[B]$ we note that any distribution in $D[B]$ is a limit of a sequence of discrete distributions. Thus if g_p and h_p are any two distributions in $D[B]$ such that $g_pI^mh_p$, then there exist sequences $\{g_p^n\}$ and $\{h_p^n\}$ of discrete distributions with finite number of values that converge weakly to g_p and h_p, respectively. Furthermore, $g_p^nI^mh_p^n$ for all n. But this implies $g_p^nN^mh_p^n$, hence $g_pN^mh_p$.

(b) $N^m \Rightarrow R^m$. Let Y and X be random variables defined on B such that YN^mX. We need to show that $\Sigma_{s\in S}p(s)E\{u(Y_s,s) - u(X_s,s)\} \leqq 0$, where for all $s \in S$ $u(\cdot,s)$ is concave. Let Z be a random variable defined by Eqs. (5.5)–(5.7). Then from Jensen's inequality for all $x_s \in [a,b]$,

$$E\{u(x_s + Z_s,s)|x_s\} \leqq u(x_s + E\{Z_s|x_s\},s).$$

But

$$\begin{aligned}u(x_s + E\{Z_s|x_s\},s) &= u(x_s,s) \\ &\quad + u'(x_s + \theta_sE\{Z_s|x_s\},s)E\{Z_s|x_s\}, \qquad \theta_s \in [0,1].\end{aligned}$$

Let $\lambda = u'(x_s^*,s) > 0$. Then

$$\begin{aligned}
&\sum_{s\in S} p(s) \int_a^b u(x_s + E\{Z_s|x_s\},s)dG(x_s) \\
&\quad = \sum_{s\in S} p(s)E\{u(x_s,s) + u'(x_s + \theta_s E\{Z_s|x_s\},s)E\{Z_s|x_s\}] \\
&\quad = \sum_{s\in S} p(s)E\{u(x_s,s)\} \\
&\qquad + \sum_{s\in S} p(s)E[(u'(x_s + \theta_s E\{Z_s|x_s\},s) - \lambda)E\{Z_s|x_s\}] \\
&\quad \leqq \sum_{s\in S} p(s)E\{u(x_s,s)\},
\end{aligned}$$

where use has been made of the facts that (a) by Eq. (5.7), $\lambda\Sigma_{s\in S}p(s)E_x[E\{Z_s|x_s\}] = 0$, and (b) by (5.6), $u'(x_s + \theta_s E\{Z_s|x_s\},s) - \lambda \gtreqless 0$, $E\{Z_s|x_s\} \lesseqgtr 0$. Hence

$$\sum_{s\in S} p(s)E\{u(x_s + E\{Z_s|x_s\},s\} \leqq \sum_{s\in S} p(s)E\{u(x_s,s)\}.$$

5.6.5 Proof of Proposition 5.1

Since the denominator in Eq. (5.17) is positive, the sign of $d\alpha^*/dt$ is the same as that of the numerator. To determine the sign of the numerator we begin by noting that, since on the reference set the marginal utility of wealth is equal across states of nature, we have

$$\begin{aligned}
(5.35)\qquad &\sum_{s\in S} p(s) \int_a^b u'(w_s^* + \alpha^* z_s,s)z_s\beta_s G_{zr}(z_s,r^s)dz_s \\
&\quad = \int_a^b u'(f_s(w_t^* + \alpha^* z_t),s) \sum_{s\in S} p(s)g_s(z_t)G_{zr}[g_s(z_t),r^s]\beta_s g_s'(z_t)dz_t,
\end{aligned}$$

where for all $s \in S$, $g_s(z_t) = [f_s(w_t^* + \alpha^* z_t) - w_s^*]/\alpha^*$, and the superscript m is suppressed to simplify the notation. Notice that if the reference set is linear, then $g_s(z_t) = \delta_s z_t$, $\delta_s > 0$. (Note that for all $s \in S\, f_s^m(w) = A_s + \delta_s w$. Hence $g_s(z_t) = [A_s + \delta_s(w_t^* + \alpha^* z_t) - w_s^*]/\alpha^*$. But $w_s^* = A_s + \delta_s w_t^*$. Consequently, $g_s(z_t) = \delta_s z_t$.) Next we observe that

$$\begin{aligned}
(5.36)\qquad &\int_a^x \sum_{s\in S} p(s)g_s(z_t)G_{zr}[g_s(z_t),r^s]\beta_s g_s'(z_t)dz_t \\
&\quad = \sum_{s\in S} p(s) \int_{g_s(a)}^{g_s(x)} z_s G_{zr}(z_s,r^s)\beta_s dz_s
\end{aligned}$$

$$= \sum_{s \in S} p(s)\left[-\int_{g_s(a)}^{g_s(x)} G_r(z_s,r^s)\beta_s dz_s + \beta_s z_s G_r(z_s,r^s)\Big|_{g_s(a)}^{g_s(x)}\right]$$
$$= -T(x) + \sum_{s \in S} p(s) g_s(x) G_r(g_s(x),r^s)\beta_s,$$

where we made use of the fact that for all $s \in S$, $G_r(g_s(a),r^s) = 0$. Hence, integrating the right side of Eq. (5.35) by parts and using Eq. (5.36) we get

$$\text{(5.37)} \quad \int_a^b u''(f_s(w_t^* + \alpha^* z_t),s) f_s'(w_t^* + \alpha^* z_t)\alpha^* T(z_t) dz_t$$
$$- \int_a^b u''(f_s(w_t^* + \alpha^* z_t),s) f_s'(w_t^* + \alpha^* z_t)\alpha^*$$
$$\sum_{s \in S} p(s) g_s(z_t) G_r(g_s(z_t),r^s)\beta_s dz_t$$
$$+ u'(f_s(w_t^* + \alpha^* z_t),s)[-T(z_t) + \sum_{s \in S} p(s) g_s(z_t) G_r(g_s(z_t),r^s)\beta_s]\Big|_a^b .$$

The last term in Eq. (5.37) is zero, since $T(b) = T(a) = G_r(g_s(b),r^s) = G_r(g_s(a),r^s) = 0$.

Assume that the reference set is linear. Then

$$\text{(5.38)} \quad \int_a^x \sum_{s \in S} p(s) g_s(z_t) G_r(g_s(z_t),r^s)\beta_s dz_t$$
$$= -\int_a^x \sum_{s \in S} p(s) \int_{g_s(a)}^{g_s(z_t)} G_r(z_s,r^s)\beta_s dz_s dz_t$$
$$+ z_t \sum_{s \in S} p(s) \int_{g_s(a)}^{g_s(z_t)} G_r(z_s,r^s)\beta_s dz_s \Big|_a^x$$
$$= -\int_a^x T(z_t) dz_t + xT(x).$$

Integrating the second term in Eq. (5.37) by parts and using Eq. (5.38) we obtain

$$\text{(5.39)} \quad \int_a^b \left\{u'''(f_s(w_t^* + \alpha^* z_t),s)(\alpha^*\delta_s)^2 \left[\int_a^{z_t} T(x)dx - z_t T(z_t)\right]\right\} dz_t$$
$$+ u_s''(f_s(w_t^* + \alpha^* z_t),s)\alpha^*\delta_s \left[-\int_a^{z_t} T(x)dx + z_t T(z_t)\right]\Big|_a^b .$$

But $T(a) = T(b) = 0$. Hence Eq. (5.39) may be written as

$$-\int_a^b [u'''(f_s(w_t^* + \alpha^* z_t),s)(\alpha^*\delta_s)^2 z_t T(z_t)]\,dz_t + \int_a^b u''(f_s(w_t^* + \alpha^* z_t),s)\alpha^*\delta_s T(z_t)\,dz_t, \tag{5.40}$$

where, to obtain the second term in Eq. (5.40), we reverse the integration by parts of the terms

$$\int_a^b u'''(f_s(w_t^* + \alpha^* z_t),s)(\alpha^*\delta_s)^2 \int_a^{z_t} T(x)\,dx\,dz_t - u''(f_s(w_t^* + \alpha^* z_t),s)\alpha^*\delta_s \int_a^{z_t} T(x)\,dx \Big|_a^b$$

in (5.39).

Substituting Eq. (5.40) in (5.38) and collecting terms we get

$$\int_a^b [2u''(f_s(w_t^* + \alpha^* z_t),s)\alpha^*\delta_s + u'''(f_s(w_t^* + \alpha^* z_t),s)(\alpha^*\delta_s)^2 z_t]\,T(z_t)\,dz_t. \tag{5.41}$$

But the expression in the square brackets of the integrand is the second derivative of $u'(f_s(w_t^* + \alpha^* z_t),s)z_t$ with respect to z_t. Since by definition $T(z_t) \geqq 0$ for all z_t, the sign of Exp. (5.41) is negative (positive) if $u'(f_s(w_t^* + \alpha^* z_t),s)z_t = \partial u[f_s(w_t^* + \alpha z_t),s]/\partial\alpha|_{\alpha=\alpha^*}$ is concave (convex) in z_t.

6 Multivariate Risk Aversion and Risk Aversion with State-Dependent Preferences

6.1 Introduction

The successful application of the Arrow–Pratt measures of risk aversion to the analysis of decision problems involving univariate state-independent utility functions inspired the development of similar measures for a broader class of utility functions. Research in this area has focused on the development of risk-aversion measures for utility functions of several variables and multiple sources of risk, and the development of measures of risk aversion for state-dependent utility functions. The multivariate case turns out to be qualitatively different from the univariate case, whether the preference relations are state-dependent or not. Whereas all monotonic increasing univariate utility functions represent in general the same ordinal preferences, multivariate utility functions represent different ordinal preferences. The Arrow–Pratt measures of absolute and relative risk aversion capture only cardinal properties of the utility functions, and as a result are inadequate for the comparative statics analysis of risk aversion when the attitudes toward a given risk depend on the ordinal properties of the decision maker's preferences. The following example is from Kihlstrom and Mirman (1974). Let u^1 and u^2 be two distinct utility functions defined on the two-dimensional commodity space. Denoting the quantities of the two commodities by x_1 and x_2, let $\bar{u}^1$ and $\bar{u}^2$ in Figure 6.1 depict indifference curves that correspond, respectively, to the two utility functions. Consider the bundles $\boldsymbol{x}' = (x_1', x_2')$ and $\boldsymbol{x}'' = (x_1'', x_2'')$ such that $u^1(\boldsymbol{x}'') < u^1(\boldsymbol{x}')$ and $u^2(\boldsymbol{x}'') > u^2(\boldsymbol{x}')$, as illustrated in Figure 6.1. Suppose that two individuals whose preferences are represented by u^1 and u^2 face a choice between a lottery that offers $\boldsymbol{x}'$ and $\boldsymbol{x}''$ as prizes and the certainty of receiving $\boldsymbol{x}'$. Clearly the individual whose utility function is u^1 prefers the sure outcome $\boldsymbol{x}'$ over any lottery with $\boldsymbol{x}'$ and $\boldsymbol{x}''$ as its prizes, while the individual whose preferences are represented by u^2 prefers any such lottery over the sure outcome. It would be a mistake,

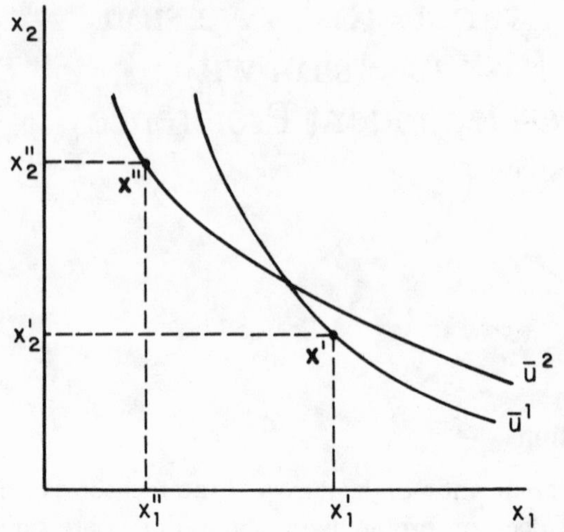

Figure 6.1 Multivariate Risk

however, to conclude that the second individual is less risk averse in the usual sense, since the choices reflect the difference between the preference orderings rather than between the utility functions representing them. Put differently, there exists another lottery and a certain outcome such that the first individual, namely the individual who preferred the certain outcome before, will prefer the lottery over the certain outcome, while the second individual facing the same choice will prefer the sure outcome over the lottery.

This consideration led Kihlstrom and Mirman to conclude that a prerequisite for interpersonal comparison of attitudes toward multivariate risk is that the decision makers being compared have identical ordinal preferences on the commodity space. Since the differences among individual preferences are then reduced to differences in the cardinal properties of the respective utility functions, restricting comparability in this manner permits the use of the Arrow–Pratt measures for interpersonal comparison of risk aversion. The restriction on the class of individuals who may be compared in terms of their attitudes toward multivariate risks is not confined to the case of state-independent preferences. Indeed, the analysis in Chapter 4 indicates that the same restriction must be imposed in the case of state-dependent preferences.

This discussion and the analysis in Chapter 2 demonstrate that, except in the relatively simple case of univariate, state-independent utility functions, interpersonal comparisons of risk aversion based on the Arrow–Pratt measures must necessarily be confined to subsets of decision makers, those with identical preference orderings in the case of state-independent, multivariate utility functions and those with identical reference sets in the case of state-dependent, univariate utility functions. In the case where the utility functions are both multivariate and state-dependent, both restrictions must be imposed (see Definition 4.2). To explore the relationships between multivariate risk aversion and risk aversion with state-dependent preferences I present the former as a special case of the latter.

The essential difference between decision problems involving multivariate preferences and those involving state-dependent preferences is that the latter involve an attribute of the ultimate outcome, namely the state of nature, which is unalterable and cannot be traded against the other attributes, say wealth. In addition, situations where the direct ultimate outcome is a bundle of goods are rare. Instead multivariate risks typically pertain to the level of income and the relative prices, while the uncertainty regarding the ultimate consumption is an indirect result. It is natural, therefore, to capture individual attitudes toward such risks using the properties of the indirect utility function. Since the prices are an unalterable attribute, the formal structure of decision problems involving multivariate risks is the same as that of decision problems with state-dependent preferences. In fact, the former problems may be regarded as a special case of decision problems with state-dependent preferences where the set of states of nature coincides with the set of prices.

6.2 The Reference Set for Utility Functions with Many Commodities

The definition of reference sets for indirect utility functions that can serve as a basis for comparability of attitudes toward multivariate risks calls for new measures of income and prices.

6.2.1 A Difficulty with the Measurement of Income and Prices

Conceptually, the notion of a reference point is the same whether the set of states of nature is the set of the decision maker's states of health or the set of prices. In both instances a reference point represents optimal allocations of wealth, or income, across states among all such allocations that are actuarially equivalent. The conceptual difficulty encountered in developing a definition of a reference point when the set of states of nature coincides with the set of prices has to do with the definition of income and prices. To illustrate the difficulty, I define reference points in terms of nominal income and prices. Consider two decision makers A and B whose utility functions u_A and u_B respectively, represent the same ordinal preferences over the commodity space. Let u_0 and u_1 in Figure 6.2 depict the indifference curves of these individuals. Let $\boldsymbol{x}^0$ and $\boldsymbol{x}^1$ depict the optimal consumption bundles when the price vectors (states of nature) are $\boldsymbol{p}^0$ and $\boldsymbol{p}^1$, respectively, and the corresponding money incomes are y^0 and y^1. Suppose further that the marginal utility of income for individual A is the same at $\boldsymbol{x}^0$ and $\boldsymbol{x}^1$.

Since A and B have the same ordinal preferences, they are comparable in terms of their attitudes toward risk. They need not have the same reference set, however. Suppose that A is globally strictly more risk-averse than B. Then there exists a monotonic increasing and strictly concave transformation $T[\cdot]$ such that $u_A = T[u_B]$. Let $\boldsymbol{p}^0$ and $\boldsymbol{p}^1$ be the only states of nature. If the reference set is defined as the set of income distributions such that the marginal utility of the nominal income is equal across states, then (y_0, y_1) is by definition a reference point of u_A. By construction, $T'[u_B(\boldsymbol{x}^1)] < T'[u_B(\boldsymbol{x}^0)]$, and $du_A(\boldsymbol{x}^i)/dy = T'[u_B(\boldsymbol{x}^i)]du_B(\boldsymbol{x}^i)/dy$, $i = 0,1$. Since the marginal utility of income of A is equal at $\boldsymbol{x}^0$ and $\boldsymbol{x}^1$, the marginal utility of income of B at $\boldsymbol{x}^1$ must exceed that at $\boldsymbol{x}^0$ and (y_0, y_1) is not a reference point of u_B. If the reference set is to serve as a basis for comparability it must be defined using different concepts of income and prices.

6.2.2 *Indexed Income and Price Functions*

Let X be the commodity space given by the nonnegative orthant of the Euclidean n-space. Let $\gtrsim$ be a preference ordering on X that has the proper-

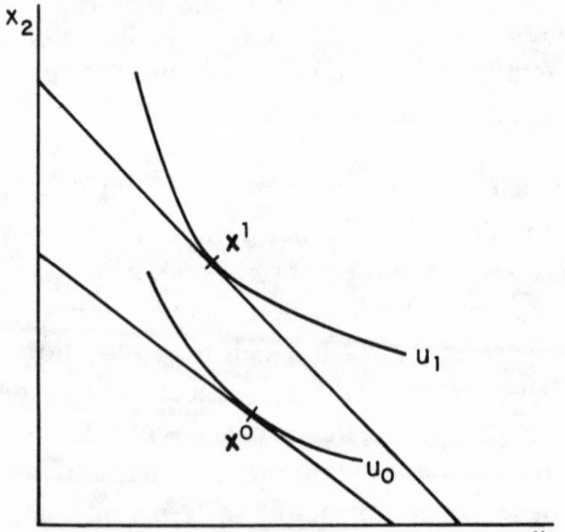

Figure 6.2 The difficulty in defining the reference set for utility functions with many commodities

ties of continuity (for all $\boldsymbol{x}^0 \in X$ the sets $\{\boldsymbol{x} \in X | \boldsymbol{x} \gtrsim \boldsymbol{x}^0\}$ and $\{\boldsymbol{x} \in X | \boldsymbol{x}^0 \gtrsim \boldsymbol{x}\}$ are closed); convexity (for all $\boldsymbol{x}^0 \in X$ the set $\{\boldsymbol{x} \in X | \boldsymbol{x} \gtrsim \boldsymbol{x}^0\}$ is convex); and monotonicity (if $x_i \geqq x_i^0$, $i = 1, \ldots, n$ with strict inequality for some i, then $\boldsymbol{x} = (x_1, \ldots, x_n) \gtrsim (x_1^0, \ldots, x_n^0) = \boldsymbol{x}^0$). Then there exists a real-valued continuous and monotonic increasing function u on X which represents the preference ordering. Let R^n_{++} be the interior of the nonnegative orthant of the Euclidean n-space and denote by $\bar{y}$ and $\bar{\boldsymbol{p}} \in R^n_{++}$ the money income and the n-dimensional vector of money prices, respectively.

PROPOSITION 6.1. *For every continuous convex preference ordering $\gtrsim$ on X there exists an index function $I: R_+ \times R^n_{++} \to R_{++}$ such that:*
(i) I is homogeneous of degree one in nominal income and prices.
(ii) If we normalize $\bar{y}$ and $\bar{\boldsymbol{p}}$ by I (if we define the new variables $y = \bar{y}/I$, $p_i = \bar{p}_i/I$, $i = 1, \ldots, n$), then the marginal utility of the normalized income y is constant on every equivalence class of $\gtrsim$.

A real-valued function on $R_+ \times R^n_{++}$, U, is said to be the indirect utility representation of the preference ordering $\gtrsim$ on X if and only if $U(y,\boldsymbol{p}) = u[\boldsymbol{x}^*(y,\boldsymbol{p}))]$, where $\boldsymbol{x}^*(y,\boldsymbol{p})$ denotes the optimal solution to the problem "Maximize $u(\boldsymbol{x})$ on X subject to $\Sigma_{i=1}^n p_i x_i = y$." Let $U_y(\cdot, \cdot)$ denote the partial derivative of $U(\cdot, \cdot)$ with respect to y. Then by Proposition 6.1, $U_y(y,\boldsymbol{p}) \equiv \lambda$ is constant on every equivalence class of $\gtrsim$. Notice also that for any level of nominal income $\bar{y}$ and all positive nominal price vectors $\bar{\boldsymbol{p}}$, $I(\bar{y},\bar{\boldsymbol{p}}) = U_y(y,\boldsymbol{p})/U_{\bar{y}}(\bar{y},\bar{\boldsymbol{p}})$(the index function is the ratio of the marginal utility of the indexed income and the marginal utility of money income).

6.2.3 The Reference Set

Consider the indirect utility function $U(y,\boldsymbol{p})$. If we interpret the price vector $\boldsymbol{p}$ as a state of nature, then the set of states of nature coincides with the interior of the nonnegative orthant of the Euclidean n-space. Assume that $U(\cdot, \cdot)$ is a twice continuously differentiable and strictly concave function of y for all $\boldsymbol{p}$. Suppose further that $U_y(0,\boldsymbol{p}) = \lambda_0$ for all $\boldsymbol{p} \in R^n_{++}$, where $\lambda_0 > 0$. Thus at zero income the marginal utility of income is bounded away from zero for all prices. This assumption seems reasonable, especially if we recall that the prices were normalized. Thus, even if the nominal prices tend to infinity the normalized prices remain finite.

To define the reference set we begin by considering the following problem: A decision maker is facing a joint probability distribution F on R^n_{++}, and a function $y': R^n_{++} \to R_+$ which assigns to every realization of $\boldsymbol{p}$ in R^n_{++} a level of income $y'(\boldsymbol{p})$. He is allowed to rearrange his income across states, provided that the actuarial value of the ultimate income distribution does not exceed the actuarial value of his initial income distribution. Formally the decision maker chooses among $y(\boldsymbol{p})$ the particular income distribution that maximizes

$$\text{(6.1)} \qquad \int_{R^n_{++}} U(y(\boldsymbol{p}),\boldsymbol{p})\, dF(\boldsymbol{p})$$

subject to

$$\text{(6.2)} \qquad \int_{R^n_{++}} [y(\boldsymbol{p}) - y'(\boldsymbol{p})]\, dF(\boldsymbol{p}) \leqq 0,$$

where $F(\boldsymbol{p})$ is the joint cumulative distribution function of $\boldsymbol{p}$. Let c be the actuarial value of the initial income distribution and denote by $y^*(\boldsymbol{p})$ the solution to (6.1)–(6.2). Then the optimality conditions are

$$\text{(6.3)} \qquad U_y(y^*(\boldsymbol{p}),\boldsymbol{p}) = \lambda(c,F) \text{ for all } \boldsymbol{p} \in R^n_{++},$$

such that $F'(\boldsymbol{p}) > 0$, where $\lambda(c,F)$ is the Lagrangian multiplier corresponding to the constraint (6.2). The multiplier $\lambda(c,F)$ is independent of $\boldsymbol{p}$.

Given c, the function $y^*(\boldsymbol{p})$ defined by Eqs. (6.3) is a reference point. Unlike the case where the set of states of nature is finite and therefore reference points are vectors, the set of states in the present case is a continuum and reference points are functions. As before, the reference set is the set of all reference points.

DEFINITION 6.1. *Given a cumulative distribution function $F(\cdot)$ on R^n_{++} such that for all $\boldsymbol{p} \in R^n_{++}$ $F'(\cdot) > 0$, the reference set of U is*

$$RS_U = \{y^*(\boldsymbol{p},c) \mid U_y(y^*(\boldsymbol{p},c),\boldsymbol{p}) = \lambda(c,F),\ c \geqq 0,\ \boldsymbol{p} \in R^n_{++}\}.$$

The reference set is not empty, since $0 \leqq U_y(y,\boldsymbol{p}) \leqq \lambda_0$ for all $\boldsymbol{p} \in R^n{}_{++}$ and $y \geqq 0$. Furthermore, it is clear from the definition that the reference set is independent of the probability distribution F.

6.3 Interpersonal Comparisons of Attitudes toward Risk

The correspondence between multivariate risk aversion and risk aversion with state-dependent preferences consists of two main points. (a) Two indirect utility functions U and V are comparable in the sense of having identical reference sets if and only if they are the indirect representations of the same ordinal preferences on the commodity space. (b) The expectation of U is a concave transformation of the expectation of V on the reference set if and only if u, the direct utility function corresponding to U, is a concave transformation of v, the direct utility function corresponding to V.

6.3.1 Comparability and Its Consequences

Two indirect utility functions are comparable if they have identical reference sets. Formally,

DEFINITION 6.2. *Let U and V be two indirect utility functions. Then U and V are said to be comparable if and only if* $RS_U = RS_V$.

Implicit in Definition 6.2 is the assumption that the index function corresponding to the two utility functions is the same. Without this assumption the indirect utility functions do not have the same arguments and the equality of the reference sets becomes a meaningless proposition.

Theorem 6.1 will establish that the prerequisite for comparability of risk aversion with state-dependent utility functions, namely equality of the reference sets, is the same as the prerequisite for comparability of risk aversion with multivariate utility functions, namely identical ordinal preferences.

THEOREM 6.1. *Let* $U(y,\mathbf{p}) \equiv u(\mathbf{x}^*(y,\mathbf{p}))$ *and* $V(y,\mathbf{p}) \equiv v(\mathbf{x}^*(y,\mathbf{p}))$ *be two indirect utility functions. Then* $U(y,\mathbf{p})$ *and* $V(y,\mathbf{p})$ *are comparable (in the sense of Definition 6.2) if and only if* $u(\mathbf{x})$ *and* $v(\mathbf{x})$ *represent the same preference ordering on X.*

6.3.2 Comparative Risk Aversion

To establish the correspondence between the measure of absolute risk aversion for utility functions with many commodities and that for indirect utility functions we must first define formal measures of risk aversion for both cases.

Given $\mathbf{x} \in X$ let $\mathbf{z}$ be a random variable that takes values in R^n and for $i = 1, \ldots, n$, $z_i \geqq -x_i$. Suppose, without loss of generality, that $\bar{\mathbf{z}} = 0$, where $\bar{\mathbf{z}}$ is the mean of $\mathbf{z}$. The risk premium correspondence, $\boldsymbol{\pi}^u(\mathbf{x},\mathbf{z})$, is a vector-valued function defined by the equation

$$(6.4) \qquad u(\mathbf{x} - \boldsymbol{\pi}^u) = E\{u(\mathbf{x} + \mathbf{z})\},$$

where the expectation on the right side of Eq. (6.4) is assumed to exist. Thus, every element of the risk premium correspondence represents a maximal bundle of commodities that a decision maker would be willing to give up to avoid the risk represented by $\mathbf{z}$. We say that $\boldsymbol{\pi}^u$ is larger than $\boldsymbol{\pi}^v$ ($\boldsymbol{\pi}^u > \boldsymbol{\pi}^v$) if and only if for every element in the correspondence $\boldsymbol{\pi}^u(\mathbf{x},\mathbf{z})$ there exists an element in the correspondence $\boldsymbol{\pi}^v(\boldsymbol{x},\boldsymbol{z})$ such that $\pi_i^u \geqq \pi_i^v$ for $i = 1, \ldots, n$ and $\pi_i^u > \pi_i^v$ for at least one i. Similarly, $\boldsymbol{\pi}^u = \boldsymbol{\pi}^v$ if for every element in the correspondence $\boldsymbol{\pi}^u(\boldsymbol{x},\boldsymbol{z})$ there is an element in $\boldsymbol{\pi}^v(\boldsymbol{x},\boldsymbol{z})$ such that $\pi_i^u = \pi_i^v$, $i = 1, \ldots, n$. The notion of a risk premium with many commodities is illustrated in Figure 6.3, where the curve $\bar{u}$ depicts the multivariate certainty equivalent, or the indifference curve corresponding to the utility level $E\{u(\boldsymbol{x} + \boldsymbol{z})\}$.

The relative position of $\bar{u}$ and $\boldsymbol{x}$ reflects that the decision maker is risk averse and therefore would prefer receiving $\boldsymbol{x}$ with certainty over a gamble with the bundle $\boldsymbol{x}$ as its mean outcome. The difference $(\boldsymbol{x} - \boldsymbol{y}) = \boldsymbol{\pi}_A^u$ and $(\boldsymbol{x} - \boldsymbol{w}) = \boldsymbol{\pi}_B^u$ represent two alternative solutions of Eq. (6.4). Let the curve $\bar{v}$ depict the multivariate certainty equivalent corresponding to a utility function v. The points $\boldsymbol{w}'$ and $\boldsymbol{y}'$ define the risk premium vectors $\boldsymbol{\pi}_A^v = (\boldsymbol{x} - \boldsymbol{y}')$ and $\boldsymbol{\pi}_B^v = (\boldsymbol{x} - \boldsymbol{w}')$, respectively, and as is apparent, since $y_i' < y_i$, $i = 1,2$, $\boldsymbol{\pi}_A^u < \boldsymbol{\pi}_A^v$, and since $w_i' < w_i$, $i = 1,2$, $\boldsymbol{\pi}_B^u < \boldsymbol{\pi}_B^v$. Since this holds for any point on $\bar{u}$, according to our definition, v displays a higher degree of risk aversion than u. Notice that it is crucial for this result that the indifference curves do not intersect, or that u and v represent the same preference ordering on R_+^2.

Next consider the notion of a risk premium for indirect utility functions. For any given $y(\boldsymbol{p})$ let $c = \int_{R_{++}^n} y(\boldsymbol{p})dF(\boldsymbol{p})$. Let $y^*(\boldsymbol{p},c) \in \mathrm{RS}_u$ be such that $\int_{R_{++}^n} y^*(\boldsymbol{p},c)dF(\boldsymbol{p}) = c$. Thus $y(\boldsymbol{p}) - y^*(\boldsymbol{p},c)$ represents actuarially neutral deviations from the reference point $y^*(\boldsymbol{p},c)$. The risk premium $\pi_U(y(\,\cdot\,),F)$

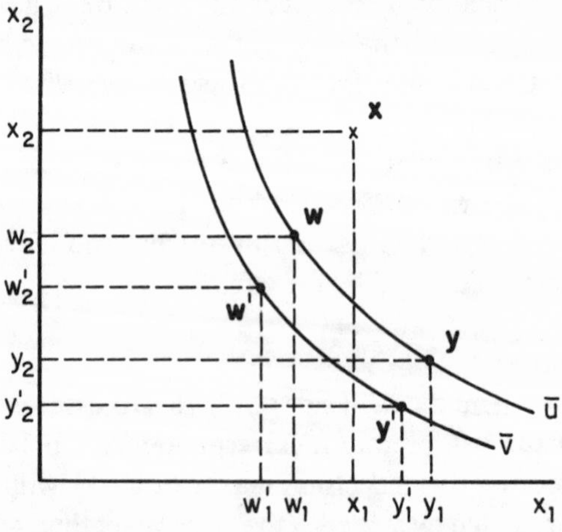

Figure 6.3 Multivariate risk premium

is defined by

(6.5) $$\int_{R^n_{++}} U(y^*(\mathbf{p},c-\pi_U(y(\mathbf{p}),F)),\mathbf{p}) = \int_{R^n_{++}} U(y(\mathbf{p}),\mathbf{p})dF(\mathbf{p}).$$

Thus the risk premium represents the largest actuarial value of income that the decision maker is willing to forgo for the opportunity to rearrange the distribution of his income across prices or states of nature to attain a point in his reference set.

Using these definitions, Theorem 6.2 will establish the equivalence of these and other measures of risk aversion.

THEOREM 6.2. *Let $U(y,\mathbf{p}) \equiv u(\mathbf{x}^*(y,\mathbf{p}))$ and $V(y,\mathbf{p}) \equiv v(\mathbf{x}^*((y,\mathbf{p}))$ be comparable. Suppose that $V(y,\mathbf{p})$ is concave in y for every $\mathbf{p}$ in R^n_{++}. Then the following conditions are equivalent in either the strict form or the weak form.*

(a) $-u_{11}(\mathbf{x})/u_1(\mathbf{x}) \geqq -v_{11}(\mathbf{x})/v_1(\mathbf{x})$ *for all* $\mathbf{x} \geqq 0$, *where* $u_{11} = \partial^2 u/\partial x_1^2$ *and* $u_1 = \partial u/\partial x_1$.

(b) *There exists a transformation T such that* $u(\mathbf{x}) = T[v(\mathbf{x})]$, $T' > 0$, $T'' \leqslant 0$.

(c) $\pi^u(\mathbf{x},\mathbf{z}) \geqslant \pi^v(\mathbf{x},\mathbf{z})$ *for all random variables* $\mathbf{z}$ *that take values in* R^n, *where for* $i = 1, \ldots, n$, $z_i \geqq -x_i$, *and all* $\mathbf{x} \geqslant 0$.

(d) $-U_{yy}(y^*(\mathbf{p},c),\mathbf{p})/U_y(y^*(\mathbf{p},c),\mathbf{p}) \geqslant -V_{yy}(y^*(\mathbf{p},c),\mathbf{p})/V_y(y^*(\mathbf{p},c),\mathbf{p})$ *for all* $\mathbf{p} \in R^n_{++}$ *and* $c \geqslant 0$.

(e) *For every joint cumulative distribution function* $F(\mathbf{p})$ *on* R^n_{++} *there exists a transformation* H_F *such that*

(6.6) $$\int_{R^n_{++}} U(y^*(\mathbf{p},c),\mathbf{p})dF(\mathbf{p}) = H_F\left[\int_{R^n_{++}} V(y^*(\mathbf{p},c),\mathbf{p})dF(\mathbf{p})\right],$$

$H'_F > 0, \quad H''_F \leqslant 0.$

(f) $\pi_U(y(\cdot),F) \geqslant \pi_V(y(\cdot),F)$ *for all* $y(\cdot)$ *and all* $F(\mathbf{p})$ *on* R^n_{++}.

Conditions (a)–(c) in Theorem 6.2 describe equivalent characterizations of the relation "more risk-averse" for comparable multivariate utility functions. Conditions (d)–(f) describe equivalent characterizations of the same relation for comparable indirect utility functions. By Theorem 6.1 the condition of comparability is the same in both cases. Thus, taken together, Theorems 6.1 and 6.2 establish that the relation "more risk-averse" is exactly the same whether it is defined in terms of multivariate utility functions or in terms of indirect utility functions where the prices are interpreted as states of nature.

6.4 Changing Attitudes toward Risk

Interpersonal comparisons of attitudes toward multivariate risks require that the ordinal preferences of the persons whose attitudes are being compared be identical. This suggests that to compare the attitudes toward risk of a given individual at different levels of income, the preference ordering must, in some sense, be autocomparable. Kihlstrom and Mirman (1981) studied the restrictions that must be imposed on a preference ordering for the utility function to display decreasing (increasing, constant) risk aversion. According to their analysis, autocomparability in the case of multivariate risks is implied by homotheticity of the preference ordering. The analysis in Chapter 2 established that linearity of the reference set implies autocomparability in the case of state-dependent preferences. It should come as no surprise, therefore, that when we treat multivariate preferences as a special case of state-dependent preferences, linearity of the reference set turns out to be equivalent to homotheticity of the ordinal preferences on the commodity space.

6.4.1 Homothetic Preferences and Their Least Concave Representations

A preference relation $\succsim$ on X is said to be homothetic if for any $\boldsymbol{x}, \boldsymbol{x}' \in X$, $\boldsymbol{x} \sim \boldsymbol{x}'$ implies $\alpha\boldsymbol{x} \sim \alpha\boldsymbol{x}'$ for any real number $\alpha \geqq 0$.

Debreu (1976) has shown that a convex preference ordering that can be represented by a concave utility function has a least concave representation. Homothetic preference orderings can be shown (see Kihlstrom and Mirman, 1979) to have least concave representations that are linear homogeneous. Thus any concave homothetic utility function $u(\cdot)$ that represents the preference ordering $\succsim$ on X may be expressed as $u(\boldsymbol{x}) = h[u^*(\boldsymbol{x})]$ where $u^*(\boldsymbol{x})$ is a linear homogeneous representation of $\succsim$ on X and h is concave. A utility function $u(\boldsymbol{x})$ is said to display decreasing (increasing, constant) risk aversion if and only if $h(\cdot)$ as a function of u^* displays decreasing (increasing, constant) risk aversion in the sense of Arrow and Pratt.

6.4.2 Autocomparability and Homotheticity of the Preference Ordering

A reference set RS_U is said to be linear if and only if for all $y^*(\boldsymbol{p},\delta c)$ and $y^*(\boldsymbol{p},c)$ in RS_U and $\delta \geqq 0$, $y^*(\boldsymbol{p},\delta c) = \delta y^*(\boldsymbol{p},c)$. This means that the optimal income in each state varies equiproportionally with the actuarial value.

DEFINITION 6.3. *A preference ordering $\succsim$ on X represented by the indirect utility function U is said to be autocomparable if and only if RS_U is linear.*

Autocomparability and homotheticity of a preference ordering are equivalent.

THEOREM 6.3. *The preference ordering $\succsim$ on X is homothetic if and only if it is autocomparable.*

Theorem 6.3 establishes correspondence between the notions of autocomparability for multivariate utility functions and state-dependent utility functions. Again we see that, given the special interpretation of the indirect utility functions as state-dependent utility functions, the prerequisite for defining decreasing (increasing, constant) risk aversion in the case of state-dependent preferences (see Section 2.5) is equivalent to the prerequisite for defining these notions in the multivariate case.

6.5 Related Work

Various aspects of the notion of multivariate risk aversion have been studied in great detail. Scalar measures of risk aversion were introduced and their economic consequences explored in Kihlstrom and Mirman (1974), and in Diamond and Stiglitz (1974). Further discussion of scalar measures appears in Biswas (1983). Matrix measures of multivariate risk aversion were defined and their implications studied in Duncan (1977) and Karni (1979). Paroush (1975) examined the definition of risk premium for utility functions with many commodities. The definition and consequences of decreasing multivariate risk aversion were explored in the work of Kihlstrom and Mirman (1981). Hanoch (1977) studied the relationship between relative risk aversion with respect to income and with respect to prices, and Stiglitz (1969) examined the relationships between aversion to income risk and the demand for commodities that would obtain under certainty. The discussion and the results contained in the first three sections of this chapter are based on Karni (1983a).

6.6 Proofs

6.6.1 Proof of Proposition 6.1.

The existence of I is proved by construction. Let $\bar{\boldsymbol{p}}^0$ be the unit vector in R^n_{++}. For any given $\bar{y}^0 \in R_+$, let $\boldsymbol{x}^0(\bar{y}^0, \bar{\boldsymbol{p}}^0) \in X$ be determined jointly with λ by the solution of

$$(6.7) \qquad u_i(\boldsymbol{x}) = \lambda, \qquad i = 1, \ldots, n,$$

$$\sum_{i=1}^{n} x_i = \bar{y}^0.$$

Thus λ is a well-defined function of $\bar{y}^0$. For any $\bar{\boldsymbol{p}} \in R^n_{++}$ and $\bar{y} \in R_+$ let $\{I(\bar{y},\bar{\boldsymbol{p}}),\boldsymbol{x}(\bar{y},\bar{\boldsymbol{p}}),y^0(\bar{y},\bar{\boldsymbol{p}})\}$ be the solution of

(6.8) (a) $u_i(\boldsymbol{x}) = \lambda(\bar{y}^0)\bar{P}_i/I \qquad i = 1, \ldots, n,$

(b) $\sum_{i=1}^{n} \bar{p}_i x_i = \bar{y},$

(c) $u(\boldsymbol{x}^0) = u(\boldsymbol{x}).$

Repeating this construction for all $\bar{y} \in R_+$ and $\bar{\boldsymbol{p}} \in R^n_{++}$ we obtain $I(\bar{y},\bar{\boldsymbol{p}})$.

For any $\bar{\boldsymbol{p}} \in R^n_{++}$ and $\bar{y} \in R_+$ consider the vector of money prices $\bar{\boldsymbol{p}}(m) = m\bar{\boldsymbol{p}}$ and nominal income $\bar{y}(m) = m\bar{y}$, $m > 0$. Since $\boldsymbol{x}$ is homogeneous of degree zero in prices and nominal income, it follows that substitution of $\bar{\boldsymbol{p}}(m)$ for $\bar{\boldsymbol{p}}$ and $\bar{y}(m)$ for $\bar{y}$ in Eqs. (6.8)(a) and (6.8)(b) will not alter the solution to (6.8) if and only if $I(\bar{y}(m),\bar{\boldsymbol{p}}(m)) = I(m\bar{y},m\bar{\boldsymbol{p}}) = mI(\bar{y},\bar{\boldsymbol{p}})$ and (i) is proved.

By construction Eqs. (6.7) and (6.8) imply that λ, the marginal utility of the normalized income, is constant if and only if u is constant, which is part (ii) of the conclusion.

6.6.2 Proof of Theorem 6.1

(a) Sufficiency. Suppose that u and v are two representations of $\succsim$ on X. Then by Proposition 6.1 the index function is identical for both of them, and consequently the normalized variables y and $\boldsymbol{p}$ are the same for both u and v. Furthermore, there exists a positive transformation $H[\,\cdot\,]$ such that $u(\boldsymbol{x}) = H[v(\boldsymbol{x})]$. Let $y^*(\boldsymbol{p},c) \in RS_U$. Then by Definition 6.1, for any $\boldsymbol{p}', \boldsymbol{p}'' \in R^n_{++}$,

(6.9) $U_y(y^*(\boldsymbol{p}',c),\boldsymbol{p}') = U_y(y^*(\boldsymbol{p}'',c),\boldsymbol{p}'') = \lambda(c,F).$

But

(6.10) $U(y,\boldsymbol{p}) \equiv H[V(y,\boldsymbol{p})].$

Hence, differentiating Exp. (6.10) with respect to y and using Eq. (6.9) we get

(6.11) $H'[V(y^*(\boldsymbol{p}',c),\boldsymbol{p}')]V_y(y^*(\boldsymbol{p}',c),\boldsymbol{p})$
$= H'[V(y^*(\boldsymbol{p}'',c),\boldsymbol{p}'')]V_y(y^*(\boldsymbol{p}'',c),\boldsymbol{p}'').$

But by Proposition 6.1 for any given c and F, U is constant for all $y^* \in RS_U$. Hence

(6.12) $H[V(y^*(\boldsymbol{p}',c),\boldsymbol{p}')] = H[V(y^*(\boldsymbol{p}'',c),\boldsymbol{p}'')]$ and

(6.13) $H'[V(y^*(\boldsymbol{p}',c),\boldsymbol{p}')] = H'[V(y^*(\boldsymbol{p}'',c),\boldsymbol{p}'')].$

Equations (6.13) and (6.11) imply that for all $\boldsymbol{p}'$ and $\boldsymbol{p}''$ in R^n_{++},

(6.14) $$V_y(y^*(\boldsymbol{p}',c),\boldsymbol{p}') = V_y(y^*(\boldsymbol{p}'',c),\boldsymbol{p}'').$$

Thus by Definition 6.1, $y^*(\boldsymbol{p},c) \in RS_V$. Since this is true for all $c \geqq 0$, it follows from Definition 6.1 that $RS_U = RS_V$.

(b) Necessity. Let U and V be comparable. Then for every $\boldsymbol{p} \in R^n_{++}$ and $c \geqslant 0$ there exists a well-defined transformation $G_{\boldsymbol{p}}$ such that

$$U(y^*(\boldsymbol{p},c),\boldsymbol{p}) = G_{\boldsymbol{p}}[V(y^*(\boldsymbol{p},c),\boldsymbol{p})] \qquad G'_{\boldsymbol{p}} > 0.$$

The existence of $G_{\boldsymbol{p}}$ follows from the comparability of U and V and can be shown as follows. Let $t = V(y^*(\boldsymbol{p},c),\boldsymbol{p})$. Since V is continuous and monotonic increasing in y^* there exists an inverse function V^{-1} such that $y^*(\boldsymbol{p},c) = V^{-1}(t,\boldsymbol{p})$. Because $RS_U = RS_V$, $U(y^*(\boldsymbol{p},c),\boldsymbol{p}) = U(V^{-1}(t,\boldsymbol{p}),\boldsymbol{p}) \equiv G_{\boldsymbol{p}}[V(y^*(\boldsymbol{p},c),\boldsymbol{p})]$.

Differentiating with respect to y^* we get

$$G'_{\boldsymbol{p}}[V(y^*(\boldsymbol{p},c),\boldsymbol{p})] = U_y(y^*(\boldsymbol{p},c),\boldsymbol{p})/\,V_y(y^*(\boldsymbol{p},c),\boldsymbol{p}) > 0.$$

Furthermore, since by definition of RS, V_y and U_y are constant for all $\boldsymbol{p} \in R^n_{++}$, it follows that for a given c,

$$G'_{\boldsymbol{p}}[V(y^*(\boldsymbol{p},c),\boldsymbol{p})] = G'[V(y^*(\boldsymbol{p},c),\boldsymbol{p})] \quad \text{for all } \boldsymbol{p} \in R^n_{++}.$$

Hence for every given c and all $\boldsymbol{p} \in R^n_{++}$,

$$u_i(\boldsymbol{x}^u(y^*(\boldsymbol{p},c),\boldsymbol{p})) = G'[V(y^*(\boldsymbol{p},c),\boldsymbol{p})]v_i(\boldsymbol{x}^v(y^*(\boldsymbol{p},c),\boldsymbol{p})), \qquad i = 1, \ldots, n,$$

where $\boldsymbol{x}^u$ and $\boldsymbol{x}^v$ denote the optimal consumption bundles corresponding to u and v, respectively, and u_i and v_i are the partial derivatives of u and v with respect to x_i. Thus, for any given $c \geqslant 0$ and $\boldsymbol{p} \in R^n_{++}$,

$$\begin{aligned} x^u_j &= \frac{-\sum_{i=1}^{n} u_i(\boldsymbol{x}^u)(\partial x^u_i/\partial p_j)}{U_y[y^*(\boldsymbol{p},c),\boldsymbol{p}]} \\ &= \frac{-G'[V(y^*(\boldsymbol{p},c),\boldsymbol{p})]\sum_{i=1}^{n} v_i(\boldsymbol{x}^v)(\partial x^v_i/\partial p_j)}{G'[V(y^*(\boldsymbol{p},c),\boldsymbol{p})]V_y(y^*(\boldsymbol{p},c),\boldsymbol{p})} \\ &= x^v_j, \qquad j = 1, \ldots, n, \end{aligned}$$

where the first and last equalities are properties of the indirect utility function. (See Katzner, 1970, Theorem 3.5.)

Finally, since for every $y \geqslant 0$ and all $\boldsymbol{p} \in R^n_{++}$, $U_y(y,\boldsymbol{p}) \in [0,\lambda_0]$, it follows that every y belongs to some element of RS. Thus $\{y^*(\boldsymbol{p},c),\boldsymbol{p} | c \geqslant 0, \boldsymbol{p} \in R^n_{++}\}$ coincides with the domain of U and V. This implies that $u(\boldsymbol{x})$ and $v(\boldsymbol{x})$ represent the same ordinal preferences over X.

6.6.3 Proof of Theorem 6.2

(a) ⟺ (b) ⟺ (c) ⟺ (d) follows from Kihlstrom and Mirman (1974) and Paroush (1975).

I shall prove the equivalence of (d), (e), and (f).

(d) ⟹ (e). Differentiating Eq. (6.6) with respect to c and using the fact that (6.6) is an identity in c, we get

$$U_y(y^*(\boldsymbol{p},c),\boldsymbol{p}) \int_{R^n_{++}} \frac{\partial y^*(\boldsymbol{p},c)}{\partial c}\, dF(\boldsymbol{p})$$
$$= H'_F[\,\cdot\,] V_y(y^*(\boldsymbol{p},c),\boldsymbol{p}) \int_{R^n_{++}} \frac{\partial y^*(\boldsymbol{p},c)}{\partial c}\, dF(\boldsymbol{p}).$$

Since U and V are comparable it follows that

$$H'_F\left[\int_{R^n_{++}} V(y^*(\boldsymbol{p},c),\boldsymbol{p})dF(\boldsymbol{p})\right] = U_y(y^*(\boldsymbol{p},c),\boldsymbol{p})/\,V_y(y^*(\boldsymbol{p},c),\boldsymbol{p}) > 0. \tag{6.15}$$

Differentiating ln H'_F with respect to c we get

$$-\frac{H''_F}{H'_F}\left[\int_{R^n_{++}} V(y^*(\boldsymbol{p},c),\boldsymbol{p})dF(\boldsymbol{p})\right] V_y(y^*(\boldsymbol{p},c),\boldsymbol{p}) \int_{R^n_{++}} \frac{\partial y^*(\boldsymbol{p},c)}{\partial c}\, dF(\boldsymbol{p})$$
$$= \left\{\left[-\frac{U_{yy}(y^*(\boldsymbol{p},c),\boldsymbol{p})}{U_y(y^*(\boldsymbol{p},c),\boldsymbol{p})}\right] - \left[-\frac{V_{yy}(y^*(\boldsymbol{p},c),\boldsymbol{p})}{V_y(y^*(\boldsymbol{p},c),\boldsymbol{p})}\right]\right\} \frac{\partial y^*(\boldsymbol{p},c)}{\partial c}.$$

From the concavity of $V(y,\boldsymbol{p})$ in y it follows that $\partial y^*(\boldsymbol{p},c)/\partial c > 0$. Hence

$$H''_F[\,\cdot\,] \leqslant 0 \Leftrightarrow -\frac{U_{yy}[y^*(\boldsymbol{p},c),\boldsymbol{p}]}{U_y[y^*(\boldsymbol{p},c),\boldsymbol{p}]} \geqslant -\frac{V_{yy}[y^*(\boldsymbol{p},c),\boldsymbol{p}]}{V_y[y^*(\boldsymbol{p},c),\boldsymbol{p}]}.$$

Therefore (d) ⟹ (e). Notice also that in the degenerate case (e) implies $U[y(c),\boldsymbol{p}] = H_{\boldsymbol{p}}[V(y(c),\boldsymbol{p})]$ for all $c \geqslant 0$. But in this case $c = y$. Hence this result holds for all $y \geqslant 0$ and $\boldsymbol{p} \in R^n_{++}$.

(e) ⟹ (f). Let $l(\boldsymbol{p},c) \equiv y^*(\boldsymbol{p},c) - y(\boldsymbol{p})$. Then from Eq. (6.5) we have

$$\begin{aligned}
&\int_{R^n_{++}} U(y^*(\boldsymbol{p},c-\pi_U),\boldsymbol{p})dF(\boldsymbol{p})\\
&\quad=\int_{R^n_{++}} U(y^*(\boldsymbol{p},c)-l(\boldsymbol{p},c),\boldsymbol{p})dF(\boldsymbol{p})\\
&\quad=\int_{R^n_{++}} H_{\boldsymbol{p}}[V(y^*(\boldsymbol{p},c)-l(\boldsymbol{p},c),\boldsymbol{p})]dF(\boldsymbol{p})\\
&\quad\leqslant H_F\left[\int_{R^n_{++}} V(y^*(\boldsymbol{p},c)-l(\boldsymbol{p},c),\boldsymbol{p})dF(\boldsymbol{p})\right]\\
&\quad=H_F\left[\int_{R^n_{++}} V(y^*(\boldsymbol{p},c-\pi_V),\boldsymbol{p})dF(\boldsymbol{p})\right]\\
&\quad=\int_{R^n_{++}} U(y^*(\boldsymbol{p},c-\pi_V),\boldsymbol{p})dF(\boldsymbol{p}),
\end{aligned}$$

where use has been made of the definition of risk premium and Lemma 6.1. Since U is monotonic increasing in c, it follows that

$$\pi_U(y(\cdot),F)\geqslant\pi_V(y(\cdot),F).$$

(f) ⇒ (d). Let F be any probability distribution on R^n_{++} and let $l(\boldsymbol{p},c)\equiv hw(\boldsymbol{p},c)$ where $\int_{R^n_{++}} w(\boldsymbol{p},c)dF(\boldsymbol{p})=0$. Differentiating π_U with respect to h we obtain

$$\frac{d\pi_U}{dh}=\frac{\int_{R^n_{++}} U_y(y^*(\boldsymbol{p},c)-hw(\boldsymbol{p},c),\boldsymbol{p})w(\boldsymbol{p},c)dF(\boldsymbol{p})}{U_y(y^*(\boldsymbol{p},c-\pi_U),\boldsymbol{p})\int_{R^n_{++}}(\partial y^*(\boldsymbol{p},c-\pi_U)/\partial c)dF(\boldsymbol{p})}.$$

Since $\int_{R^n_{++}} w(\boldsymbol{p},c)dF(\boldsymbol{p})=0$ and U_y is constant on RS_U,

$$\left.\frac{d\pi_U}{dh}\right|_{h=0}=0.$$

The same result is obtained for V. Hence (f) implies that

$$\left.\frac{d^2\pi_U}{dh^2}\right|_{h=0}\geqslant\left.\frac{d^2\pi_V}{dh^2}\right|_{h=0}.$$

But

$$\left.\frac{d^2\pi_U}{dh^2}\right|_{h=0} = \frac{-\displaystyle\int_{R^n_{++}} U_{yy}(y^*(\boldsymbol{p},c),\boldsymbol{p})[w(\boldsymbol{p},c)]^2 dF(\boldsymbol{p})}{U_y(y^*(\boldsymbol{p},c),\boldsymbol{p}) \displaystyle\int_{R^n_{++}} (\partial y^*(\boldsymbol{p},c)/\partial c) dF(\boldsymbol{p})}.$$

Hence

$$\text{(6.16)} \qquad \int_{R^n_{++}} \left[-\frac{U_{yy}}{U_y}(y^*(\boldsymbol{p},c),\boldsymbol{p}) + \frac{V_{yy}}{V_y}(y^*(\boldsymbol{p},c),\boldsymbol{p}) \right] [w(\boldsymbol{p},c)]^2 dF(\boldsymbol{p}) \geqslant 0$$

for all $w(\boldsymbol{p},c)$ such that $\int_{R^n_{++}} w(\boldsymbol{p},c) dF(\boldsymbol{p}) = 0$. Thus $-(U_{yy}/U_y)(y^*(\boldsymbol{p},c),\boldsymbol{p}) \geqslant -(V_{yy}/V_y)(y^*(\boldsymbol{p},c),\boldsymbol{p})$, otherwise we can choose $w(\boldsymbol{p},c)$ so as to reverse Inequality (6.16).

LEMMA 6.1. *For any given $F(\boldsymbol{p})$ and all $hw(\boldsymbol{p},c)$ such that $\int_{R^n_{++}} w(\boldsymbol{p},c) dF(\boldsymbol{p}) = 0$,*

$$\text{(6.17)} \qquad \int_{R^n_{++}} H_{\boldsymbol{p}}[V(y^*(\boldsymbol{p},c) - hw(\boldsymbol{p},c),\boldsymbol{p})] dF(\boldsymbol{p}) \leqslant H_F\left[\int_{R^n_{++}} V(y^*(\boldsymbol{p},c) - hw(\boldsymbol{p},c),\boldsymbol{p}) dF(\boldsymbol{p}) \right].$$

where $H_{\boldsymbol{p}}$ is H_F for F such that $\Pr\{\boldsymbol{p}\} = 1$.

Outline of Proof of Lemma 6.1 The proof is similar to that of Lemma 2.1, and appears in full detail in Karni (1983a).

For a given $w(\boldsymbol{p},c)$ such that $\int_{R^n_{++}} w(\boldsymbol{p},c) dF(\boldsymbol{p}) = 0$, define the two functions

$$\text{(6.18)} \qquad I(h) = \int_{R^n_{++}} H_{\boldsymbol{p}}[V(y^*(\boldsymbol{p},c) - hw(\boldsymbol{p},c),\boldsymbol{p})] dF(\boldsymbol{p}),$$

$$\text{(6.19)} \qquad J(h) = H_F\left[\int_{R^n_{++}} V(y^*(\boldsymbol{p},c) - hw(\boldsymbol{p},c),\boldsymbol{p}) dF(\boldsymbol{p}) \right].$$

Clearly, $I(0) = J(0)$. It can be shown, following the procedure in the proof of Lemma 2.1, that $J'(h) \geqq I'(h)$ for all $h > 0$. Thus $J(h) \geqq I(h)$ for all h.

6.6.4 Proof of Theorem 6.3

(a) Suppose that $\succsim$ on X is homothetic. Then for each $\boldsymbol{p} \in R^n_{++}$, $y \in R_+$, and $\alpha \geqq 0$,

(6.20) $\quad x^*(\alpha y,p) = \alpha x^*(y,p),$

where $x^*(y,p)$ denotes the optimal consumption bundle, given y and p. For all $y^*(p,c) \in RS_U$,

$$U(y^*(p,c),p) = u(x^*(y^*(p,c),p)) = h[u^*(x^*(y^*(p,c),p))],$$

where $u^*(\cdot)$ is homogeneous of degree one. Hence, by the definition of the indirect utility and Eq. (6.3),

$$U_y(y^*(p,c),p) = h'[u^*(x^*)] \sum_{i=1}^{n} u_i^*(x^*)(\partial x_i^*/\partial y) = \lambda(c,F)$$

and

$$U_y(\delta y^*(p,c),p) = h'[\delta u^*(x^*)] \sum_{i=1}^{n} u_i^*(x^*)(\partial x_i^*/\partial y) = \lambda(\delta c,F),$$

where we made use of (6.20), the homogeneity of degree 1 of u^*, and the homogeneity of degree zero of u_i^*. Consequently,

(6.21) $$U_y(\delta y^*(p,c),p) = \frac{h'[\delta u^*(x^*)]}{h'[u^*(x^*)]} \lambda(c,F).$$

Since, by the definition of the reference set and the index function, $u^*(x^*(y^*(p,c),p))$ is independent of p, it follows that Eq. (6.21) holds for all p. Thus $\delta y^*(p,c) \in RS_U$. But $\int_{R^n_{++}} \delta y^*(p,c) = \delta c$. Hence $\delta y^*(p,c) = y^*(p,\delta c) \in RS_U$.

(b) Suppose that for all $p \in R^n_{++}$, $y^*(p,\delta c) = \delta y^*(p,c) \in RS_U$. Given $c \geqslant 0$ the set $\{x^*(y^*(p,c),p) \in X | p \in R^n_{++}\}$ is an equivalent class of the preference ordering (depicted by u^0 in Figure 6.4). For $\delta \geqq 0$, define the surface $\mu(\delta c) = \{\delta x^*(y^*(p,c),p) \in X | p \in R^n_{++}\}$ (see Figure 6.4). By the linearity of the reference set for each $p \in R^n_{++}$ and $y^*(\delta c,p)$, the point $\delta x^*(y^*(c,p),p)$ is attainable. Suppose by way of negation that it is not optimal—that $\delta x^*(y^*(p,c),p) \neq x^*(\delta y^*(p,c),p)$ for some $p \in R^n_{++}$. Given such p and $\delta x^*(y^*(p,c),p)$ define the (budget) hyperplane $H(p,\delta x^*) = \{x \in X | \Sigma_{i=1}^n p_i x_i = \delta \Sigma_{i=1}^n p_i x_i^*\}$. Since the preference ordering is strictly convex, the upper contour set defined by the surface $\mu(\delta c)$ is in the half-space defined by $H(p,\delta x^*)$. Thus, by supposition, the equivalence class corresponding to $x^*(\delta y^*(p,c),p)$ (depicted by u_1 in Figure 6.4) does not coincide with $\mu(\delta c)$. This implies that there exists some $p' \in R^n_{++}$ such that the intersection of $H(p',\delta x^*(y^*(p',c),p'))$ and the equivalence class of $x^*(\delta y^*(p,c),p)$ is empty.

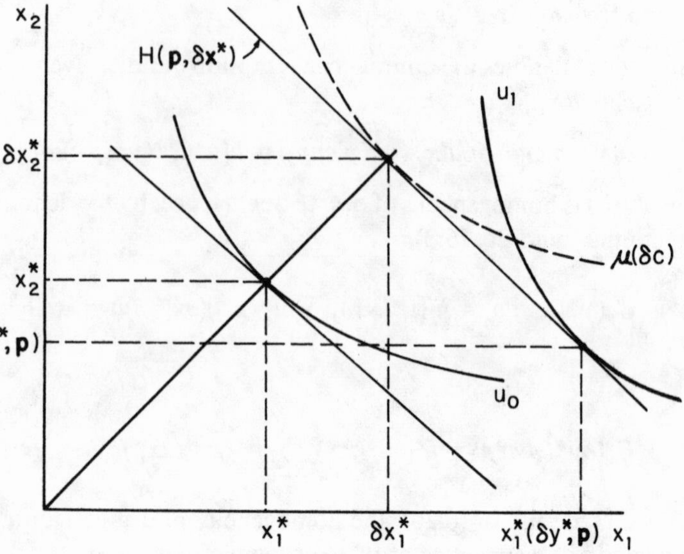

Figure 6.4 Part (b) of the proof of Theorem 6.3

Thus, $\boldsymbol{x}^*(\delta y^*(\boldsymbol{p}',c),\boldsymbol{p}') \in H(\boldsymbol{p}',\delta \boldsymbol{x}^*(y^*(\boldsymbol{p}',c),\boldsymbol{p}'))$ does not belong to the equivalence class of $\boldsymbol{x}^*(\delta y^*(\boldsymbol{p},c),\boldsymbol{p})$. Since, by definition, $U_y(y^*(\boldsymbol{p},c),\boldsymbol{p})$ is constant on every equivalence class, then for utility functions that are not linear homogeneous, U_y varies across equivalence classes. This implies that $U_y(\delta y^*(\boldsymbol{p},c),\boldsymbol{p}) \neq U_y(\delta y^*(\boldsymbol{p}',c),\boldsymbol{p}')$. Hence $\{\delta y^*(\boldsymbol{p},c) | \boldsymbol{p} \in R^n_{++}\}$ is not a reference point of U. This is a contradiction, and $\boldsymbol{x}^*(\delta y^*(\boldsymbol{p},c),\boldsymbol{p}) = \delta \boldsymbol{x}^*(y^*(\boldsymbol{p},c),\boldsymbol{p})$ for all $\boldsymbol{p}$. Thus the preference ordering is homothetic.

Finally, if the utility function is linear homogeneous, then the preference ordering is homothetic.

References

Anscombe, F. J., and R. J. Aumann. 1963. "A Definition of Subjective Probability." *Annals of Mathematical Statistics,* 34: 199–205.

Arrow, K. J. 1965. "The Theory of Risk Aversion." *Aspects of the Theory of Risk Bearing,* Lecture 2. Helsinki: Yrjo Jahnsson Foundation. (Reprinted in Arrow, *Essays in the Theory of Risk Bearing.*)

——— 1971. *Essays in the Theory of Risk Bearing.* Chicago: Markham.

——— 1974. "Optimal Insurance and Generalized Deductibles." *Scandinavian Actuarial Journal,* 1–42.

Bernoulli, D. 1738. "Specimen Theoriae Novae de Mensura Sortis." *Commentarii Academiae Scientiatum Imperalas Petropolitanae,* 5: 175–192. Translated as "Exposition of a New Theory on the Measurement of Risk." *Econometrica,* 22 (1954): 23–26.

Biswas, T. 1983. "A Note on the Generalized Measures of Risk Aversion." *Journal of Economic Theory,* 29: 347–352.

Debreu, G. 1976. "Least Concave Utility Functions." *Journal of Mathematical Economics,* 3: 121–129.

Demers, M. 1983. "Mean Utility Preserving Increases in Risk for State-Dependent Utility Functions." Manuscript.

Diamond, P. A., and J. E. Stiglitz. 1974. "Increases in Risk and in Risk Aversion." *Journal of Economic Theory,* 8: 337–360.

Duncan, G. T. 1977. "A Matrix Measure of Multivariate Local Risk Aversion." *Econometrica,* 45: 895–903.

Eisner, R., and R. H. Strotz. 1961. "Flight Insurance and the Theory of Choice." *Journal of Political Economy,* 69: 350–368.

Fishburn, P. C. 1970. *Utility Theory for Decision Making.* New York: John Wiley and Sons.

——— 1973. "A Mixture-Set Axiomatization of Conditional Subjective Expected Utility." *Econometrica,* 41: 1–25.

——— 1974. "On the Foundations of Decision Making under Uncertainty." In M. S. Balch, D. L. MacFadden, and S. Y. Wu, eds., *Essays on Economic Behavior under Uncertainty.* New York: American Elsevier Publishing Co.

Hanoch, G. 1977. "Risk Aversion and Consumer Preferences." *Econometrica,* 45: 413–426.

Hardy, G. H., Littlewood, J. E., and G. Polya. 1934. *Inequalities.* Cambridge: Cambridge University Press.

Herstein, I. N., and J. Milnor. 1953. "An Axiomatic Approach to Measurable Utility." *Econometrica,* 21: 291–297.

Karni, E. 1979. "On Multivariate Risk Aversion." *Econometrica,* 47: 1391–1401.

——— 1983a. "On the Correspondence between Multivariate Risk Aversion and Risk Aversion for State-Dependent Preferences." *Journal of Economic Theory,* 30: 230–242.

——— 1983b. "Risk Aversion in the Theory of Health Insurance." In E. Helpman, A. Razin, and E. Sadka, eds., *Social Policy Evaluation: An Economic Perspective.* New York: Academic Press, pp. 97–106.

——— 1983c. "Risk Aversion for State-Dependent Utility Functions: Measurement and Applications." *International Economic Review,* 24: 637–647.

——— In press. "Increasing Risk with State-Dependent Preferences." *Journal of Economic Theory.*

Karni, E., and D. Schmeidler. 1981. "An Expected Utility Theory for State-Dependent Preferences." Working Paper 48–80, Foerder Institute for Economic Research, Tel-Aviv University.

Karni, E., Schmeidler, D., and K. Vind. 1983. "On State Dependent Preferences and Subjective Probabilities." *Econometrica,* 51: 1021–32.

Karni, E., and I. Zilcha. 1983. "Risk Aversion in the Theory of Life Insurance: The Fisherian Model." Manuscript.

——— 1985. "Uncertain Lifetime, Risk Aversion and Life Insurance" *Scandinavian Actuarial Journal.*

Katzner, D. W. 1970. *Static Demand Theory.* London: MacMillan Co.

Kihlstrom, R. E., and L. J. Mirman. 1974. "Risk Aversion with Many Commodities." *Journal of Economic Theory,* 8: 337–360.

——— 1981. "Constant, Increasing and Decreasing Risk Aversion with Many Commodities." *Review of Economic Studies,* 48: 271–280.

Moffet, D. 1978. "A Note on Yaari's Life Cycle Model." *Review of Economic Studies,* 45: 385–388.

Paroush, J. 1975. "Risk Premium with Many Commodities." *Journal of Economic Theory,* 11: 283–286.

Pratt, J. W. 1964. "Risk Aversion in the Small and in the Large." *Econometrica,* 32: 122–136.

Ramsey, F. P. 1931. "Truth and Probability." In *The Foundation of Mathematics and other Logical Essays.* London: K. Paul, Trench, Trubner and Co.

Röell, A. 1983. "Essays in the Theory of Risk Aversion with Special Reference to State-Dependent Preferences." Ph.D. diss., Johns Hopkins University.

Ross, S. A. 1981. "Some Stronger Measures of Risk Aversion in the Small and in the Large with Applications." *Econometrica,* 49: 621–638.

Rothschild, M., and J. E. Stiglitz. 1970. "Increasing Risk: I. A Definition." *Journal of Economic Theory,* 3: 225–243.

——— 1971. "Increasing Risk: II. Its Economic Consequences." *Journal of Economic Theory,* 4: 66–84.

——— 1972. "Addendum to 'Increasing Risk: I. A Definition.'" *Journal of Economic Theory,* 5: 306.

Savage, L. J. 1954. *The Foundations of Statistics.* New York: John Wiley and Sons.

Schmeidler, D. 1979. "A Bibliographical Note on a Theorem of Hardy, Littlewood and Polya." *Journal of Economic Theory,* 20: 125–128.

Stiglitz, J. E. 1969. "Behavior Towards Risk with Many Commodities." *Econometrica,* 37: 660–667.

von Neumann, J., and O. Morgenstern. 1947. *Theory of Games and Economic Behavior,* 2nd ed. Princeton: Princeton University Press.

Yaari, M. E. 1965. "Uncertain Lifetime, Life Insurance and the Theory of the Consumer." *Review of Economic Studies,* 52: 137–150.

——— 1969. "Some Remarks on Measures of Risk Aversion and Their Uses." *Journal of Economic Theory,* 1: 315–329.

Index